A History of
JAPANESE LITERATURE

A History of

JAPANESE LITERATURE

by W. *william* G. ASTON, C.M.G., D.Lit.

with an introduction to the new edition by
TERENCE BARROW, Ph.D.

CHARLES E. TUTTLE COMPANY
Rutland, Vermont & Tokyo, Japan

Representatives

Continental Europe: BOXERBOOKS, INC., *Zurich*

British Isles: PRENTICE-HALL INTERNATIONAL, INC., *London*

Australasia: BOOK WISE (AUSTRALIA) PTY. LTD.
104-108 Sussex Street, Sydney 2000

*Published by the Charles E. Tuttle Company, Inc.
of Rutland, Vermont & Tokyo, Japan
with editorial offices at
Suido 1-chome, 2-6, Bunkyo-ku, Tokyo, Japan*

© *1972 by Charles E. Tuttle Co., Inc.*

Library of Congress Catalog Card No. 73-157264

International Standard Book No. 0-8048-0997-6

*First Tuttle edition, 1972
Fifth printing, 1981*

0291-000287-4615
PRINTED IN JAPAN

TABLE OF CONTENTS

V

TABLE OF CONTENTS

TABLE OF CONTENTS

ERRATA

Page 113, near bottom, *read* 'the birth of a succession of female children.'

Page 114, *for* ' carriage,' &c., *read* ' people who ride in a creaking carriage. Such people must be deaf and are very detestable. When you ride in such a carriage yourself it is the owner who is detestable.'

INTRODUCTION TO THE
NEW EDITION

THE literature of Japan presents a rich source of beauty and new ideas highly significant to the West. It is widely recognized that in traditional modes of expression the Western mind is aggressive and masculine while the Eastern mind, on the other hand, is inclined to passivity and feminine receptiveness. It is as if this division of mankind were a preparation for human progress. When East and West meet, as history illustrates, men conceive most fruitful ideas. This is particularly true in the field of literature of the nineteenth and twentieth centuries in Europe and to some degree in America (books of Oriental philosophy had a profound influence on Emerson, Whitman, and Thoreau). Japanese writers have been very susceptible to Western literature over the past century; so the West also has its fertilizing effect.

The Western discovery of Japanese literature was aided by William George Aston's *A History of Japanese Literature*. First published in New York in 1899, this book is a milestone in such study. When it was written, as the author reminds us, knowledge of the Japanese language and Japanese books was a recent acquirement in the West. Forty years before, he says, no Englishman could read a single page of Japanese.

At the pioneering nineteenth-century stage of Japanese studies no man was better qualified, or more favorably situated, than was Professor Aston. Born in Northern Ireland in 1841, he had early distinguished himself as a gifted linguist when he was a student at the Queen's University of Ireland (this university was later to honor him with the degree of Doctor of Literature). His practical knowledge of the Far East was based on a quarter of a century in government service, mainly in Japan, where he was first an interpreter in the British Consular Service and later a staff member of the British Legation in Tokyo. From 1880 to 1883 he was consul at Hyogo.

Aston pioneered the translation of Japanese into English. Armando Martins Janeira in his recent *Japanese and Western Literature: A Comparative Study* (Charles E. Tuttle, Co., Inc., 1970) refers to Aston as the "first English historian of Japanese literature." Aston also performed the incredibly difficult tasks of compiling the first European grammar of the Japanese language and translating (for the first time in English) the classic chronicle of Japanese history entitled *Nihongi* (Charles E. Tuttle Co., Inc., 1972). An impression of the extent of Aston's scholarship may be gained from the library of 9,500 Japanese books which he bequeathed to the University of Cambridge in England. Professor Aston was recognized by his contemporaries as a great Orientalist and scholar, a reputation which has remained undiminished.

We must remember, however, that *A History of Japanese Literature* was written when there was little critical writing on the subject. This book was the first substantial presentation of Japanese literature to the English-speaking world. Subsequent decades of scholarship have of course provided many studies of Japanese literature, as well as the translation into English of original Japanese works. We may regard the above-noted book by Armando Martins Janeira as complementary to Aston's work. Both books are landmarks in the field, Janeira being modern and moving in realms more or less inaccessible to scholars of Aston's time—for example, the field of Zen thought. Meiji movements in Japanese literature, contemporary with Aston, are seen in perspective by Janeira. Aston has little to say concerning the scene of his own time.

Chinese elements must be regarded as a true part of Japanese literature, just as the literature and languages of Greece and Rome are an integral part of Western literature. Almost every aspect of Japanese culture contains foreign elements. Aston points out: "There is no department of Japanese national life and thought, whether material civilization, religion, morals, political organization, language, or literature, which does not bear traces of Chinese influence." The historical origins of Chinese influence are now well understood—for example, Buddhism, a Chinese import, gained a footing in Japan's mid-sixth century under the scholarly sponsorship of Shotoku Taishi.

With early Buddhism came the knowledge of writing and literature. The Japanese, at first attentive copyists of Chinese written characters and literature, soon proved themselves innovators rather than imitators. They remained learners only so long as it was necessary. From their native ability there soon emerged a distinct tradition in verse, drama, the novel, and the other Japanese literary arts. Some forms, such as the poetic haiku and the Noh drama, are uniquely Japanese and have no exact Chinese equivalents.

The literary forms of China, as well as Chinese ideographic characters, are at the root of Japanese literature. The Japanese had a native independence similar to that found in the English character (a quality that is now somewhat withered in both England and Japan). Comparison can be extended to include the geographical situations of both countries—that is, both looked to nearby continents for the resources of writing and culture.

Indeed the literary traditions of Britain and Japan can be paralleled in the millennium of their formation and over the same period of time. Both traditions, which are in so many ways alike, were created by the inhabitants of islands adjacent to restless continental civilizations superior to them in both technology and civilization. Japan and Britain were populated, in early times, by refugees fleeing before pursuers, the pursuers themselves, the footloose, and the needy. From a heterogeneous assortment of people representing all sorts of ethnic differences these great nations were born. However, both Englishmen and Japanese continued for centuries to look to the continents for knowledge and culture—England to Greece and Rome, Japan to China (via Korea). The dwellers on the continents, in both cases, regarded these neighboring islanders as barbarians. Paradoxically, England proved to be the singular preserver of European culture just as Japan became the great preserver of things Chinese. Their respective literatures are among the richest known to mankind.

The Meiji Restoration of 1868 gave a new face to

Japan—a face somewhat shocking to the contemporary Western nations. Western-style capitalism was nurtured, feudal ideas were eventually revivified, and the ground was laid for the conflict of World War II. The times also gave birth to a new Japanese literature not found in the pages of *A History of Japanese Literature*. Professor Aston's view takes us up to the end of the nineteenth century. However, the Western reading public no longer regards Japan as an exotic novelty. Today, traditional stories like Lady Murasaki's *Tale of Genji* are as well known as the writings of Nobel prize winner Yasunari Kawabata. The scene is changing, but Professor Aston's little classic, *A History of Japanese Literature*, can continue to serve as a gateway to the riches of Japan's literature just as it has done over the past seven decades of the twentieth century.

Terence Barrow, Ph.D.

PREFACE

THE Japanese have a voluminous literature, extending over twelve centuries, which to this day has been very imperfectly explored by European students. Forty years ago no Englishman had read a page of a Japanese book, and although some Continental scholars had a useful acquaintance with the language, their contributions to our knowledge are unimportant. Much has been done in the interval, by writers of grammars and dictionaries, to facilitate the acquirement of this most difficult language, and translations by Sir E. Satow, Messrs. Mitford, Chamberlain, Dickins, and others, have given us interesting glimpses of certain phases of the literature. But the wider field has hitherto remained untouched. Beyond a few brief detached notices, there is no body of critical opinion on Japanese books in any European language, and although the Japanese themselves have done more in this direction, their labours are for various reasons in a great measure unserviceable.

The historian of their literature is therefore thrown mainly upon his own resources, and must do his best, by a direct examination of those works which the verdict of posterity has marked out as most worthy of notice, to ascertain their character and place in literature, and to grasp as far as possible the ideas which inspired them. In the following pages comparatively little space has been devoted to what is necessarily a record of personal impressions and opinions, the outcome of rough pioneer work, and having little claim to be considered as mature literary criticism. It seemed preferable, especially in the case of a literature so little known to the English public as that of Japan, to allot ample room to translated extracts, and to such biographical notices as are necessary to show what manner of men the authors were.

The general plan, however, of this series has not been lost sight of. Important writers have been treated at comparatively greater length, to the neglect of many lesser notabilities, and an attempt has been made, in so far as the state of our knowledge permits, to follow the movement of the literature, and to trace the causes which determined its character at particular periods.

Writers on European literatures are entitled to take for granted, on the part of their readers, a previous acquaintance with the leading facts of the political and religious history of the country with which they are dealing. In the case of Japan, however, it has been thought not superfluous to add a few data of this kind, without a knowledge of which it is impossible to understand the course of the literary development.

In justice to Japanese literature, it is right to draw attention to some obstacles which prevent any translations from giving an adequate idea of its merits. The Italian adage is particularly applicable to translators from the Japanese. Even when they have a competent knowledge of the language they cannot possibly reproduce all the metaphors, allusions, quotations, and illustrations which form the stock of the Japanese author, and which are in great part unintelligible without a profusion of explanatory notes intolerable to the reader.

Another difficulty arises from the fact that a Japanese word frequently covers a meaning which is only approximately the same as that of the corresponding English term, or calls up quite different associations. The *karasu*, for example, is not exactly a crow, but a *corvus Japonensis*, a larger bird than our species, with different cries and habits. The cherry is, in Japan, the queen of flowers, and is not valued for its fruit, while the rose is regarded as a mere thorny bush. Valerian, which to us is suggestive principally of cats, takes the place of the rosebud as the recognised metaphor for the early bloom of womanhood. And what is the translator to do with the names of flowers as familiar to the Japanese as daisy or daffodil to ourselves, but for which he can offer no better equivalents than such clumsy inventions as *Lespedeza*, *Platycodon grandiflorum*, and *Deutzia scabra*?

In the world of thought and sentiment, the differences, though less tangible, are even more important. Take the Japanese word for conscience, namely, *honshin*. It means "original heart," and implies a theory that man's heart is originally good, and that conscience is its voice speaking within him. The words for justice, virtue, chastity, honour, love, and many more ideas of this class, although meaning substantially the same as with ourselves, must yet be taken with differences which are necessarily lost in a translation.

When to these are added the ordinary difficulties which beset the task of rendering thought from one language into another, and which are incomparably greater in the case of an idiom so different from our own, it will be seen that it is not possible to do justice to Japanese literature by translation. In the present volume it has often been necessary to pass over the best and most characteristic passages of an author in favour of others which lent themselves more readily to presentation in an English form.

With one or two stated exceptions the translations are my own.

My best thanks are due to Sir Ernest Satow, Her Majesty's Minister to Japan, for lending me most of his extensive library of Japanese books, and also for supplying me from time to time with recent native publications, which have been of much service to me.

I cordially associate myself with previous contributors to this series of histories, by acknowledging the benefit which the present volume has derived from the editorial care of Mr. Edmund Gosse.

Japanese words and proper names have been introduced as sparingly as possible. The system of spelling adopted is that of the Royal Geographical Society. It may be described briefly as "Consonants as in English, vowels as in Italian ; no silent letters."

W. G. ASTON.

BOOK THE FIRST

ARCHAIC PERIOD (BEFORE A.D. 700)

BOOK THE FIRST

ARCHAIC PERIOD (before a.d. 700)

THERE are a few geographical and other facts which it is useful to bear in mind in tracing the history of Japanese literature. If we glance at a map of Eastern Asia we see that Japan forms a group of islands somewhat larger in superficial area than Great Britain and Ireland, separated by a narrow strait from the adjoining continent. Here lies the peninsula of Corea, inhabited by a nation distinct from the Chinese in race and language, but from ancient times dependent both politically and intellectually on its powerful neighbour. Corea has shown little originality in the development of its literature or civilisation, and its chief importance in connection with Japan depends on its geographical position, which, in the infancy of the art of navigation, made it the natural intermediary between Japan and China.

China, with its ancient civilisation, its copious and in many respects remarkable literature, and a history which goes back for more than two thousand years, has for many centuries exercised a commanding influence over all its neighbours. What Greece and Rome have been to Europe, China has been to the nations of the far East. Japan, in particular, is very deeply indebted to it. There is no department of Japanese national life and thought, whether material civilisation, religion, morals, political organisation, language, or literature, which does not bear traces of Chinese influence.

Beyond China lies India, which has furnished one important factor in moulding the literature of Japan, namely, Buddhism. If, in regard to Japan, China takes the place of Greece and Rome, Buddhism, with its softening and humanising influences, holds a position similar to that of Christianity in the Western World. The alternate preponderance of these two powers is an interesting feature of Japanese history, and we shall see that it has not been without effect upon the literature.

We must not, however, forget the native genius of the Japanese nation, which, in spite of numerous external obligations, has yet retained its originality. The Japanese are never contented with simple borrowing. In art, political institutions, and even religion, they are in the habit of modifying extensively everything which they adopt from others, and impressing on it the stamp of the national mind. It is the same with the literature. Though enormously indebted to China, and at times hindered in its natural development by a too implicit reliance on foreign guidance, it has remained nevertheless a true index of the national character. It is the literature of a brave, courteous, light-hearted, pleasure-loving people, sentimental rather than passionate, witty and humorous, of nimble apprehension, but not profound ; ingenious and inventive, but hardly capable of high intellectual achievement ; of receptive minds endowed with a voracious appetite for knowledge ; with a turn for neatness and elegance of expression, but seldom or never rising to sublimity.

The insular position and political independence of

Japan no doubt account partially for the literature retaining its native originality of character. But more is no doubt due to a fundamental difference of race from the nations to which the Japanese have been indebted. There is reason to believe that the Japanese nation contains an aboriginal polynesian element (which some writers call Malay), but the evidence of language and anthropology is conclusive that it is in the main a continental race, quite distinct, however, from the Chinese. It must have come from a more northerly region, and geographical considerations point distinctly to Corea as the point of embarkation. Beyond this it is safer not to go. Nor need we attempt to fix any date for their migration. Native tradition is silent on the subject, or rather assumes that the Japanese are aborigines. The process of colonisation probably extended over centuries, and the numerous immigrations from Corea to Japan in historical times are no doubt simply a continuation of the same movement.

The first historical fact to be gleaned from the legendary stories which have been preserved to us in the ancient Japanese annals is an invasion of the central part of the country, already settled by men of Japanese race, by a conquering army from the western island of Kiushiu. Their leader, Jimmu Tennō, who is recognised as the first Mikado, established his capital in the province of Yamato at a time which it is best to indicate vaguely as a few centuries before the Christian epoch. Here, or in one of the adjoining provinces, his successors reigned for many centuries, each Mikado building himself a palace and founding a capital in a fresh locality. A semi-nomad arrangement of this kind is obviously incompatible with much advance in civilisation. It was not until the capital was established on a more permanent footing at Nara, in the beginning of the eighth century, that any substantial progress was made in literature and the arts.

Although the Archaic period has left us but few literary monuments, it is marked by two events of prime importance for the development of literature in Japan. One is the introduction of the art of writing, with which was associated an acquaintance with the literature and history of China ; and the other the first propagation of the Buddhist religion. Both came, in the first place, from Corea, which had received them from China no long time before. Until they became acquainted with Chinese the Japanese had no written character. It is probable that individuals had acquired some knowledge of the Chinese language and script early in the Christian era, but the first actual mention of the study of Chinese in Japan belongs to A.D. 405. In this year a Corean named Wangin was appointed tutor in Chinese to a Japanese Imperial Prince. He was the first of a succession of teachers from Corea whose instructions paved the way for a revolution in Japanese customs and institutions, not less profound and far-reaching than that which we have witnessed in our own day as the result of an acquaintance with Western civilisation and science.

Buddhism was introduced about one hundred and fifty years later—in the middle of the sixth century—but it was not until the seventh that it made much progress. Its real founder in Japan was the Imperial Prince Shōtoku Daishi, who died A.D. 621.

In the scanty remains of the period with which we are now dealing, there is scarce any trace either of Buddhist or of Chinese influences. It may be said that the *Kiujiki*, a historical work attributed to the Prince just mentioned, should be reckoned an exception to this statement. But its authenticity has been questioned ; and, in any case, it is in the Chinese language, and therefore, properly speaking, forms no part of Japanese literature.

SONGS.

The oldest relics of the genuine native literature of Japan are a series of songs contained in the ancient annals known as the *Kojiki* and *Nihongi*, and the *Norito* or liturgies of the Shinto, or native Japanese religion.

These songs are associated with some historical or quasi-historical incident, and are ascribed to Mikados or other distinguished personages. Several of them are attributed to Jimmu Tennō, who is said to have founded the Japanese monarchy in 660 B.C., and equally fictitious accounts are given of others. Probably we shall not be far wrong if we assign most of the poems of the *Kojiki* and *Nihongi* to the latter part of the Archaic period, namely, to the sixth and seventh centuries of our era.

The poetry of this time possesses a certain philological and archæological interest, but its merit as literature is small. The language is still unformed, and there is a plentiful lack of imagination and of the other higher qualities of poetry. What, for example, can be more primitive than the following war-song, which is supposed to have been chanted by Jimmu Tennō's soldiers, and which, the author of the *Nihongi* informs us, was still sung by the Imperial Guards in his own day ?

> " *Ho! now is the time;*
> *Ho! now is the time;*
> *Ha! Ha! Psha!*
> *Even now*
> *My boys!*
> *Even now*
> *My boys!*"

Or this, which is dated 90 B.C. ?

> " *The Hall of Miwa*
> (*Of sweet saké fame*),
> *Even at morn its door*
> *Let us push open—*
> *The door of the Hall of Miwa.*"

Saké, it ought, perhaps, to be explained, is an intoxicating liquor brewed from rice. The sentiment of this song therefore recalls our own "We won't go home till morning."

The following, which is said to have been composed by the Mikado Ōjin, A.D. 282, but which more probably belongs to the sixth century, may serve to indicate the highest level to which poetry attained during this period. This Mikado was about to add to his harem a beautiful woman named Kami-naga-hime, or the " long-haired maid," when he discovered that his son had fallen violently in love with her. He invited them both to a banquet, and then surprised his son by resigning to him the lady with the following words :—

> " *Lo! my son!*
> *On the moor, garlic to gather,*
> *Garlic to gather,*
> *On the way as I went,*
> *Pleasing of perfume*
> *Was the orange in flower.*
> *Its branches beneath*
> *Men had all plundered,*
> *Its branches above*
> *Birds perching had withered,*
> *Midway its branches*
> *Held in their hiding*
> *A blushing maiden.*
> *Lo! my son, for thee*
> *Let her burst into blossom.*"

The *Kojiki* and *Nihongi* have preserved to us more than two hundred of these poems. Their study tends to correct ideas such as that of Macaulay, who, doubtless reasoning from the now exploded premiss that Homer is a primitive poet, argued that "in a rude state of society we may expect to find the poetical temperament in its highest perfection." Judging from this early poetry of Japan, a want of culture by no means acts as a stimulus to the poetic faculty. We nowhere find "the agony, the ecstasy, the plenitude of belief," which Macaulay would have us look for in this product of an age and country which were certainly far less advanced than those of Homer in intellectual culture. Instead of passion, sublimity, and a vigorous imagination, we have little more than mild sentiment, word-plays, and pretty conceits. Moreover, a suspicion will not be banished that even for such poetical qualities as they possess, these poems are in some degree indebted to the inspiration of China. Of this, however, I cannot offer any definite proof.

SHINTO RITUALS.

The prose of the Archaic period is represented by a series of Norito,[1] or prayers to the deities of the Shinto religion, which were recited with much ceremony by the Nakatomi, a hereditary corporation of court officials whose especial function it was to represent the Mikado in his capacity of high priest of the nation. Their precise date and authorship are unknown. In their essence they are no doubt of very great antiquity, but there is reason

[1] Vide *Transactions of the Asiatic Society of Japan*, March 1879, &c., for a translation of some of these by Sir Ernest Satow.

to believe that they did not assume their present form until the seventh century, some of them perhaps even later. The Norito are not known to have been committed to writing before the period Yengi (901–923), when the preparation was begun of the work entitled *Yengishiki* or "Institutes of Yengi," a collection of the ceremonial regulations in force at this time. The *Yengishiki* enumerates seventy-five of these prayers, and gives the text of twenty-seven, which, no doubt, comprise all the most important. There are prayers for a good harvest, deprecating fire and pestilence, invoking blessings on the palace, services in honour of the Food Goddess, the Wind Deities, and so on. The most famous of all is the Ōharai or General Purification Service. It is not devoid of literary quality, as the following translation may perhaps indicate. The other Norito which I have read are much inferior in merit.

"Give ear, all ye Imperial Princes, Ministers of State, and high functionaries, who are here assembled, and hearken to the great purification by which at this interlune of the sixth month are purged and washed away all sins which may have been committed by Imperial officials and attendants—whether they wear the scarf [women] or the shoulder strap [stewards]; whether they bear on their back the bow, or gird on them the sword.

"Of yore, our Imperial ancestors who dwell in the plain of high heaven, summoned to an assembly the eight hundred myriads of deities, and held divine counsel with them. And they gave command, saying, 'Let our August Grandchild hold serene rule over the land of fair rice-ears—the fertile reed-plain.' But in the land thus delivered to him there were savage deities. These they chastised with a divine chastisement, and expelled with a divine expulsion. Moreover, the rocks, trees, and leaves of grass which had the power of speech, were silenced. Then they despatched him downward from his celestial, everlasting throne, cleaving as he went with an awful way-cleaving the many-piled clouds of heaven. Here at the middle point of the land entrusted to him—in Yamato, the High Sun Land—the August Grandchild established his peaceful rule and built a fair palace, basing deep on the nethermost rock the massy pillars, and upraising to high heaven the timbers of the roof wherewithal to shelter him from sun and sky.

"Now, of the various offences to be committed by the celestial race destined more and more to people this land of peaceful rule, some are of heaven and others of earth. Heavenly offences are the breaking down of divisions between rice-fields, filling up of water-courses, removing water-pipes, flaying alive, flaying backwards. . . . Earthly offences are the cutting of living bodies, the cutting of dead bodies, leprosy, incest, calamities from creeping things, from the high gods and from high birds, killing of cattle, bewitchments.

"Whensoever these offences are committed, for committed they will be, let the great Nakatomi clip heavenly twigs at the top and clip them at the bottom, making thereof a complete array of one thousand stands for offerings. Having trimmed rushes of heaven at the top and trimmed them at the bottom, let them split them into a manifold brush. Then let them recite this great liturgy.

"When they do so, the gods of heaven, thrusting open the adamantine doors of heaven and cleaving the many-piled clouds of heaven with an awful way-cleaving, will approach and lend ear. The gods of earth, ascending to the tops of the high mountains and the tops of the low mountains, sweeping aside the mists of the high mountains and the mists of the low mountains, will approach and lend ear.

"Then shall no offences remain unpurged, from the court of the august child of the gods even to the remotest ends of the realm. As the many-piled clouds of heaven are scattered at the breath of the Wind Gods; as the morning breezes and the evening breezes disperse the morning vapours and the evening vapours; as a huge ship moored in a great harbour, casting off its stern moorings, casting off its bow moorings, drives forth into the vast ocean; as yonder thick brushwood is smitten and cleared away by the sharp sickle forged in the fire— so shall all offences be swept utterly away. To purge and purify them, let the goddess Seoritsu-hime, who dwells in the rapids of the swift stream whose cataracts tumble headlong from the high mountains and from the low mountains, bear them out into the great sea plain. There let the goddess Haya-akitsu-hime, who dwells in the myriad ways of the tides of the raging sea, and in the myriad meeting-places of the tides of the myriad sea paths, swallow them up, and let the god Ibukido Nushi [the master of the spurting-out place], who dwells in Ibukido, spurt them out away to the nether region. Then let the goddess Haya-sasura-hime, who dwells in the nether region, dissolve and destroy them.

"They are now destroyed, and all, from the servants of the Imperial court down to the people in the four quarters of the realm, are from this day forth void of offence.

"Attend, all of you, with ears pricked up to the plain of high heaven, to this great purification by which, on this interlune of the sixth month as the sun goes down, your offences are purged and purified."

The Norito, although prose, are in some respects more poetical than much of the contemporary poetry. This is not the place to discuss the general question whether literature begins with prose or poetry. It may be noted, however, that the earliest Japanese literature presents two imperfectly differentiated types—a poetry which in metrical form, thought, and diction, is not far removed from prose ; and prose compositions which contain an appreciable element of poetry.

BOOK THE SECOND

NARA PERIOD (EIGHTH CENTURY)

BOOK THE SECOND

NARA PERIOD[1] (EIGHTH CENTURY)

CHAPTER I

PROSE OF THE NARA PERIOD—THE "KOJIKI"

STRICTLY speaking, this period begins A.D. 710, when Nara was made the seat of the Mikado's government, and ends A.D. 794, when the capital was removed to Nagaoka, in the province of Yamashiro, a site which was abandoned a few years later for that of the existing city of Kiōto. For the present purpose it is sufficiently accurate to make the Nara period coincide with the eighth century.

With the establishment of the capital at Nara, the old system by which every Mikado built himself a new palace in a fresh locality was discontinued. This was not only in itself an important progressive measure, but it was an evidence of the advance in civilisation which had been made during the previous two centuries. Under the influence of Chinese political ideas, the

[1] I have followed the convenient Japanese practice of calling the periods of history by the names of the places which were the seat of government at the time.

authority of the crown had become greatly extended, the power of the hereditary local chieftains broken, and a system of government instituted under prefects who held office subject to the control of the central authority. Learning, by which in Japan is, or rather was, meant the study of the masterpieces of Chinese antiquity, had made great progress. The Mikado Tenchi (662–671) established schools, and we hear later of a university under government auspices which comprised four faculties, viz., history, the Chinese classics, law, and arithmetic.

This, it should be observed, was for the benefit of the official classes only. It was not until many centuries later that education reached the common people. There were also teachers (mostly Coreans) of painting, medicine, and the glyptic arts. The colossal bronze statue of Buddha and some remarkable sculptures in wood which are still to be seen at Nara, testify to the skill which the Japanese had then acquired in the last-named arts.

Of even greater importance was the advance in the art of architecture. This was intimately associated with Buddhism, a cult which demanded stately temples and pagodas for its due exercise. The increased authority of the court also required edifices more befitting its dignity and more in consonance with the gorgeous costumes and ceremonial adopted from China than the old one-reign palaces.

The first written book which has come down to us in the Japanese, or indeed in any Turanian tongue, is the *Kojiki*[1] or "Records of Ancient Matters," which was completed A.D. 712. It contains the early traditions of the Japanese race, beginning with the myths which form

---

[1] Translated by B. H. Chamberlain in the *Transactions of the Asiatic Society of Japan*, 1882; vol. x., Supplement.

the basis of the Shinto religion, and acquiring more and more of a historical character as it proceeds, until it comes to a close in A.D. 628.

The *Kojiki*, however valuable it may be for research into the mythology, the manners, the language, and the legends of early Japan, is a very poor production, whether we consider it as literature or as a record of facts. As history it cannot compare with the *Nihongi*, a contemporary work in Chinese; while the language is a strange mixture of Chinese and Japanese, which there has been little attempt to endue with artistic quality. The circumstances under which it was composed are a partial explanation of the very curious style in which it is written. We are told that a man named Yasumaro, learned in Chinese, took it down from the lips of a certain Hiyeda no Are, who had such a wonderful memory that he "could repeat with his mouth whatever was placed before his eyes, and record in his heart whatever struck his ears." Yasumaro's task was not an easy one. He himself in his preface describes his embarrassment. The phonetic syllabaries, known as the Katagana and Hirakana, which correspond to our alphabet, had not then been invented. The only choice open to him was to use the Chinese ideographic symbols, giving them their proper meaning and construction—in other words, to write pure Chinese—or to make each Chinese character represent merely the sound associated with it regardless of its meaning. The result of this latter course would be a Japanese text.

By the former method it was impossible to write down Japanese poetry, proper names, and a quantity of phrases and expressions for which there existed no adequate Chinese equivalent; while if a separate Chinese character had to be used for every syllable of the polysyllabic Japanese words, a prolixity intolerable to a mind formed by Chinese study would be the result. In this dilemma Yasumaro resorted to a compromise, and mixed up the two systems in a way which is fatal to style. Even in the same sentence we often find a purely Japanese construction interrupted by a phrase which it is impossible to consider as anything but clumsy Chinese ; while, *vice versâ*, his Chinese contains expressions not to be understood without a knowledge of Japanese.

At the time of the compilation of the *Kojiki* there existed at the court of Nara a hereditary corporation of Kataribe or "reciters," whose function it was to recite "ancient words" before the Mikado on certain solemn State occasions, such as the beginning of a new reign. Even if Yasumaro's informant was not himself a member of this order, he must have been well acquainted with the matter of their recitals, and there can be little doubt that the myths, legends, and quasi-history of the *Kojiki* were drawn from this source. There is no reason whatever to believe that the recitations of the Kataribe were anything but prose. We are in possession of a considerable body of poetry belonging to this period, but none of it takes the form of narrative. It consists of lyrics, not ballads, and yields no material for history, whether true or otherwise. The annals of Japanese literature therefore give no countenance to Macaulay's theory that in the natural course of things history is preceded by ballad poetry. So far from its being true of Japan, a directly opposite process is observable. At a later period, history showed some tendency to develop into poetry. It began to be treated in an ornate, romantic fashion, and with some imperfect endeavour after metrical form.

The motley character of the language of the *Kojiki* of course disappears in a translation, but the following passage may give some idea of the sort of legends which form the staple of the earlier part of the work. The student of folk-lore will recognise in it one of the numerous variants of what in its Greek form is the story of Perseus and Andromeda.

The god Haya-Susa no wo, having been banished from heaven for his misdeeds, descends to earth and alights on the bank of a river in the province of Idzumo. He observes a chopstick floating down with the current :—

"His Augustness Haya-Susa no wo, thinking that there must be people living farther up the stream, went in quest of them, and found an old man and an old woman weeping, with a young maiden set between them. He asked of them, 'Who are ye?' The old man replied, 'Thy servant is a deity of earth, and his name is Ashinadzuchi, son of the great God of the Mountain. My wife's name is Tenadzuchi, and my daughter is called Kushinada hime.' He further inquired, 'Why weep ye?' He answered, saying, 'I have had eight children, girls; but the eight-forked serpent of Koshi came year after year and devoured them. It is now the time of its coming, and therefore do we weep.' 'Describe to me this serpent,' said Haya-Susa no wo. 'Its eyes are as red as the winter cherry. It has one body with eight heads and eight tails. Moreover, its body is overgrown with moss, pines, and cedars. Its length extends over eight valleys and eight hills. Its belly is always all bloody and inflamed to look upon.' Then his Augustness Haya-Susa no wo said to the old man, 'If this be thy daughter, wilt thou give her unto me?' 'With reverence be it said,' replied the old man, 'I know not thy honourable name.' ' I am the elder brother of the Sun Goddess, and have now come down from heaven,' replied Susa no wo. Then the deities Ashinadzuchi and Tenadzuchi said, ' In that case, with reverence we offer her to thee.' Haya-Susa no wo straightway took that young maiden and changed her into a many-toothed comb, which he stuck into his hair, and said to the deities Ashinadzuchi and Tenadzuchi, ' Do ye brew some saké of eight-fold strength. Also make a fence round about, and in that fence let there be eight doors, at each door let there be eight stands, on each stand let there be a saké-tub, and let each saké-tub be filled with the saké of eight-fold strength. Then wait.' So having prepared everything in accordance with his august bidding, they waited, Then the eight-forked serpent came, indeed, as had been said, and bending down one head into each of the tubs, lapped up the saké. Hereupon it became drunken, and all the heads lay down to sleep, when straightway Haya-Susa no wo drew his ten-span sword from his girdle and slew the serpent, so that the river had its current changed to blood. Now, when he cut the middle part of the tail the edge of his august sword was broken. Wondering at this, he pierced it and split it open, when he found that within there was a great sharp sword. He took this sword, and thinking it a wonderful thing, reported his discovery to the Sun Goddess. This is the great sword Kusanagi (Herb-queller)."

In the early part of the eighth century the Japanese Government gave orders for the compilation of geographical descriptions of all the provinces. The mineral, vegetable, and animal productions were to be noted, with the quality of the soil, the origin of the names of places, and the local traditions. Of these works only a few have reached us, the best known of which is the *Idzumo Fudoki*, written in 733. It contains a very few interesting legendary passages, but as a whole it consists of bald statements of fact, and must be classed with Charles Lamb's *Biblia Abiblia* or "Books that are No Books." It was the forerunner of the very considerable modern topographical literature known to us as Meisho.

The only other Japanese prose compositions of this time which need be noticed are the Imperial Edicts contained in the *Shoku-nihongi*, a continuation (in Chinese) of the *Nihongi*. Their style much resembles that of the *Norito*. Motoöri has edited them in a separate form with a commentary.

CHAPTER II

JAPANESE POETRY GENERALLY—
THE "MANYŌSHIU"

BEFORE proceeding to an examination of the Nara poetry, it seems desirable to give an account of those characteristics of Japanese poetry generally which distinguish it in a conspicuous manner from that of Europe. Narrow in its scope and resources, it is chiefly remarkable for its limitations—for what it has not, rather than for what it has. In the first place there are no long poems. There is nothing which even remotely resembles an epic — no *Iliad* or *Divina Commedia* — not even a *Nibelungen Lied* or *Chevy Chase*. Indeed, narrative poems of any kind are short and very few, the only ones which I have met with being two or three ballads of a sentimental cast. Didactic, philosophical, political, and satirical poems are also conspicuously absent. The Japanese muse does not meddle with such subjects, and it is doubtful whether, if it did, the native Pegasus possesses sufficient staying power for them to be dealt with adequately. For dramatic poetry we have to wait until the fourteenth century. Even then there are no complete dramatic poems, but only dramas containing a certain poetical element.

Japanese poetry is, in short, confined to lyrics, and what,

for want of a better word, may be called epigrams. It is primarily an expression of emotion. We have amatory verse, poems of longing for home and absent dear ones, praise of love and wine, elegies on the dead, laments over the uncertainty of life. A chief place is given to the beauties of external nature. The varying aspects of the seasons, the sound of purling streams, the snow on Mount Fuji, waves breaking on the beach, seaweed drifting to the shore, the song of birds, the hum of insects, even the croaking of frogs, the leaping of trout in a mountain stream, the young shoots of the fern in spring, the belling of deer in autumn, the red tints of the maple, moon, flowers, rain, wind, mist, these are among the favourite subjects which the Japanese poet delights to dwell upon. If we add some courtly and patriotic effusions, a vast number of conceits more or less pretty, and a very few poems of a religious cast, the enumeration is tolerably complete. But, as Mr. Chamberlain has observed, there are curious omissions. Sunsets and starry skies, for example, do not appear to have attracted attention. War-songs, strange to say, are almost wholly absent. Fighting and bloodshed are apparently not considered fit themes for poetry.

It is not only in its form and subject-matter that Japanese poetry is limited in its scope. The modern poet of Europe makes free use of the works of the Greek and Roman poets as models and as storehouses of poetic imagery. Much of his very language comes from the same source. But the poets of Japan have deliberately refrained from utilising in this way the only literature which was known to them. That their refinement of language and choice of subjects are in some measure due to an acquaintance with the ancient literature of China is hardly open to question, but they allow few outward signs of it to appear. Allusions to Chinese literature and history, although not wholly absent, are unfrequent, and the use of Chinese words is strictly tabooed in all poetry of the classical type. There was a substantial reason for this prohibition. The phonetic character of the two languages is quite different. Chinese is monosyllabic ; Japanese as polysyllabic as English. A Chinese syllable has far more complication and variety than those of Japanese words. It may have diphthongs, combinations of consonants and final consonants, none of which are to be found in Japanese, where every syllable consists of a single vowel or of a single consonant followed by a single vowel. It is true that the Japanese, in adopting Chinese vocables, modify them to suit their own phonetic system. But the process of assimilation is incomplete. The two elements harmonise no better than brick and stone in the same building. It was most natural, therefore, for the Japanese to refuse these half-naturalised aliens admission to the sacred precincts of their national poetry, although by so doing they sacrificed much in fulness and variety of expression, and deprived themselves of a copious store of illustration and allusion to which their prose writers resort even too freely.

The acknowledged euphony and ease of pronunciation of the Japanese language is greatly owing to that property of the syllable which has just been described. Even a reader who knows no Japanese may appreciate the euphonic quality of the following :—

> " *Idete inaba*
> *Nushi naki yado to*
> *Narinu tomo*
> *Nokiba no ume yo*
> *Haru wo-wasuruna.*"[1]

But it is at the same time a source of weakness. It makes smooth versification almost a matter of course, but it also renders impossible much variety or force of rhythm. The Japanese poet can hardly do otherwise than obey Pope's precept :—

> " *Then all your Muse's softer art display,*
> *Let Carolina smooth the tuneful lay,*
> *Lull with Amelia's liquid name the line.*"

The whole language is composed of words made up, like Carolina and Amelia, of syllables with open vowels preceded by single consonants or none. Nor is he under any temptation to

> " *Rend with tremendous sound your ears asunder*
> *With gun, drum, trumpet, blunderbuss, and thunder.*"

His phonetic resources simply will not admit of it. Pope further advises that

> " *When loud surges lash the sounding shore,*
> *The hoarse rough verse should like a torrent roar.*
> *When Ajax strives some rock's vast weight to throw,*
> *The line too labours and the words move slow.*"

---

[1] The initial *i* of *inaba* is elided.

Translation :—

> " When I am gone away,
> Masterless my dwelling
> Though it become—
> Oh ! plum tree by the eaves,
> Forget not thou the spring."

But it is vain for the Japanese poet to strive to adopt this counsel. With a language like the old Japanese it is only within the narrowest limits that it is possible to make the sound an echo to the sense. It is probably in some measure to the want of variety of rhythm which results from this quality that the preference of the national genius for short poems is due.

The mechanism of Japanese verse is simple in the extreme. Unlike Chinese, it has no rhyme, a want which is plainly owing to the nature of the Japanese syllable described above. As every syllable ends in a vowel, and as there are only five vowels, there could only be five rhymes, the constant reiteration of which would be intolerably monotonous.

In the Japanese poetical language all the vowels are of the same length, so that quantity, such as we find in the poetry of Greece and Rome, is unknown. Nor is there any regular succession of accented and un-accented syllables as in the poetry of modern Europe, the Japanese laying hardly any greater stress on one part of a word than on another. In short, the only thing in the mechanism of Japanese poetry which distinguishes it from prose is the *alternation of phrases of five and seven syllables each*. It is, in fact, a species of blank verse.

Some Japanese critics seem to think that the numbers five and seven were suggested by the Chinese Book of odes, where many of the poems consist of lines of five, and others of lines of seven syllables. This does not seem very probable.

The best known metre constructed on this principle is what is known as " Tanka " or " short poems." When poetry is spoken of in Japan it is usually this kind of

verse which is meant. It consists of five phrases or
lines of 5, 7, 5, 7, and 7 syllables—31 syllables in all.[1]
Each of these stanzas constitutes an entire poem. The
Tanka is the most universal and characteristic of the
various forms of poetry in Japan. The oldest examples
date back to the seventh century, or possibly earlier.
Ever since there has been a continual and copious
stream of this kind of composition. Even at the present
day the Mikado gives out themes at the New Year for
his courtiers to show their skill upon, and the pages of
the magazines give evidence that Tanka are still produced
in considerable quantity.

It may be thought that in the compass of 31 syllables,
and with the other limitations to which the poet in Japan
is subject, nothing of much value can be the result.
This, however, is far from being the case. Although no
great qualities can be claimed for the Tanka, it must be
admitted that the Japanese poets have made the most of
their slender resources. It is wonderful what felicity of
phrase, melody of versification, and true sentiment can
be compressed within these narrow limits. In their way
nothing can be more perfect than some of these little
poems. They remind us of those tiny carvings known
to us as Netsuke, in which exquisite skill of workmanship
is displayed in fashioning figures an inch or two in
height, or of those sketches where the Japanese artist has
managed to produce a truly admirable effect by a few
dexterous strokes of the brush.

Next to the Tanka, the most common kind of classical
metre is the Naga-uta or " long poetry." The Naga-uta
has the same alternation of five and seven syllable
phrases, with an additional line of seven syllables at the

---

[1] See specimen on page 27.

end, as the Tanka, and only differs from it in having no limit in regard to length.

Some of the best poetry which Japan has produced is in this metre. But it has never been a great favourite, and after the Nara period was almost completely neglected, the preference of the national genius being evidently for the shorter kind of verse.

Notwithstanding the name, Naga-uta are by no means long poems. Few of them are nearly so long as "Locksley Hall," and the majority are effusions of a few dozen lines only.

A feature which strikingly distinguishes the Japanese poetic muse from that of Western nations is a certain lack of imaginative power. The Japanese are slow to endow inanimate objects with life. Shelley's "Cloud," for example, contains enough matter of this kind for many volumes of Japanese verse. Such lines as

> " *From my wings are shaken*
> *The dews that waken*
> *The sweet buds every one,*
> *When rocked to rest*
> *On their mother's breast*
> *As she dances about the sun,*"

would appear to them ridiculously overcharged with metaphor, if not absolutely unintelligible. Still more foreign to their genius is the personification of abstract qualities. Abstract words are comparatively few, and it does not occur to the Japanese poet (or painter) to represent Truth, Justice, and Faith as comely damsels in flowing robes, or to make Love a chubby naked boy with wings and a bow and arrows. Muses, Graces, Virtues, Furies—in short, the host of personifications without which Western poetry would be only a shadow of itself—have little counterpart in Japanese literature.

This impersonal habit of the Japanese mind is shared by them with other races of the Far East, notably China. It is not confined to poetry, or even to literature, but is profoundly characteristic of their whole mental attitude, showing itself in their grammar, which is most sparing of personal pronouns ; in their art, which has no school of portrait-painting or monumental sculpture worth mentioning ; in the late and imperfect development of the drama ; and in their religious temper, with its strong bent towards rationalism, and its hazy recognition of a ruling personal power in the universe. To their minds things happen, rather than are done ; the tides of fate are far more real to them than the strong will and the endeavour which wrestles with them. The significance of this fact in regard to the moral and psychological development of these races may be left to others to determine. It is sufficient here to note its influence on the literature, and especially on the poetry.

Some rhetorical devices which are peculiar to Japanese poetry require a brief notice. One of these is the Makura-Kotoba, or "pillow-word" as it is called, because it usually stands at the beginning of the verse, serving, as it were, as a pillow upon which it rests. The Makura-Kotoba is a stock conventional epithet prefixed to certain words something after the fashion of Homer's "swift-footed" Achilles or "many-fountained" Ida. These words are survivals from a very archaic stage of the language, and the meaning of some of them is now extremely doubtful, a circumstance which forms no obstacle whatever to their continued use. Others are still intelligible and appropriate enough, such as the "house-bird" cock, the "rain-enshrouded" Mount Mikasa, the "ever-firm" heaven, "morning-mist" thought-wandering. But even although a Makura-Kotoba may be sufficiently apt if it is rightly applied, some Japanese poets take a perverse pleasure in wresting it from its proper sense in a way which to us is nothing short of ludicrous. "Whale-catching," for example, may pass as an epithet of the sea. But what shall we say of the poet who uses it as a prefix to the inland sea of Ōmi, now called Lake Biwa, where, needless to observe, whales are an unknown phenomenon? "Creeper-clad" is well enough as an epithet of a rock, but it tries one's patience a little to find it applied to the province of Iwami, simply because *Iwa* means rock.

From the versifier's point of view the Makura-Kotoba is a very useful institution. It consists almost invariably of five syllables, and therefore supplies him without any trouble with a first line ready made, no unimportant consideration when the entire poem consists of only thirty-one syllables. These epithets are several hundreds in number, and are collected into dictionaries which serve the purpose of a *Gradus ad Parnassum*. They are most useful in a country where the composition of Tanka has been for centuries little more than a mere mechanic art.

Another trick of the Japanese poet is what Mr. Chamberlain[1] has aptly termed "pivot-words." In these a word or part of a word is used in two senses, one with what precedes, the other with what follows. Thackeray has something of the kind in *The Newcomes*, where he speaks of the tea-pot presented to Mr. Honeyman by the devotees attending his chapel as the "devotea-pot." Here the syllable "tea" is contrived a double debt to

[1] In his *Classical Poetry of the Japanese*.

pay. It represents at the same time the final syllable of "devotee" and the first syllable of "tea-pot." Perhaps a better example is the following from Butler's *Hudibras :*—

> " *That old Pyg—what d'ye call him—malion,*
> *Who cut his mistress out of stone,*
> *Had not so hard a hearted one.*"

"What is this but a kind of pun?" the reader will not unnaturally say. Yet it would be hardly fair to stigmatise these *jeux de mots* as puns. They are meant not to provoke laughter, but as ornament, and the effect is sometimes not unpleasing.

At its best, however, the "pivot" word is an ornament of doubtful taste, and poets of the classical period indulge in this figure of speech but sparingly. More remains to be said of it when we come to the dramatists of a later age, who have used it in an extravagant, and, at least to us Europeans, exasperating manner.

Parallelism, or the correspondence between each word of two successive lines or clauses, noun for noun and verb for verb, is an occasional ornament of Japanese, as it is of Chinese poetry. It is familiar to us in the Psalms of David, and is a favourite with Longfellow, whose *Hiawatha* contains numerous such pairs of parallel lines, as—

> " *Filled the marshes full of wild-fowl,*
> *Filled the river full of fishes.*"

Some Japanese examples of this figure will be found in the poems quoted on page 37.

NARA POETRY

While the eighth century has left us little or no prose literature of importance, it was emphatically the golden age of poetry. Japan had now outgrown the artless effusions described in a preceding chapter, and during this period produced a body of verse of an excellence which has never since been surpassed. The reader who expects to find this poetry of a nation just emerging from the barbaric stage of culture characterised by rude, untutored vigour, will be surprised to learn that, on the contrary, it is distinguished by polish rather than power. It is delicate in sentiment and refined in language, and displays exquisite skill of phrase with a careful adherence to certain canons of composition of its own.

The poetry of this and the following period was written by and for a very small section of the Japanese nation. The authors, many of them women, were either members of the Mikado's court, or officials temporarily stationed in the provinces, but looking to the capital as their home. We hear nothing of any popular poetry. On the other hand, the faculty of writing verse was universal among the higher classes. Nearly every educated man and woman could indite a Tanka upon occasion. There were no voluminous writers. It was not the custom to publish the poems of individual authors separately. Had it been so, very thin volumes indeed would have been the result. Collections were made at intervals by Imperial authority, in which the choice poems of the preceding period were brought together, and if twenty or thirty Tanka of one poet found a place there, it was sufficient to give him or her a distinguished position among the multitude of contributors.

The poetry of the Nara period has been preserved to us in one of these anthologies, known as the *Manyōshiu*, or "Collection of One Thousand Leaves." According to the usual account, it was completed early in the ninth century. The poems contained in it belong chiefly to the latter half of the seventh and the first half of the eighth century of the Christian era, and cover a period of about 130 years. They are classified as follows : poems of the four seasons ; poems of the affections ; elegiac, allegorical, and miscellaneous poems. They number in all more than 4000 pieces, of which the great majority are Tanka, or short poems of thirty-one syllables. The remainder are for the most part Naga-uta or so-called "long poems." As for the authors, their name is legion. Among them, however, two poets stand out with some degree of eminence—viz., Hitomaro and Akahito. The former flourished at the end of the seventh century, the latter in the reign of Shōmu (724–756). Little is known of either, further than that they were officials of the Mikado's court, and attended him on some of his progresses through the provinces.

The Riakuge edition of the *Manyōshiu* in thirty volumes, which was formerly the best, has now been totally eclipsed and superseded by the magnificent *Manyōshiu Kogi*, recently published under official auspices. It extends to 122 volumes, and contains everything (and more) in the way of commentary and indexes that the most ardent student can desire. The print is admirable, and the text a great improvement on that of the Riakuge edition.

The following translations, inadequate as they are, may help to give some idea of the character of the *Manyōshiu* poetry. The first specimen is by Hitomaro. It is an elegy on Prince Hinami, son of the Mikado Temmu, who died A.D. 687, before succeeding to the throne.

The poet begins by relating the appointment, at a council of the gods, of the deity Ninigi no Mikoto as the first divine sovereign of Japan. In the second part allusion is made to the death of the late Mikado ; while in the third the poet gives expression to the disappointment of the nation that Prince Hinami did not live to succeed him, and laments the loneliness of his tomb, which he represents as a palace where the Prince dwells in silence and solitude.

> " When began the earth and heaven,
> By the margin of the River
> Of the firmament eternal,
> Met the Gods in high assembly,
> Met the gods and held high counsel,
> Myriads upon myriads gathered.
> Then to each high charge was given ;
> On the Goddess of the Sunlight,
> Her who fills the sky with radiance,
> They bestowed the realm of Heaven.
> To her grandchild they delivered
> This, the land of Ashihara,
> This, the land of fairest rice-ears,
> His with god-like sway to govern,
> Long as heaven and earth endurèd.
> Downward sped, he swept asunder
> Heaven's clouds, the many-pilèd,
> Earthward gloriously descending.
>
> In the Palace of Kiyomi,
> The great seat of power Imperial,
> God-like ruled his true descendant,
> The august High-shining-sun-Prince,
> Till he rose on high divinely,
> Flinging wide the gates eternal
> On the plain of heaven that open.
>
> Mighty Prince, if thou hadst deignèd
> This sublunar world to govern,
> Thou hadst been to all thy people
> Dear as are the flowers in spring-time,
> As the full moon, soul-contenting.
> As in a great ship the seaman,
> So our trust in thee we rested ;

As the welcome rain from heaven,
All the nation did await thee.
Thou hast chosen—why we know not—
By the hill of lone Mayumi
There to raise the massy pillars,
There to build a lofty palace,
But at morn thy voice is heard not;
Months and days have passed in silence,
Till thy servants, sad and weary,
Have departed, none knows whither."

The next specimen is also by Hitomaro.   It is an elegy on a lady of the court.

" In her face were the tints of the autumn woods,
Buxom was her form as the graceful bamboo.
Unknown to us are her thoughts of the future;
We hoped for her a cable-long life,
Not transitory like the dew which falls at morn
And vanishes before evening,
Or the mist which rises at even
And is dispersed in the morning.
Even we, who knew her by report—
We, who had seen her but by glimpses,
Are filled with deep regret.
What then must be the sorrow
Of her youthful spouse
Who shared her couch—
Their white arms interlaced for pillows ?
Desolate indeed must be his thoughts as he lies down,
Despairing must be his longings for her.
Ah me ! she who has passed away from us
By so untimely a fate,
Did indeed resemble the morning dews
Or the mists of evening."

The following illustrates the Japanese poet's use of parallelism.   It is dated A.D. 744.

" By the Palace of Futagi,
Where our great king
And divine lord
Holds high rule,

Gentle is the rise of the hills,
Bearing hundreds of trees;
Pleasant is the murmur of the rapids
As downward they rush.

So long as in the spring-time
(When the nightingale comes and sings)
On the rocks
Brocade-like flowers blossom,
Brightening the mountain-foot;
So long as in the autumn
(When the stag calls to his mate)
The red leaves fall hither and thither,
Wounded by the showers,
The heaven be-clouding—

For many thousand years
May his life be prolonged,
To rule over all under heaven
In the great palace
Destined to remain unchanged
For hundreds of ages."

IN PRAISE OF JAPAN

" The land of Yamato
Has mountains in numbers,
But peerless among them
Is high Kaguyama.
I stand on its summit
My kingdom to view.
The smoke from the land-plain
Thick rises in air,
The gulls from the sea-plain
By fits soar aloft.
O land of Yamato!
Fair Akitsushima!
Dear art thou to me."

THE LEGEND OF URASHIMA

This is one of the most ancient and popular of Japanese legends. In its original version it is much older than the *Manyōshiu*.

" *On a hazy day in spring*
  I went forth and stood upon the beach of Suminoye;
  And as I watched the fishing-boats rock to and fro,
  I bethought me of the tale of old,
  How Urashima of Midzunoye,
  Proud of his skill in catching the bonito and the tai,
  Did not return even for seven days,
  But rowed on beyond the bounds of ocean,[1]
  Where with a daughter of the Sea God
  It was his fortune to meet as he rowed onwards.
  When, after mutual courtship, they had come to an understanding,
  They plighted their troths, and went to the immortal land.
  Hand in hand they two entered
  Into a stately mansion within the precincts
  Of the Palace of the Sea God.
  Here he might have dwelt for ever,
  Never growing old, and never dying.
  But the foolish man of this world
  Thus addressed his spouse:
  ' *For a little while I would return home*
  And speak to my father and my mother;
  To-morrow I will come again.'
  Thus he spake, and his wife replied:
  ' *If thou art to return again to the immortal land*
  And live with me as now,
  Beware how thou openest this casket.'
  Strongly did she enjoin this on him.
  But having returned to Suminoye,
  Though he looked for his house, no house could he see;
  Though he looked for the village, no village could he see.
  Wondering at this, the thought occurred to him:
  ' *In the space of three years, since I left my home,*

---

[1] The horizon.

> *Can my home have vanished, leaving not even the fence?*
> *Were I now to open this casket,*
> *Might it not appear as before?'*
> *So saying, he opened a little the precious casket,*
> *Whereupon a white cloud issued from it*
> *And spread away towards the immortal land.*
> *He ran, he shouted, he waved his sleeves,*
> *He writhed upon the earth, and ground his feet together.*
> *Of a sudden his heart melted away;*
> *Wrinkles covered his body, that had been so youthful;*
> *His hair, that had been so black, became white.*
> *By-and-by his breath also failed;*
> *At last his life departed.*
> *And, lo! here once stood the cottage*
> *Of Urashima of Midzunoye."*

Like most Naga-uta the above is followed by a thirty-one syllable poem known as a Hanka. The Hanka sometimes echoes the principal idea of the poem which precedes, and is at others employed as a sort of poetical save-all to utilise any stray scrap of thought or imagery which it may not have been convenient to include in the principal poem. Some Naga-uta have several Hanka appended to them.

HANKA

> " *In the immortal land*
> *He might have gone on to dwell;*
> *But by his nature*
> *How dull was he, this wight!"*

The authors of the two following lyrics are unnamed.

MOUNT FUJI (FUJIYAMA)

> " *Where on the one hand is the province of Kai,*
> *And on the other the land of Suruga,*
> *Right in the midst between them*
> *Stands out the high peak of Fuji.*
> *The very clouds of heaven dread to approach it;*
> *Even the soaring birds reach not its summit in their flight.*

Its burning fire is quenched by the snow;
The snow that falls is melted by the fire.
No words may tell of it, no name know I that is fit for it,
But a wondrous deity it surely is!
That lake we call the Sea of Se
Is contained within it;
That river which men, as they cross it, call the Fuji
Is the water which flows down from it;
Of Yamato, the Land of Sunrise,
It is the peace-giver, it is the god, it is the treasure.
On the peak of Fuji, in the land of Suruga,
I never weary of gazing."

POVERTY

The following is exceptional, as giving a glimpse of the condition of the poorer classes. It contains lines in which Buddhist influence is traceable.

" 'Tis night: mingled with the storm the rain is falling;
Mingled with the rain the snow is falling.
So cold am I, I know not what to do.
I take up and suck coarse salt [fish ?]
And sip a brew of saké dregs;
I cough, I sneeze and sneeze, I cannot help it.
I may stroke my beard, and think proudly to myself,
Who is there like me?
But so cold am I, I pull over me the hempen coverlet,
And huddle upon me all the nuno cloaks I have got.

Yet even this chilly night
Are there not others still poorer,
Whose parents are starving of cold and hunger,
Whose wife and children are begging their food with tears?

(The poet fancies himself addressing such a person.)

' At such a time how do you pass your days?'

(Answer.)

' Heaven and earth are wide, but for me they have become narrow;
The sun and moon are bright, but for me they yield no radiance.

Is it so with all men, or with me alone?
Born a man by the rarest of chances,
I am made in human shape like another,
Yet on my shoulders I wear a nuno cloak void of padding,
Which hangs down in tatters like seaweed—
A mere mass of rags.
Within my hut, twisted out of shape,
Straw is strewn on the bare floor of earth.
Father and mother at my pillow,
Wife and children at my feet,
Gather round me weeping and wailing,
With voices as from the throat of the nuye bird.
For no smoke rises from the kitchen furnace,
In the pot spiders have hung their webs,
The very art of cooking is forgotten.
To crown all—cutting off the end, as the proverb has it,
Of a thing that is too short already—
Comes the head man of the village with his rod,
His summons [to forced labour] penetrates to my sleeping-place.
Such helpless misery is but the way of the world.' "

It is characteristic of the difference between the Japanese and English languages, that this poem in the original contains only seven personal (including possessive and relative) pronouns.

SOME TANKA

No Edward FitzGerald has yet come to give us an English metrical version of the best Tanka of the *Manyō-shiu* and *Kokinshiu*. A prose rendering must serve in the meantime. The translations correspond mostly line for line to the original.

The following are ten of a set of thirteen Tanka composed in praise of saké by Ōtomo-no-Yakamochi (died 785), after Hitomaro and Akahito, the most distinguished poet of his day. This is not a very common theme of the Japanese poet, and its choice is probably due to Chinese influence.

> " *Ah! how true was that saying*
> *Of the great sage*
> *Of the times of old,*
> *Who gave to saké*
> *The name of ' Sage.'* "

> " *It was saké*
> *That was the thing most loved,*
> *Even by the seven wise men*
> *Of the days of old.*"

> " *Better than talk*
> *That would be wise,*
> *Were it even to drink saké*
> *Until you weep tears*
> *Of drunkenness.*"

> " *More than I can say,*
> *More than I can do to show it,*
> *An exceeding noble thing*
> *Is saké.*"

> " *If it turned out*
> *That I were aught else but man,*
> *I would be*
> *A saké-jar,*
> *For then I should get soaked.*"

> " *Hateful in my eyes*
> *Is the sententious prig*
> *Who will not drink saké.*
> *When I look on such a one*
> *I find him to resemble an ape.*" [1]

> " *Talk of priceless treasures!*
> *Can they be more precious*
> *Than a single cup*
> *Of thick saké?*"

---

[1] The official edition of the *Manyōshiu* has bestowed eight pages of commentary on this last stanza.

> " *Talk of jewels*
> *Which shine by night!*
> *Can they give so much pleasure*
> *As drinking saké*
> *To drive away one's care?*"

> " *Many are the ways*
> *Of this world's pleasures;*
> *But none to my mind*
> *Is like that of getting mellow,*
> *Even to tears.*"

> " *So long as in this world*
> *I have my pleasure,*
> *In the future existence*
> *What care I though I become*
> *An insect or a bird?*"

Spring is a more favourite subject. The following are by various authors :—

> " *On the plum blossoms*
> *Thick fell the snow;*
> *I wished to gather some*
> *To show to thee,*
> *But it melted in my hands.*"

> " *The plum blossoms*
> *Had already been scattered,*
> *But notwithstanding*
> *The white snow*
> *Has fallen deep in the garden.*"

> " *Among the hills*
> *The snow still lies—*
> *But the willows*
> *Where the torrents rush together*
> *Are in full bud.*"

> " *O thou willow*
> *That I see every morn,*
> *Hasten to become a thick grove*
> *Whereto the nightingale* [1]
> *May resort and sing.*"

---

[1] The bird which it is necessary in an English translation to call the nightingale is not our songster, but an allied species, the Uguisu or Cettia cantans.

" *Before the wind of spring*
  Has tangled the fine threads
  Of the green willow—
  Now, I would show it
  To my love."

" *The time of the cherry blossoms*
  Is not yet past—
  Yet now they ought to fall
  Whilst the love of those who look on them
  Is at its height."

" *Fall gently*
  O thou rain of spring!
  And scatter not
  The cherry flowers
  Until I have seen them."

" *When I went out*
  Over the moor,
  Where the haze was rising,
  The nightingale sang;
  Spring, it seems, has come."

" *My days pass in longing,*
  And my heart melts
  Like the hoar-frost
  On the water-plants
  When spring has come."

" *In yearning love*
  I have endured till night.
  But to-morrow's long spring day
  With its rising mists,
  How shall I ever pass it?"

It is not without some resemblance to the English bird, being of the same size, and of a plain greyish colour. Its habits are not specially nocturnal, but when singing it seeks the deepest shade of a bush or thicket, a condition which the Japanese simulate by covering its cage with paper so as to produce an artificial gloom. The repertory of the Uguisu is by no means so varied as that of the nightingale, but for liquid melody of note it is unsurpassed by any songster whatever. Its brief melodious utterances are no inapt emblem of the national poetry.

" *My love is thick*
  As the herbage in spring,
  It is manifold as the waves
  That heap themselves on the shore
  Of the great ocean."

" *No more will I plant for thee*
  Tall trees,
  O cuckoo ! [1]
  Thou comest, and with thy resounding cry
  Dost increase my yearnings."

" *This morn at dawn*
  The cuckoo's cry I heard.
  Didst thou hear it, my lord,
  Or wast thou still asleep ?"

" *I will plant for thee*
  A whole grove of orange-trees,
  O thou cuckoo !
  Where thou mayst always dwell,
  Even until the winter."

" *It is dawn ;*
  I cannot sleep for thoughts of her I love.
  What is to be done
  With this cuckoo
  That goes on singing ?"

" *Were only thy hand*
  Lying in mine,
  What matter though men's words
  Were copious as the herbage
  Of the summer meads."

" *Since we are such things*
  That if we are born
  We must some day die,
  So long as this life lasts
  Let us enjoy ourselves."

---

[1] The Japanese have quite different associations with the cuckoo from ourselves. They hear in its cry the longings of unsatisfied love. It is true that it is not the same bird as ours, but an allied species with a different note. Its name (in Japanese, Hototogisu) is onomatopoetic.

> " *To what shall I compare*
> *This life of ours?*
> *It is like a boat*
> *Which at daybreak rows away*
> *And leaves no trace behind it.*" [1]

> " *I would go to some land*
> *Where no cuckoos are,*
> *I am so melancholy*
> *When I hear*
> *Their note.*"

> " *The rippling* [2] *wistaria*
> *That I planted by my house*
> *As a memento*
> *Of thee whom I love,*
> *Is at length in blossom.*"

> " *When the cuckoo sang,*
> *Straightway I drove him off,*
> *Bidding him go to you.*
> *I wonder did he reach you?*"

> " *Go, thou cuckoo,*
> *And tell my lord,*
> *Who is too busy*
> *To come to see me,*
> *How much I love him.*"

> " *Granted that I*
> *Am hateful to you,*
> *But the flowering orange,*
> *That grows by my dwelling,*
> *Will you really not come to see it?*"

> " *I wear no clothing*
> *Drenched with dew*
> *From wending my way through the summer herbage;*
> *But yet the sleeve of my garment*
> *Is never for a moment dry [from tears].*"

---

[1] The sentiment of this poem is Buddhist. The transitoriness of life is a constant refrain all through Japanese literature.

[2] The flowers are supposed to resemble waves.

"'Tis the sixth month,
The sun is shining,
So that the very ground is cracked ;
But even so, how shall my sleeve become dry
If I never meet thee ?"

" On the spring moor
To gather violets
I went forth ;
Its charm so held me
That I stayed¹ till morn."

—AKAHITO.

" Oh ! the misery of loving,
Hidden from the world
Like a maiden-lily
Growing amid the thick herbage
Of the summer plain ! "

" The sky is a sea
Where the cloud-billows rise ;
And the moon is a bark ;
To the groves of the stars
It is oaring its way."

" Oh ! that the white waves far out
On the sea of Ise
Were but flowers,
That I might gather them
And bring them as a gift to my love ! "

—PRINCE AKI, A.D. 740.

Although the *Nihongi*,² being in the Chinese language, does not fall within the proper scope of this work, it occupies so conspicuous a position among books written in Japan, that it deserves a passing notice. In it we have a collection of the national myths, legends, poetry, and history from the earliest times down to A.D. 697, prepared

¹ No doubt to be understood metaphorically of a visit to his love.
² Translated by W. G. Aston in the *Transactions of the Japan Society*, 1896.

under official auspices and completed A.D. 720. It is the first of a long series of official histories in Chinese. They are for the most part dreary compilations in which none but students of history, anthropology, and kindred subjects are likely to take much interest. The writers were content to record events in their chronological sequence from month to month and from day to day, without any attempt to trace the connection between them or to speculate upon their causes. The attention to Chinese composition and studies, which the use of this language necessitated, had, however, some important effects. It served to engross the attention of the men, the cultivation of the native literature being left in a great measure to the women, and it helped to familiarise the Japanese with better models of style than they could find in their own country.

BOOK THE THIRD

HEIAN (CLASSICAL) PERIOD (800–1186)

BOOK THE THIRD

HEIAN (CLASSICAL) PERIOD (800-1186)

CHAPTER I

INTRODUCTORY

IN 794 the capital was removed to the site of the present city of Kiōto. It received the name of Heian-jō, or the "City of Peace." The Mikados continued to make it their residence until the revolution of 1868, but the term "Heian period" is restricted to the time when Kiōto was the real seat of government, namely, about four centuries. When Yoritomo, at the end of this period, established the Shōgunate, or rule of the military caste, at Kamakura, in the east of Japan, all practical authority was transferred thither.

With the founding of Heian-jō (Kiōto) the wave of progress which received its impulse from the combined influences of Chinese learning and the Buddhist religion reached its height, and a period of great material prosperity ensued. But the usual results were not long in manifesting themselves. The ruling classes became indolent and luxurious, and neglected the arts of government for the pursuit of pleasure. There was great laxity of morals, as the literature of the period abundantly shows ; but learning flourished, and a high state of refinement prevailed in that narrow circle which surrounded the Mikado and his court.

The Heian period is the classical age of Japanese literature. Its poetry may not quite reach the standard of the *Manyōshiu*, but it contains much that is of admirable quality, while in the abundance and excellence of its prose writings it leaves the Nara period far behind. The language had now attained to its full development. With its rich system of terminations and particles, it was a pliant instrument in the writer's hands, and the vocabulary was varied and copious to a degree which is astonishing when we remember that it was drawn almost exclusively from native sources. The few words of Chinese origin which it contains seem to have found their way in through the spoken language, and are not taken straight from Chinese books, as at a later stage when Japanese authors loaded their periods with alien vocables to an extent for which our most Johnsonian English affords a feeble parallel.

The literature of the Heian period reflects the pleasure-loving and effeminate, but cultured and refined character of the class of Japanese who produced it. It has no serious, masculine qualities. History, theology, science, law—in short, all learned and thoughtful works were composed in the Chinese language, and were of poor literary quality. The native literature may be described in one word as belles-lettres. It consists of poetry, fiction, diaries, and essays of a desultory kind, called by the Japanese Zuihitsu, or "following the pen," the only exceptions being a few works of a more or less historical character which appeared towards the close of the period.

The lower classes of the people had no share in the literary activity of this time. Culture had not as yet penetrated beyond a very narrow circle. Both writers and readers belonged exclusively to the official caste. The people from time to time showed their dissatisfaction with oppression and misgovernment, but their discontent found no expression in literature. It took the form of outbreaks and rebellions, robbery and piracy.

It is a remarkable and, I believe, unexampled fact, that a very large and important part of the best literature which Japan has produced was written by women. We have seen that a good share of the Nara poetry is of feminine authorship. In the Heian period the women took a still more conspicuous part in maintaining the honour of the native literature. The two greatest works which have come down to us from this time are both by women. This was no doubt partly due to the absorption of the masculine intellect in Chinese studies, and to the contempt of the stronger sex for such frivolous pursuits as the writing of poetry and romances. But there was still a more effective cause. The position of women in ancient Japan was very different from what it afterwards became when Chinese ideas were in the ascendant. The Japanese of this early period did not share the feeling common to most Eastern countries, that women should be kept in subjection, and, as far as possible, in seclusion. Feminine chieftains are frequently mentioned in the old histories, and several even of the Mikados were women. Indeed the Chinese seem to have thought that the "monstrous regiment of women" was the rule in Japan at this time; at least they often styled it the "Queen-country." Many instances might be quoted of Japanese women exercising an influence and maintaining an independence of conduct quite at variance with our preconceived notions of the position of women in the East. It is this which gives their literary work an air of freedom and originality which it would be vain to expect in the writings of inmates of a harem.

The fact that the Heian literature was largely the work of women no doubt accounts partly for its gentle, domestic character. It abounds in descriptions of scenes of home and court life, and of amours and sentimental or romantic incidents. Though the morality which it reveals is anything but strait-laced, the language is uniformly refined and decent, in this respect resembling the best literature of China, upon which the Japanese taste was formed, and contrasting strongly with the pornographic school of popular fiction which disgraced Japan in the eighteenth and nineteenth centuries.

The Heian period witnessed an important advance in the art of writing, the invention of the phonetic script known as Kana. The ancient Japanese had no writing. When they began to write their own language phonetically they had no alternative but to use Chinese ideographs for the purpose. This system was open to two objections. A Chinese character is a complicated contrivance, consisting of numerous strokes, and as a complete character was required for each syllable of the polysyllabic Japanese words, an intolerable cumbersomeness was the result. The second objection was that a given Japanese syllable might be represented by any one of several Chinese characters. Some hundreds were actually in use to write the forty-seven syllables of which the language consists. It was no easy matter to remember so many, either in reading or in writing. To meet these difficulties the Japanese did two things : they restricted themselves to a limited number of characters for use as phonetic signs, and they wrote these in an abbreviated or cursive form. There are two varieties of the script thus produced, which are known as the Katakana and Hiragana. No exact date can be assigned for their introduction, but for the present purpose it is sufficient to know that both had come into use by the end of the ninth century. They simplified writing enormously. It is hardly too much to say that without them the labour of committing to paper the lengthy compositions of this period would have given pause to the most industrious scribes.

CHAPTER II

POETRY—THE "KOKINSHIU"

FOR seventy or eighty years after the establishment of the capital at Heian or Kiōto, Chinese learning monopolised the attention of the nation. No prose writings of importance in the Japanese language have come down to us from this period. The native poetry also languished. Chinese verse composition was the fashion, Mikados and even princesses being numbered among the adepts in this accomplishment. The end of the ninth century, however, saw a revival of Japanese poetry. We now meet with the names of Yukihira, Narihira, Ōtomo no Kuronushi, and others, followed in the early part of the tenth by Ki no Tsurayuki, Ōshi Kōji, Henjō, and Ono no Komachi (a poetess).

In A.D. 905 the Mikado Daigo instructed a committee of officials of the Department of Japanese Poetry, consisting of Ki no Tsurayuki and other poets, to make a collection of the best pieces which had been produced during the previous one hundred and fifty years. The Anthology known as the *Kokinshiu* (Poems, Ancient and Modern) was the result of their labours. It was completed about 922, and contains over eleven hundred poems, arranged under the headings of Spring, Summer, Autumn, Winter, Felicitations, Partings, Journeys, Names of Things, Love, Sorrow, and Miscellaneous. Only five of this number are in the longer metre called Naga-uta, the rest being Tanka of thirty-one syllables, with a few in somewhat similar short metres.

The neglect of the Naga-uta for the Tanka which is indicated by these figures was no passing phase of Japanese poetry. It has continued up to our own day, with fatal consequences, and has been a bar to all real progress in the poetic art. How a nation which possessed in the Naga-uta an instrument not unfitted, as there are examples to show, for the production of narrative, elegiac, and other poems, could practically confine itself for many centuries to a form of poetic expression within whose narrow limits nothing more substantial than aphorisms, epigrams, conceits, or brief exclamations can be contained, is a question which it is more easy to ask than to answer.

Much of the poetry of this time was the outcome of poetical tournaments, at which themes were proposed to the competitors by judges who examined each phrase and word with the minutest critical care before pronouncing their verdict. As might be expected, the poetry produced under these circumstances is of a more or less artificial type, and is wanting in the spontaneous vigour of the earlier essays of the Japanese muse. Conceits, acrostics, and untranslatable word-plays hold much too prominent a place; but for perfection of form, the poems of this time are unrivalled. It is no doubt to this quality that the great popularity of this collection is due. Sei Shōnagon, writing in the early years of the eleventh century, sums up a young lady's education as consisting of writing, music, and the twenty volumes of the *Kokinshiu*. Subsequent poetry is evidently modelled on it rather than on the more archaic poems of the *Manyōshiu*. Even at the present day the *Kokinshiu* is the best known and most universally studied of all the numerous anthologies of Japanese poetry.

SOME TANKA FROM THE "KOKINSHIU"

> " Who could it have been
> That first gave love
> This name?
> 'Dying' is the plain word
> He might well have used."

Neatly rendered by Mr. Chamberlain :—

> " O love! who gave thee thy superfluous name?
> Loving and dying—is it not the same?"

The personification of love, however, is hardly in the Japanese style.

> " Do I forget thee
> Even for so brief a space
> As the ears of grain
> On the fields of autumn
> Are lit up by the lightning's glare?"

> " I fell asleep while thinking of thee;
> Perchance for this reason
> I saw thee in a dream!
> Had I only known it to be one
> I would not have awaked."

> " Shall we call that only a dream
> Which we see
> While asleep:
> This vain world itself
> I cannot regard as a reality."

> " I know that my life
> Has no assurance of to-morrow;
> But to-day,
> So long as darkness has not yet fallen,
> I will grieve for him who has passed away."

> ' *O thou cuckoo*
> *Of the ancient capital*
> *Of Iso no Kami!* [*Nara*]
> *Thy voice alone*
> *Is all that is left of the olden time.*"

Tsurayuki, having met with a cool reception at his native place, plucks a branch of flowering plum, and exclaims—

> " *Its people? Ah well!*
> *I know not their hearts,*
> *But in my native place*
> *The flowers with their ancient*
> *Fragrance are odorous.*"

> " *The hue of the flowers*
> *Mingles with the snow,*
> *So that it cannot be seen;*
> *But their presence may be known*
> *Were it only by the perfume.*"

> " *I came and found thee not:*
> *Wetter far is my sleeve*
> *Than if I had threaded my way at morn*
> *Through the bamboo-grass*
> *Of the autumn plain.*"

> " *This night of spring,*
> *Of formless gloom,*
> *The colour of the plum-flowers*
> *Cannot, indeed, be seen;*
> *But how can their perfume be hidden?*"

> " *What is it that makes me feel so desolate*
> *This evening*
> *While I wait*
> *For one who comes not?*
> *Can it be the blowing of the* [*chill*] *autumn wind?*"

> " *I would that thy heart*
> *Were melted unto me,*
> *As when spring comes*
> *The ice thaws away*
> *And leaves no remainder.*"

> " *For many a year*
> *The fire in me of love*
> *Has not been quenched,*
> *Yet my frozen sleeve* [*soaked with tears*]
> *Is still unthawed.*"

> " *It is I alone*
> *Who am most miserable,*
> *For no year passes*
> *In which even the ' Cow-herd'*
> *Does not meet his love.*"

There is here an allusion to the Chinese story, according to which the Cow-herd, one of a group of stars near the River of Heaven (the Milky Way), is the lover of a star on the other side called the Spinster. They are separated all the year round except on the seventh day of the seventh month, when magpies bridge over the River of Heaven, so as to allow the pair to meet. Both Chinese and Japanese poetry contain numberless allusions to this legend.

The most convenient of the many editions of the *Kokinshiu* is Motoöri's *Tō-Kagami*. It contains a modern colloquial paraphrase of the original.

CHAPTER III

PROSE—"KOKINSHIU" PREFACE, "TOSA NIKKI,"
"TAKETORI MONOGATARI," "ISE MONOGA-
TARI," MINOR WORKS

The "Kokinshiu" Preface

ABOUT two centuries elapsed after the *Kojiki* was written
without any substantial addition being made to the prose
literature of Japan. Some of the Norito and Imperial
edicts described in a previous chapter belong to this
period, but it was not until the early part of the tenth
century that Japanese writers took up in earnest the
practice of prose composition in their native language.
KI NO TSURAYUKI, the poet and editor of the *Kokinshiu*,
was the first in the field.

But few details of his life have reached us. He was
a court noble who traced his descent in a direct line
from one of the Mikados, and his history is little more
than the record of the successive offices which he held
at Kiōto and in the provinces. He died A.D. 946.

His famous preface to the *Kokinshiu* was written
about 922. It has to this day a reputation in Japan as
the *ne plus ultra* of elegance in style. Later literature is
full of allusions to it, and it has served as the model for
countless similar essays. It is interesting as the first
attempt to discuss such a philosophical question as the

nature of poetry in a thoughtful spirit. I transcribe the
more important passages :—

"The poetry of Yamato (Japan) has the human heart
for its seed, and grows therefrom into the manifold forms
of speech. Men are full of various activities, among
which poetry is that which consists in expressing the
thoughts of their hearts by metaphors taken from what
they see or hear.

"Listening to the nightingale singing among the
flowers or to the cry of the frog which dwells in the
water, we recognise the truth that of all living things
there is not one which does not utter song. It is poetry
by which, without an effort, heaven and earth are moved,
and gods and demons invisible to our eyes are touched
with sympathy. By poetry the converse of lovers is
made gentler, and the hearts of fierce warriors soothed.

"Poetry began when heaven and earth were created.
But of that which has been handed down to our day, the
first was made in everlasting heaven by Shita-teru-hime,
and on the ore-yielding earth by Susa-no-wo. In the
age of the swift gods it would seem that as yet there was
no established metre. Their poetry was artless in form
and hard of comprehension. It was in the age of man
that Susa-no-wo made the first poetry of thirty and one
syllables. And so by the varied multiplication of
thoughts and language we came to express our love
for flowers, our envy of birds, our emotion at the sight
of the hazes which usher in the spring, or our grief at
beholding the dew.[1] As a distant journey is begun by
our first footstep and goes on for months and years, as a
high mountain has its beginning in the dust of its base
and at length rises aloft and extends across the sky like

[1] Dew with the Japanese poets suggests tears, and is associated with grief.

the clouds of heaven, so gradual must have been the rise of poetry.

. . . .

" In the present day love has seduced men's hearts into a fondness for ornament. Hence nothing is produced but frivolous poetry without depth of feeling. In the houses of those given to a life of gallantry, poetry is like a tree buried in the ground and unknown to men ; while with more serious people it is regarded as a flowering suzuki [1] which will never bear ears of grain. If we consider its origin, this ought not to be. The Mikados of former times, on a morning when the spring flowers were in blossom, or on a night when the autumn moon was shining, used to send for their courtiers and demand from them verses suitable to the occasion. Some would represent themselves as wandering in trackless places in search of the flowers they loved ; others would describe their groping in the guideless dark and longing for the moon. The Mikado would then examine all such fancies, and pronounce this to be clever, that to be stupid.

" Or else they wished prosperity to their lord, using the metaphors of pebbles [2] or of Mount Tsukuba.[3] When joy was too much for them, when their hearts overflowed with pleasure, when they felt their love to be eternal as

---

[1] A kind of grass.

[2] " *May our lord*
Live for a thousand ages,
Until the pebbles
Become a rock
Overgrown with moss."

[3] " *Mount Tsukuba [which has two peaks]*
Has a shadow
On this side and on that,
But the shadow of Our Lord
Has no shadow to excel it."

the smoke which rises from Mount Fuji, when they longed for a friend with the yearning of the cry of the matsumushi [a kind of cicada], when the sight of the pair of fir-trees of Takasago and Suminoye suggested a husband and wife growing old together, when they thought of their bygone days of manly vigour, or grudged to the past the one time of maiden bloom, it was with poetry that they comforted their hearts. Again, when they looked upon the flowers shed from their stalks on a spring morning, or heard the leaves falling on an autumnal eve, or every year lamented the snow and waves [*i.e.* grey hairs] reflected in a mirror ; or, seeing the dew upon the grass or the foam upon water, were startled to recognise in them emblems of their own lives ; or else, but yesterday in all the pride of prosperity, to-day, with a turn of fortune, saw themselves doomed to a wretched life, those dear to them estranged ; or again drew metaphors from the waves and the fir-clad mountain or the spring of water in the midst of the moor, or gazed on the under leaves of the autumn lespedeza, or counted the times a snipe preens its feathers at dawn, or compared mankind to a joint of bamboo floating down a stream, or expressed their disgust with the world by the simile of the river Yoshino, or heard that the smoke no longer rises from Mount Fuji, or that the bridge of Nagara had been repaired—in all these cases poetry it was by which they soothed their hearts."

The above are allusions to well-known poems. Tsurayuki traces briefly the history of Japanese poetry in the Nara period, and then goes on to speak of the more recent poets whose effusions find a place in the collection he had made. The following may have some interest as the earliest example of literary criticism in Japan :—

" Henjō excels in form, but substance is wanting. The emotion produced by his poetry is evanescent, and may be compared to that which we experience at the sight of a beautiful woman in a painting. Narihira overflows with sentiment, but his language is deficient. His verse is like a flower which, although withered and without bloom, yet retains its fragrance. Yasuhide is skilful in the use of words, but they match ill with his matter, as if a shopkeeper were to dress himself in fine silks. Kisen is profound, but the connection between the beginning and the end is indistinct. He may be compared to the autumn moon, which, as we gaze on it, is obscured by the clouds of dawn. We have not much of his poetry, so that we gain little towards understanding it by a comparison of one poem with another. Ono no Komachi belongs to the school of Soto-ori-hime of ancient times. There is feeling in her poems, but little vigour. She is like a lovely woman who is suffering from ill health. Want of vigour, however, is only natural in a woman's poetry. Kuronushi's verse is poor in form. He resembles a woodman burdened with faggots resting in the shade of flowers."

" TOSA NIKKI "

Another work of Tsurayuki's is the *Tosa Nikki* or Tosa Diary. It was written on a journey back to Kiōto after having completed his term of four years' service as Prefect of that province.

The first entry bears date the 21st day of the twelfth month, and we learn from other sources that the year was the fourth year of Shōhei. This would be, according to the European reckoning, some time in the months of January or February A.D. 935.

Tsurayuki begins by telling his readers that diaries being commonly written by men, this is an attempt to write a woman's diary ; meaning, that it was in the Japanese language and written character, not in Chinese. He then records his departure from the Government House of Tosa, and his arrival at the port from which he was to sail.   He was accompanied hither by large numbers of people who came to take leave of him. Most brought with them parting presents, usually of eatables or saké.   The result was that in Tsurayuki's words, "Strange to say, here we were all fresh by the shore of the salt sea."   He did not actually set sail till the 27th, the intervening six days being chiefly taken up in disposing of the presents, and in a visit to the newly appointed Prefect, with whom he spent a day and night in drinking and verse-making, after which he took a final leave.   Tsurayuki's successor in office shook hands with him at the bottom of the steps leading up to the house, and they bade each other farewell with many cordial but tipsy expressions of good-will on both sides. On the following day, however, we find Tsurayuki in a different frame of mind.   He tells us that during his stay in Tosa a girl had died who was born in Kiōto, and that amid all the bustle and confusion of leaving port, her friends could think of nothing but her.   Some one, he says, composed this verse of poetry on the occasion : " With the joyful thought, ' Home to Kiōto,' there mingles the bitter reflection that there is one who never will return."   We are informed by another writer that Tsurayuki here deplores the loss of his own daughter, a little girl of nine years of age.

But the jollifications had not yet come to an end.   The new Prefect's brother made his appearance at a projecting cape on their way to the first stopping-place, and they were accordingly obliged to land on the beach, where there was more drinking and composing of verses. Of these Tsurayuki seems to have had no great opinion. He says that it required the united efforts of two of the party to make one bad verse, and compares them to two fishermen labouring along with a heavy net on their shoulders. Their jollity was interrupted by the master of the junk, who summoned them on board. There was a fair wind, he said, and the tide served ; and Tsurayuki maliciously adds that there was no more saké to drink. They accordingly embarked, and proceeded on their voyage.

On the 29th they had got no farther than Ominato, a harbour only a few miles distant from their starting-point. Here they were detained for ten days waiting for a fair wind. Presents of eatables and drinkables still came in, but more sparingly, and Tsurayuki records regretfully the fate of a bottle of saké which he had fastened on the roof of the cabin, but which was displaced by the rolling of the junk and fell overboard. One of these presents was a pheasant, which, according to the old Japanese custom, was attached to a flowering branch of plum. Some brought verses with their gifts. Here is a specimen : " Louder than the clamour of the white surges on your onward path will be the cry of me weeping that I am left behind." Tsurayuki remarks that if that were really so, he must have a very loud voice.

On the 9th of the second month they at last sailed from Ominato. As they passed Matsubara, they admired a large grove of ancient firs which grew by the sea-shore. Tsurayuki mentions the pleasure with which they watched the cranes flying about among their tops,

and gives us this verse composed on the occasion:
"Casting my glance over the sea, on each fir-tree[1] top
a crane has his dwelling. They have been comrades for
a thousand years."

It became dark before they reached their next stopping-
place. The idea of pursuing their voyage all night long
does not seem to have occurred to them. Besides, to
judge from its having gone up the Osaka river as far as
Yamazaki, their junk must have been a very small one,
and the diary shows that it depended more on oars than
on sails. Here is Tsurayuki's description of nightfall:—

"Whilst we rowed along gazing on this scene, the
mountains and the sea became all dark, the night deep-
ened, and east and west could not be distinguished, so we
entrusted all thought of the weather to the mind of the
master of our ship. Even the men who were not accustomed to the sea became very sad, and still more the
women, who rested their heads on the bottom of the ship
and did nothing but weep. The sailors, however, seemed
to think nothing of it, and sung the following boat-song."
Tsurayuki gives a few lines of it, and then proceeds.
"There was a great deal more of this kind of stuff, but I
do not write it down. Listening to the laughter at these
verses, our hearts became somewhat calmed in spite of
the raging of the sea. It was quite dark when we at
length reached our anchorage for the night."

Three more days leisurely travelling brought them to
Murotsu, a port just to the west of the eastern of the two
horns which the island of Shikoku sends out to the
southward. The morning after their arrival here, a slight
but constant rain prevented them from starting, and the
passengers took the opportunity to go on shore for a

[1] Both the crane and the fir are, in Japan, emblems of long life.

bath. In the entry for this day, Tsurayuki mentions a curious superstition. He tells us that since the day on which they first embarked, no one wore scarlet or other rich colours or good silks, lest they should incur the anger of the gods of the sea. The next day the rain continued. It was a Buddhist fast-day, and Tsurayuki kept it faithfully till noon ; but as suitable food for fast-days was not obtainable on board, he bought with rice (not having any copper cash) a *tai* which one of the sailors had caught the day before. This was the beginning of a trade between him and the sailors, saké and rice being exchanged for fish. There was no change in the weather till the 17th, the fifth day from their arrival at Murotsu. On that day they started early in the morning with the moon, then just past the full, shining over a waveless sea, which reflected the sky so perfectly, that, as Tsurayuki said, the heaven above and the ocean beneath could not be distinguished. He composed the following stanza on this occasion : "What is this that strikes against my oar as the boat is rowed along over the moon of the sea-depths ? Is it the bush of the man in the moon ?"

The fine weather, however, did not continue. Dark clouds gathering overhead alarmed the master of the junk, and they put back to Murotsu under a pelting shower, and feeling very miserable. Three more wretched days they were obliged to remain here, endeavouring with indifferent success to while away the time by writing Chinese and Japanese verses, and every morning counting the days that had been already spent on the voyage. On the 21st they again proceeded on their way. A large number of other junks sailed at the same time, a pretty sight, which was greatly admired by Tsurayuki. " It was spring," he remarks, "but it seemed as if over the sea the leaves of autumn were being scattered." The weather was now fine, and they entered what we call the Kii Channel.

Here they were disturbed by a fresh cause of anxiety. It seems that Tsurayuki during his term of office in Tosa had had occasion to deal rather severely with the pirates of these parts, and it was thought likely that they would now try to have their revenge. One of the commentators attempts to save Tsurayuki's reputation for courage by reminding us that this diary is written in the character of a woman. The course of the narrative shows that their fears were to all appearance well grounded. Two days later we find them praying to the Kami and Hotoke [1] to save them from the pirates. On the following days there were constant alarms, and on the 26th they heard that the pirates were actually in pursuit of them, so they left their anchorage at midnight and put to sea. There was a place on their way where it was usual to make offerings to the God of the Sea. Tsurayuki made the captain offer *nusa*. [2] They were offered by being cast into the air, and allowing the wind to carry them to the sea. The *nusa* fell in an easterly direction, and the junk's course was turned to the same quarter. To the great joy of all on board, they had now a favourable wind, sail was set, and they made a good day's run. The next two days they were again storm-bound, but on the 29th they proceeded on their voyage. On the 30th they crossed the entrance to the Naruto passage, and the same night, by dint of hard rowing, they reached the strait of Idzumi. They had now reached the Gokinai, or five provinces round Kiōto, and here there was

---

[1] Shinto and Buddhist gods.
[2] The strips of white paper seen in Shinto shrines, and also called *gohei*.

no longer any fear of pirates. The 1st day of the second month they made little way, and on the 2nd we have the following entry : " The rain and wind ceased not ; a whole day and a whole night we prayed to the Kami and Hotoke." On the next day the weather was equally bad, and on the 4th the captain would not put to sea, from a fear of bad weather which proved quite groundless. There were a great many beautiful shells on the beach at this place, and Tsurayuki composed these lines in allusion to a shell which is called in Japanese the *wasure-gai* or "shell of forgetfulness:" " I would descend from my ship to gather the shell of forgetfulness of one for whom I am filled with sorrowful longing. Do ye, oh ye advancing surges, drive it forward to the strand." He afterwards says that the true wish of his heart was not to forget her whom he had lost, but only to give such respite to his sorrow that it might afterwards gain greater strength.

The following is part of the entry for the 5th, the day before they arrived in the Osaka river. They were now opposite Sumiyoshi.

" Meanwhile a sudden gale sprung up, and in spite of all our efforts we fell gradually to leeward, and were in great danger of being sent to the bottom. ' This god of Sumiyoshi,' said the captain, ' is like other gods. What he desires is not any of the fashionable articles of the day. Give him *nusa* as an offering.' The captain's advice was taken, and *nusa* were offered ; but as the wind, instead of ceasing, only blew harder and harder, and the danger from the storm and sea became more and more imminent, the captain again said, ' Because the august heart of the god is not moved for *nusa*, neither does the august ship move ; offer to him something in which he will take greater pleasure.' In compliance with this advice, I bethought me what it would be best to offer. ' Of eyes I have a pair—then let me give to the god my mirror, of which I have only one.' The mirror was accordingly flung into the sea, to my very great regret ; but no sooner had I done so than the sea itself became as smooth as a mirror."

The next day they entered the Osaka river. All the passengers, men, women, and children, were overjoyed at reaching this point of their voyage, and clasped their foreheads with their hands in ecstasies of delight. Several days were now spent in dragging the vessel laboriously against the strong current of the river. A fast-day occurred on their way up it, which Tsurayuki had this time the satisfaction of keeping properly by abstaining entirely from fish. On the 12th they reached Yamazaki, from which place a carriage (that is, one of the bullock-carts in which nobles rode) was sent for to Kiōto, and on the evening of the 16th they left Yamazaki for the capital. Tsurayuki was greatly delighted to re-cognise the old familiar landmarks as he rode along. He mentions the children's playthings and sweetmeats in the shops as looking exactly as when he went away, and wonders whether he will find as little change in the hearts of his friends. He had purposely left Yamazaki in the evening in order that it might be night when he reached his own dwelling. I translate his account of the state in which he found it :—

" When I reached my house and entered the gate the moon was shining brightly, and its condition was plainly to be seen. It was decayed and ruined beyond all description—worse even than I had been told. The heart of the man in whose charge I left it must have been in an equally dilapidated condition. The fence between the two houses had been broken down, so that both seemed but one, and he appeared to have fulfilled his charge by looking in through the gaps. And yet I had supplied him by every opportunity with the means of keeping it in repair. To-night, however, I would not allow him to be told this in an angry tone, but in spite of my vexation, offered him an acknowledgment for his trouble. There was in one place a sort of pond where water had collected in a hollow, by the side of which grew a fir-tree. It had lost half its branches, and looked as if a thousand years had passed during the five or six years of my absence. Younger trees had grown up round it, and the whole place was in a most neglected condition, so that every one said that it was pitiful to see. Among other sad thoughts that rose spontaneously to my mind was the memory—ah, how sorrowful !—of one who was born in this house, but who did not return here along with me. My fellow-travellers were chatting merrily with their children in their arms ; but I meanwhile, still unable to contain my grief, privately repeated these lines to one who knew my heart."

I shall not give the verses, but proceed to the last sentence of the diary, which is as follows : " I cannot write down all my many regrets and memories ; be it for good or for evil, here I will fling away my pen."

The *Tosa Nikki* is a striking example of the importance of style. It contains no exciting adventures or romantic situations ; there are in it no wise maxims or novel information ; its only merit is that it describes in simple yet elegant language, and with a vein of playful humour, the ordinary life of a traveller in Japan at the time when it was written. But this has proved sufficient to give it a high rank amongst Japanese classics, and has insured its being handed down to our own day as a most esteemed model for composition in the native Japanese style. It has been followed by many imitations, but has had no equal.

"TAKETORI MONOGATARI" AND "ISE MONOGATARI"

Monogatari, a word which will be frequently met with below, means "narrative." It is applied chiefly to fiction, but there are some true histories which fall under this denomination.

The date and authorship of both these books is unknown. We may, however, accept the opinion of the eminent native critic Motoöri, that they belong to a time not long after the period Yengi (901–922). Both are obviously the work of persons well versed in the literature of the day, and familiar with court life in Kiōto.

The *Taketori Monogatari*[1] is usually given the precedence in order of time. It is what we should call a fairy-tale. The scene is laid in the neighbourhood of Kiōto, and the personages are all Japanese. The language too is as nearly as possible pure Japanese. But there are abundant traces of foreign influences. The supernatural machinery is either Buddhist or Taoist, and most even of the incidents are borrowed from the copious fairy-lore of China.

An old man who earned a living by making bamboo-ware (*Taketori* means bamboo-gatherer) espied one day in the woods a bamboo with a shining stem. He split it open, and discovered in one of the joints a beautiful little maiden three inches in height. He took her home and adopted her as his daughter, giving her the name of

[1] Translated by Mr. F. V. Dickins in the *Journal of the Royal Asiatic Society*, January 1887.

Kaguyahime or the " shining damsel." She speedily grew up to womanhood, when her beauty attracted numerous admirers. To each of them she assigned a quest, promising that she would marry the suitor who successfully accomplished the task allotted to him. One lover was told to fetch Buddha's begging-bowl of stone from India; another to bring her a branch of the tree with roots of silver, stem of gold, and fruit of jewels, which grew in the fabulous island Paradise of Mount Hōrai. From the third she required a garment made of the fur of the fire-rat, supposed to be uninflammable. The fourth was to procure the shining jewel of many hues of the dragon's head, and the fifth a swallow's cowry-shell. They all failed. The maiden was then wooed by the Mikado, but equally in vain, though they remained on friendly terms and kept up an exchange of sentimental Tanka. She was eventually taken up to heaven in a flying chariot, brought by her relatives in the moon, whence it seems she had been banished to earth for an offence which she had committed.

The episode of the quest of the golden branch from Mount Hōrai may serve as a specimen of this work. Prince Kuramochi, to whom this task was allotted, having had a counterfeit branch made by cunning workmen, produces it and claims his reward. The old man asks him to tell in what manner of place he obtained this " marvellous, graceful, and lovely" branch. Prince Kuramochi thereupon relates his supposed voyage to Mount Hōrai, not, it will be observed, without some bungling and repetition natural to a man who has to make up his story as he goes along :—

" Three years ago, on the 10th day of the second month, we embarked from Osaka. We knew not what

course we should take when we put out to sea, but as
I felt that life would be valueless if I could not have my
heart's desire fulfilled, we sailed on, entrusting ourselves
to the empty winds. If we perish, thought we, there is no
help for it. So long as we live, however, we will sail on
until it may be we reach this island, called, it seems,
Mount Hōrai. With such thoughts we rowed on over
the ocean, and tossed about until we left far behind the
shores of our own land. In our wanderings we were at
one time like to go down even to the bottom of the sea
whilst the waves were raging ; at another time we were
borne by the wind to an unknown country where creatures like devils came forth and tried to kill us. At one
time, knowing neither the way we had come nor the
course we should follow, we were almost lost upon the
sea ; at another our provisions became spent, and we
used the roots of trees for food. Once beings hideous
beyond description came and attempted to devour us,
and once we sustained life by gathering shell - fish.
Under a strange sky, where there was none to render
us aid, we tossed about over the sea, a prey to diseases
of all kinds, and leaving the ship to her own spontaneous motion, for we knew not at all the course we
ought to follow. At last, when five hundred days had
passed, about the hour of the dragon a mountain became
faintly visible in the midst of the sea. All in the ship
gazed steadfastly at it, and saw that it was a very great
mountain which floated about upon the surface. Its
appearance was lofty and picturesque. This, we thought,
must be the mountain we are seeking. No wonder we
were filled with dread at its sight. We sailed round it for
two or three days. Then there came forth from amongst
the hills a woman clothed like an inhabitant of heaven,

and drew water in a silver vessel. When we saw her, we landed from the ship, and asked what might be the name of this mountain. The woman replied and said, 'This is Mount Hōrai.' Our joy was unbounded. 'And who,' we inquired, 'is she who tells us so?' 'My name is Hōkanruri,' she said, and of a sudden went away in among the hills.

"There seemed no way to climb this mountain, so we went round its side, where flowering trees unknown in this world were growing. Streams of golden, silver, and emerald hue flowed forth from it, spanned by bridges of all manner of jewels. Here stood shining trees, the least beautiful of which was that of which I brought away a branch, but, as it answered Kaguyahime's description, I plucked it and came away. That mountain is delightful beyond measure, and there is nothing in this world to compare with it. But when I had got the branch, I became impatient to return; so we embarked in our ship, and the wind being fair, arrived at Osaka after a voyage of over four hundred days. Urged by my great desire, I left for the capital yesterday, and now I present myself here without even changing my garments soaked with brine."

(I omit a verse of poetry in which the old man expresses his sympathy with the Prince's sufferings, and also the Prince's poetical reply.)

At this juncture a party of six men appeared in the courtyard. One of them, who held in his hand a cleft stick, with a paper in it, said: " I, Ayabe no Uchimaro, the head smith of your workshop, beg humbly to state— For more than a thousand days I and my men have laboured with all our strength and most heedful care in making for you the jewel-branch, but yet have received from you no wages. I pray you let me receive them, so that I may pay my men." So saying, he presented his paper. The old bamboo-cutter, with his head bowed down in thought, wondered what the words of this workman might mean, while the Prince, beside himself with dismay, felt as if his heart were melting within him. When Kagayuhime heard this, she said, " Bring me that paper." It read as follows :—

" My Lord the Prince,—When you shut yourself up for more than a thousand days with us mean workmen, and made us fashion the wonderful jewel-branch, you promised to reward us with official appointments. As we were lately thinking over this, we remembered that you had told us that the branch was required by the lady Kaguyahime, whose lord you were to be, and it occurred to us that in this palace we should receive our reward."

Kaguyahime, whose heart had been growing sadder and sadder as the sun went down, bloomed into smiles. She called the old man to her and said, " Truly I had thought that it was no other than the real tree of Mount Hōrai. Now that we know that it is but a sorry counterfeit, give it back to him at once."

Compared with the later literature of the Heian period, the style of the *Taketori* is artless and unformed, but its naïve simplicity accords well with the subject-matter, and is not without a charm of its own.

The *Ise Monogatari* is one of the most admired productions of the older Japanese literature. Its style is clear and concise, and far surpasses in elegance that of the *Taketori Monogatari*.

It consists of a number of short chapters which have little connection with each other, except that they all relate incidents in the life of a gay young nobleman of the court of Kiōto, who is usually identified with a real personage named Narihira. Narihira lived about a century before the date when the *Ise Monogatari* was written, but he is supposed to have left diaries on which this work was founded. What truth there may be in this it is now impossible to ascertain, nor does it much concern us to know. The long series of love affairs in which the hero is involved are more suggestive of fiction than of fact, and the most plausible explanation of the title of the work points to the same conclusion. It seems that the men of Ise, like the Cretans of old, were not remarkable for veracity, so that the author, by calling his work *Tales of Ise*, probably meant to convey a broad hint to his readers that they must not take everything in it for truth. A free rendering of *Ise Monogatari* would be *Tales for the Marines*—a title under which we should not expect to find a very conscientious adherence to actual fact.

It is a caprice of the author to make all his chapters begin with the word *Mukashi*, the Japanese equivalent of the "a long time ago" of our fairy tales. Each serves as a setting for one or two little poems of more than average merit which are put into the mouth of the hero and his numerous inamoratas.

The first few chapters relate some juvenile love adventures of the hero. The following may serve as a specimen :—

"A long time ago there dwelt a woman in the Western Pavilion which was occupied by the Empress in East Gojō.[1] Here she was visited by one who loved her

---

[1] The city of Kiōto is divided into sections by parallel streets somewhat in the fashion of the "Avenues" of New York. Gojō (fifth column) is one of these. It is the principal shopping street of Kiōto at the present day.

deeply, though in secret. About the 10th day of the first month she concealed herself elsewhere. He learned where she was living, but as it was a place where visits were impossible, he remained plunged in melancholy. In the first month of the following year, reminded of the previous spring by the flowering of the plum-trees before his house, he went to the Western Pavilion, and stood there gazing. But gaze as he might, there was to his mind no resemblance to the scene of the year before. At last he burst into tears, and laying himself down on the shattered floor, thought longingly of the bygone time until the moon went down. He composed this poem—

> "*Moon? There is none.*
> *Spring? 'Tis not the spring*
> *Of former days:*
> *It is I alone*
> *Who have remained unchanged*"[1]—

and then took his way homeward as the night was breaking into dawn."

A Western writer would have expanded this into a sonnet at least, but within the narrow bounds of thirty-one syllables prescribed by custom to the Japanese poet, it is hardly possible to express more forcibly the blank feeling of despair at the sight of familiar scenes which are no longer brightened by the presence of the loved one. The moon and spring flowers are there before his eyes, but as they do not move him as they did formerly,

---

[1] The following is an attempt to imitate as nearly as possible the metrical movement of the original, which, however, has no rhyme :—

> "*Moon? There is none.*
> *Where are spring's wonted flowers?*
> *I see not one.*
> *All else is changed, but I*
> *Love on unalteringly.*"

> "*Tsuki ya! aranu:*
> *Haru ya! mukashi no*
> *Haru naranu:*
> *Waga mi hitotsu wa*
> *Moto no mi ni shite.*"

he boldly denies their existence, giving emphasis by the contrast to the declaration of his own unchanging love. His subsequent adventures, it must be confessed, do not speak highly for his constancy.

After several other unfortunate love affairs, the hero found his life in Kiōto intolerable, and set out on an expedition to the east of Japan. His journey gives occasion for the introduction of a number of stanzas descriptive of the remarkable sights on the way, such as the smoking summit of Mount Asama, and the snow on Fujiyama in the height of summer. He and his people crossed the river Sumida, where Tōkio now stands, in a ferryboat at nightfall. The dismal scene made them all feel as if they had come to the end of the world, and their thoughts went back with longing to their homes in Kiōto. There were some birds on the river known to us as "oyster-catchers," but to the Japanese by the more poetical name of Miyakodori, or "birds of the capital." Narihira exclaims—

> " *O thou bird of Miyako!*
> *If such be thy name,*
> *Come! this question I would ask thee—*
> *Is she whom I love*
> *Still alive, or is she no more?* "

On hearing this, every one in the boat was moved to tears. But Narihira is not always so sentimental. Some of his adventures are intended to be more or less comical.

We soon after find him in one of the northern provinces, where a rustic beauty, eager to make the acquaintance of a fashionable young gentleman from Kiōto, sends him a poem (of course in thirty-one syllables) of invitation. He condescends to visit her, but takes his leave while it is still pitch-dark. As Juliet, under somewhat similar circumstances, reviles the lark, the lady, attributing his departure to the crowing of a cock, vents her displeasure in the following stanza, which still lingers in the popular memory :—

> " *When morning dawns*
> *I would that a fox*
> *Would devour that cock*
> *Who, by his unseasonable crowing,*
> *Has driven away my spouse!* "

I have before me two of the many editions of this work. One is by the eminent scholar and critic Mabuchi, and contains much more commentary than text. The other (dated 1608) is perhaps worthy of the attention of book-collectors whose mental horizon is not bounded by Europe. It is in two volumes, block-printed on variously-tinted paper, and adorned with numerous full-page illustrations which are among the very earliest specimens of the wood-engraver's art in Japan.

The *Utsubo Monogatari* is conjectured to have been written by the same author as the *Taketori Monogatari*, and the style and matter of the first of the fourteen stories of which it consists go far to confirm this supposition, though it may perhaps be a question whether the whole collection is by the same person. It is mentioned in the *Genji Monogatari* and in the *Makura Zōshi*, works which belong to the end of the tenth or the beginning of the eleventh century, and was probably composed some fifty or sixty years earlier. No exact date can be assigned for its composition.

The style of the *Utsubo Monogatari* is plain and straightforward; but it has unfortunately suffered greatly at the hands of copyists and editors, and also from the ravages of time, so that the text, as we now have it, is in a very unsatisfactory condition.

The title of the first story, "Toshikage," is taken from the name of the hero. It is the best known of the series, and has been published separately, as if it were the entire work. Like the *Taketori Monogatari*, it belongs to the class of fiction best described as Mährchen.

The hero is a son of a member of the Fujiwara family by an Imperial Princess. In other words, he has in his veins the bluest blood in Japan. His parents purposely allow him to grow up without any teaching, but he nevertheless learns with astonishing quickness, and at seven years of age holds a correspondence in the Chinese written character with a stranger from Corea who is on a visit to Japan. The Mikado, hearing of his remarkable talent, holds an examination, at which Toshikage far surpasses all his competitors. He subsequently receives an official appointment at the court, and later, at the age of sixteen, is made Ambassador to China. Two of the three ships in which the embassy sailed are lost during a storm, and Toshikage's own vessel drives ashore in a strange country, everybody (apparently) being drowned but Toshikage himself. On landing, he puts up a prayer to the Buddhist goddess Kwannon. A black horse, ready saddled, makes his appearance, and carries him to a spot where there are three men under a sandal-tree seated on tiger-skins and playing on lutes (*koto*). The horse vanishes. Toshikage remains here until the following spring, when hearing in the west the sound as of men felling trees, he resolves to follow it. Taking a courteous leave of his three hosts, he sets out on his quest. Seas and rivers, mountains and valleys are crossed, but it is not until the spring of the next year but one that he arrives at his destination. Here in a valley he sees a company of Asura (demons of Indian myth) engaged in cutting up an immense kiri-tree (*Paullownia Imperialis*) which they had felled. These demons "had hair like upright sword-blades, their faces burned like flames of fire, their feet and hands resembled spades and mattocks, their eyes gleamed like chargers of burnished metal." Toshikage is in danger of faring ill at their hands, when a boy comes down from the sky, riding on a dragon, amid a storm of thunder and lightning and rain, bearing a golden tablet, with instructions to the Asura to let him go, and to give him part of the tree they had felled, so that he might make it into lutes. He makes thirty lutes and goes his way, the lutes being carried for him by a whirlwind, which arises opportunely.

After other adventures of an equally wonderful kind, Toshikage returns to Japan and makes his report to the Mikado. He retires into private life, marries, and has one daughter. He and his wife die, leaving the daughter in great poverty. She lives in a secluded spot in the suburbs of Kiōto, where she is one day visited by a youth who was accompanying his father to worship at the shrine of Kamo. On his return home the next morning, his father, enraged at him for giving his parents so great anxiety by his disappearance, forbids him in future to leave his sight for a moment. When, after some years, he is able to visit the place where his lady-love dwelt, the house had completely disappeared.

Meanwhile Toshikage's daughter gives birth to a child, who, like many of the heroes of Chinese and Japanese romance, is a prodigy of precocious talent and filial devotion. At the age of five he sustains his mother by the fish which he catches, and at a later time brings her fruit and roots from the mountains. Finding, however, that this obliges him to leave her too much alone, he seeks a place in the woods where he can lodge her, and finds a great hollow[1] tree, which he thought would serve his purpose. It is already the home of a family of bears. They are about to devour the intruder, when he remonstrates with them as follows:—

"Stay a little and do not destroy my life, for I am a filial child, the support of my mother, who lives all alone in a ruined house, without parents, or brothers, or any one to attend upon her. As I could do nothing for her in the village where we live, I come to this mountain to get her fruit and roots. Having to climb up lofty peaks, and to descend into deep valleys, I leave home in the morning and return when it is dark. This is a source of great distress to us. I therefore thought of bringing her to this hollow tree, not knowing it to be the dwelling of such a king of the mountain. . . . If there is any part of me which is not useful for my mother's support, I will sacrifice it to you. But without feet how could I go about? Without hands how could I gather fruit or dig up roots for her? Without a mouth where would the breath of life find a passage? Without a breast where would my heart find a lodgment? In this body there is no part which is not of service except the lobes of my ears and the tip of my nose. These I offer to the king of the mountain."

This discourse moves the bears to tears, and they at once give up the hollow tree to him and seek a home elsewhere.

The mother and son live here for many years, being supplied with food by a number of monkeys. They are

[1] "Hollow" is in Japanese *utsubo*, whence the name of the whole work.

ultimately discovered by the father, who comes here on a hunting expedition. He builds them a fine mansion in Kiōto, in which they all live happily ever after.

The *Hamamatsu Chiunagon Monogatari* is a story of a Japanese noble who goes to China and has an amour with the Empress. He brings back to Japan with him a child who was the fruit of their union. The author is unknown. It belongs to the second half of the tenth century.

The story called *Ochikubo Monogatari* also belongs to the second half of the tenth century. Mabuchi would assign it to the period from 967 to 969. Its author is said to be one Minamoto no Shitagaü, a small official and famous scholar, who flourished in the reigns of the Mikados Murakami, Reizei, and Yenyū. The name *Ochikubo* means "underground cavity." The heroine, a young lady of noble birth, is confined in a room underground by her step-mother. She has a very miserable time, until by the help of a female servant she makes the acquaintance of a young nobleman, who assists her to escape. Of course they are married and live happily ever after.

A work named *Sumiyoshi Monogatari* is mentioned in the *Makura Zōshi*. Critics, however, are agreed that the book now known by that name is a forgery of a later date. It is also a story of a wicked step-mother (a favourite character of far-eastern fiction), and of the events which led in due course to her condign punishment.

The author of the *Yamato Monogatari* is really unknown, though it has been ascribed by some to Shigeharu, a son of Narihira, the hero of the *Ise Monogatari*, and by others to the Mikado Kwazan. It is an imitation of the *Ise Monogatari*, but is much inferior to its model, and the style is wanting in clearness and conciseness. It is a collection of stories adorned with Tanka after the manner of the earlier work. There is, however, no connecting link between them. The following is one of the best known of the series:—

"A long time ago there dwelt a maid in the province of Tsu. She was wooed by two lovers, one of whom, Mubara by name, lived in the same province ; the other, called Chinu, belonged to the province of Idzumi.

"Now these youths were of like age, and were also alike in face, form, and stature. The maid thought of accepting the one who loved her best, but here, too, no difference could be found between them. When night fell they both came together, and when they made her presents, the presents of both were alike. Neither of them could be said to surpass the other, so that the maiden was sore distressed in mind. If their devotion had been of vulgar sort she would have refused them both. But as for days and months the one and the other presented themselves at her door, and showed their love in all manner of ways, their attentions made her utterly wretched. Both persisted in coming with their like gifts of all kinds, notwithstanding that they were not accepted. Her parents said to her, 'It is a pity that month after month and year after year should pass in this unseemly manner. It is wearisome to listen to the laments of these men, and all to no purpose. If you married one, the other's love would cease.' The girl replied, 'I think so too, but I am sorely perplexed by the sameness of the men's love. What am I to do ?' Now in those days people lived in tents on the bank of the river Ikuta. Accordingly the parents sent for the two lovers and said to them, 'Our child is sorely perplexed by the equality of the love shown by you two gentlemen. But we intend to-day, in one way or another, to come to a decision. One of you is a stranger from a distant place; the other, a dweller here, has taken trouble beyond measure. The conduct of both of you has our warm sympathy.' Both heard this with respectful joy. 'Now, what we proposed to say to you,' continued the parents, 'was this: aim your arrows at one of the water-fowl floating on this river. We will give our daughter to the one who hits it.' 'An excellent plan,' said they. But when they shot at it, one hit it on the head and the other near the tail. Thereupon the maiden, more profoundly embarrassed than ever, exclaimed—

> *Weary of life,*
> *My body I will cast away*
> *Into the river Ikuta,*
> *In the land of Tsu.*
> *Ikuta !* [1] *to me a name and nothing more !'*

"With these words she plunged into the river which flowed below the tent. Amid the frantic cries of the parents, the two lovers forthwith leaped into the stream at the same place. One seized her by the foot, the other took hold of her arm, and both died along with her. The parents, wild with grief, took up her body and buried it with tears and lamentations. The parents of the lovers also came and built tombs on each side of the sepulchre of the maiden. But when the time of burial came, the parents of the youth of the land of Tsu objected, saying: 'That a man of the same province should be buried in the same place is but right and proper, but how can it be allowed that a stranger should intrude upon our soil?' So the parents of the Idzumi wooer brought over in ships

[1] *Ikuta* means "living field."

earth from the province of Idzumi, and at length buried their son. The maiden's tomb is in the middle, and those of her lovers on each side, as may be seen unto this day."

The present writer once made a pious pilgrimage to these tombs, which are still in existence not far from the treaty port of Kobe. He was not a little surprised to find that they were immense tumuli, certainly the sepulchres of much more exalted personages than the heroes of the above tale. Not only so, but the so-called lovers' tombs are a mile away each side from that of the fair lady for whom they died. On one of them, sad to say, there was growing a thriving crop of cabbages, planted by some irreverent, or more likely ignorant, Japanese. The Ikuta river must have greatly changed since the days of this story. It now sends to the sea a volume of water about equal to that of the stream which waters the public gardens at Bournemouth, and where, needless to say, death by drowning is impossible.

CHAPTER IV

"GENJI MONOGATARI"[1]

WE now come to two works which by common consent mark the highest point to which the classical literature of Japan attained, namely, the *Genji Monogatari* and the *Makura Zōshi*. The authors were contemporaries, and both of them were women.

The real name of the author of the *Genji Monogatari* has not come down to us. She is known to history as MURA-SAKI NO SHIKIBU. Critics are not agreed as to the reason why she was called Murasaki, a word which means "purple," nor does it greatly matter. Shikibu, if it meant anything, would indicate that she was in some way connected with the Board of Rites. It was, however, customary at this time for the ladies of the court to take to themselves fancy official designations which had no particular application. In her case the name was perhaps suggested by the circumstance that her father held office in that Department.

Murasaki no Shikibu belonged to a junior branch of the great Fujiwara family, or rather clan, which held so distinguished a position in Japan during many centuries of its history, and which has produced such numbers of

[1] There is a translation of the first seventeen (out of fifty-four) chapters of this work by K. Suyematsu. Although a highly creditable performance under the circumstances, it is not satisfactory. The translator had not Motoöri's commentary before him, and the Kogetsushō edition is a very uncertain guide.

Mikados, statesmen, literati, and poets. Her father had a reputation for scholarship, and others of her family were poets of some note. Murasaki no Shikibu herself displayed a love of learning at an early age. She was well versed both in Japanese and Chinese literature, and her father often wished that such talents and learning had not been wasted on a girl. Married to another Fujiwara, she lost her husband after a short time, and seems to have then attached herself to the Empress Akiko, also a Fujiwara and fond of learned pursuits. This would explain her familiarity with the ceremonies and institutions of the court of Kiōto. Her writings bear unmistakable testimony to the fact that she moved in the best circles of her time and country.

The *Genji* is generally supposed to have been finished in A.D. 1004, but this date has been disputed, and it may have been composed a few years earlier. There is a pleasing legend which associates its composition with the Temple of Ishiyama at the southern end of Lake Biwa, where the river Uji issues from it. To this beautiful spot, it is said, Murasaki no Shikibu retired from court life to devote the remainder of her days to literature and religion. There are sceptics, however, Motoöri being one, who refuse to believe this story, pointing out, after the manner of their kind, that it is irreconcilable with known facts. On the other hand, the very chamber in the temple where the *Genji* was written is shown—with the ink-slab which the author used, and a Buddhist Sutra in her hand-writing, which, if they do not satisfy the critic, still are sufficient to carry conviction to the minds of ordinary visitors to the temple.

The *Genji Monogatari* is a novel. There is nothing remarkable, it may be said, in a woman excelling in this branch of literature. But Murasaki no Shikibu did more than merely write a successful novel. Like Fielding in England, she was the creator in Japan of this kind of fiction—the prose epic of real life, as it has been called. In the quality of her genius, however, she more resembled Fielding's great contemporary Richardson. Before her time we have nothing but stories of no great length, and of a romantic character far removed from the realities of daily life. The *Genji Monogatari* is realistic in the best sense of the word. Here we see depicted men and women, especially women, as they are, in their everyday lives and surroundings, their sentiments and passions, their faults and weaknesses. The author does not aim at startling or horrifying her readers, and she has a wholesome abhorrence for all that is sensational, unnatural, monstrous, or improbable. Such a hero as the nineteenth-century novelist Bakin's Tametomo, who has two pupils to his eyes and one arm longer than the other, and who, after falling over a cliff many thousand feet high, presently picks himself up and walks home several miles as if nothing had happened, would have seemed to her as ridiculous as he does to ourselves. There are few dramatic situations in the *Genji*, and what little of miraculous and supernatural it contains is of a kind which might well be believed by a contemporary reader. The story flows on easily from one scene of real life to another, giving us a varied and minutely detailed picture of life and society at Kiōto such as we possess for no other country at the same period.

The hero is the son of a Mikado by a favourite concubine, whose colleagues are all jealous of the preference shown her, and are continually annoying her in a petty way. She takes this so much to heart that she falls ill and dies. Her death is related with much pathos. Genji grows up to be a handsome and accomplished youth of a very susceptible disposition, and his history is mainly an account of his numerous love affairs, and of his ultimate union with Murasaki, a heroine in all respects worthy of him. It continues the story up to his death at the age of fifty-one. The last ten books, which relate chiefly to one of Genji's sons, are by some considered a separate work.

The style of the *Genji* has been called ornate. The writer who applied this epithet to it was probably thinking of the courtly honorifics with which it is in many places burdened. But there is much excuse for this. The *Genji* is a novel of aristocratic life. Most of the characters are personages of rank, in describing whose sayings and actions a courtly style of speech is indispensable. To a Japanese it would be simply shocking to say that a Mikado has breakfast—he augustly deigns to partake of the morning meal, and so on. The European reader finds this irritating and tiresome at first, but he soon gets accustomed to it. In truth, such language is in entire consonance with the elaborate ceremonial, the imposing but cumbrous costumes, and much else of the rather artificial life of the Japanese court of the time. Apart from this the style of the *Genji* is not more ornate than that, let us say, of *Robinson Crusoe*, and incomparably less so than that of many Japanese books of later date. It is free from any redundance of descriptive adjectives or profusion of metaphors such as we are accustomed to associate with the word ornate.

Others have objected to the style of the *Genji* as wanting in brevity. It must be admitted that its long, involved sentences contrast strongly with the direct, concise manner of the *Ise Monogatari*. But, as Motoöri points out, a brief style may be a bad one, and lengthy sentences full of detail may best fit the subject. Murasaki no Shikibu's fulness is not prolixity. On close examination it will be found that there is nothing superfluous in the abundant details of her narrative. That is her method, and is essential to the effect she aims at producing.

The *Genji* is not intrinsically a very difficult work, and no doubt the author's contemporaries found it quite easy to understand. But since then the language, institutions, and manners and customs of Japan have changed so much as greatly to obscure the meaning, not only to European students, but to the Japanese themselves. Piles of commentary by native editors have been accumulated over it, and their interpretations are often so blundering and inadequate that Motoöri found it necessary to devote to its elucidation a critical work [1] in nine volumes, mostly taken up with correcting the errors of his predecessors.

The enormous bulk of the *Genji* will always remain another obstacle to its just appreciation by European readers. It is in fifty-four books, which in the standard (but not very satisfactory) Kogetsushō edition run to no less than 4234 pages. The genealogical tree alone of the personages which figure in it, comprising several Mikados, a crowd of Princes, Princesses, and Imperial consorts, with a host of courtiers, occupies eighty pages.

Japanese critics claim for the *Genji* that it surpasses anything of the kind in Chinese literature, and even deserves to be ranked with the masterpieces of European fiction. None, however, but an extreme Japanophile

---

[1] The *Tama no Ogushi*. It was left unfinished at his death.

(the species is not altogether unknown) will go so far as to place Murasaki no Shikibu on a level with Fielding, Thackeray, Victor Hugo, Dumas, and Cervantes. On the other hand, it is unjust to dismiss her summarily with the late M. George Bousquet as "cette ennuyeuse Scudéry japonaise," a verdict endorsed by Mr. Chamberlain. There are in the *Genji* pathos, humour, an abundant flow of pleasing sentiment, keen observation of men and manners, an appreciation of the charms of nature, and a supreme command of the resources of the Japanese language, which in her hands reached its highest point of excellence. Though never melodramatic, she gives us plenty of incident, and is seldom dull. A scholar, she abhorred pedantry and fine writing, the bane of so many of the modern novelists of Japan.

It is unnecessary to discuss here the opinion of some Japanese writers, that the *Genji* was written to inculcate Buddhist doctrine, or the notion of others, that the teaching of Confucian morality was its aim. Nor need we trouble ourselves with the suggestion that it is a novel *à clef*, and that the personages are to be identified with real persons who were alive at the time when it was written. As Motoöri very justly observes, all these ideas show an ignorance of the true object of novel-writing, which is to excite our sympathies, and to interest and amuse by the presentation of a picture of real life.

Another subject much dwelt on by native critics is the morality of the *Genji*, some denouncing it, as it deserves, while others strive to defend what even from the Japanese point of view is indefensible. Truth to say, the laxity of morals which it depicts is deplorable. It is a satisfaction to add that it belongs to the age and country in which the author lived, and that her own private life is admittedly free from any stain of this kind. Of coarseness and pruriency, moreover, there is none in the *Genji*, or indeed in the literature of this period generally. The language is almost invariably decent, and even refined, and we hardly ever meet with a phrase calculated to bring a blush to the cheek of a young person.

It is difficult to give much idea of the *Genji* by quotation. The following passages may serve as well as any others for this purpose ; but the writer is conscious that here, more perhaps than anywhere else in Japanese literature, the chasm which divides us in thought, sentiment, and language from the Far East forms an insuperable obstacle to communicating to a translation the undoubted charm of the original.

Genji, aged sixteen, discusses feminine character with a young friend :—

" It was an evening in the wet season. Without, the rain was falling drearily, and even in the Palace hardly any one was to be seen. In Genji's quarters there was an unusual sense of stillness. He was engaged in reading by the light of a lamp when it occurred to him to take out from a cupboard which was close by some letters written on paper of various tints. The Chiujō [his friend] was inordinately eager to have a look at them. 'There are a few of a kind that I can let you see,' said Genji, 'but there are others that are imperfect ;' and these he refused to show him. 'Oh ! but it is just those written without reserve and couched in moving language that I like. Commonplace ones don't count. What I wish to see are letters which reveal the various circumstances of the writers. When they are inspired by petulant jealousy or written at the hour of eve—a prey to passionate longings and the like—it is then that they are worth reading.' It was unlikely that any which demanded the strictest secrecy should be left lying about in an ordinary cupboard. Such were no doubt carefully concealed, and these were of the second order of intimacy. Genji there-fore, being thus pressed, allowed his friend to read passages from them here and there. 'What a variety!' said the Chiujō, and began to guess at the authors. 'This is from so-and-so, is it not?—that from such another?' he inquired. Sometimes he guessed right, and even when he missed the mark Genji was much amused by his infer-ences and suspicions. But he said little and maintained his reserve, putting his friend off with dubious answers. 'You must have a collection of your own,' said Genji. 'Will you not let me see a few of them? In that case, my cupboard would open its doors more cheerfully.' 'I am sure none of mine would be worth your while to read,' replied the Chiujō. 'I have at last [he was aged sixteen] discovered,' continued he, 'how hard it is to find a woman of whom it may be said, "Here at any rate is the one. Here no fault can be found." There are plenty who may be considered fairly tolerable, girls of super-ficial sensibilities, ready with their pens, and competent to give intelligent responses [1] upon occasion. But how hard it is to pitch upon any of whom you can say that here is one who compels your choice. Often they have no thought for any accomplishments but such as they themselves possess, and depreciate those of others in a most provoking way. Some, again, there are, made much of by their parents and not allowed to leave their side, who, while they remain within the lattice which bounds their future, may no doubt make an impression on the hearts of men who have had little opportunity of

[1] Probably poetical responses of thirty-one syllables are meant.

really knowing them. They may be young, attractive, and of sedate manners; and so long as they are without external distractions, they will naturally, by the assiduous imitation of others, gain some skill in frivolous pastimes. But their friends will screen their defects and represent their good qualities in the best light. How is anybody to condemn them in his own mind without a proof, and say to himself, "That is not so"? Whereas if we believe all that is said of them, we are sure to find on further acquaintance that they fall in our estimation.' Here the Chiujō paused, ashamed of his own precipitancy. Genji smiled, thinking of something of the same kind, though not absolutely so, in his own experience, and said, ' But surely they have all some good points?' 'Just so,' replied the Chiujō. 'If they had none, who would be taken in? Of those utterly sorry creatures who are beneath notice, and of the superior women for whose accomplishments we feel an unqualified admiration, the numbers are alike few. Those born in a high station are made much of by their friends, and their faults are concealed, so that in outward appearance they are naturally second to none. In the middle class, there is greater freedom of expression of individual feeling, and thus the means are afforded of distinguishing among them. As for those of the lowest station of all, they are quite unworthy of our attention.'"

Here Genji and the Chiujō are joined by two other friends. The conversation is continued at considerable length, and various types of womanhood are discussed with illustrative anecdotes drawn from the speakers' experience. This passage, known as the Shina-sadame, or Critique (of women), is much admired by the Japanese, and is considered by critics to be the kernel of the whole work, the chief idea of which is to present to the reader a picture of various types of womanhood.

Genji, having retired to a monastery in order to be exorcised for ague, espies in a neighbouring temple a young girl who is living with her grandmother, a nun, and who is destined to fix his vagrant fancy at a later period.

"At this season the days were very long, and time passed slowly ; so under cover of the deep evening mist he approached the low hedge of which he had been told. Here he sent back all his attendants, retaining with him only Koremitsu. Peeping through the hedge, he could see straight before him the western front of the house, where there was a nun performing her devotions before a private image of Buddha. She raised up the hanging screen and made an offering of flowers. Then taking her place by the middle pillar, she placed a Sutra on an arm-rest, and proceeded to read it in a voice which betrayed much suffering. This nun seemed no ordinary person. She was something over forty years of age. Her complexion was fair, and she had an air of distinction. She was thin, but her face had a puffy appearance from ill health. Whilst looking at her, Genji was struck with the beauty of her hair, which seemed rather to have gained in elegance by having been cut. [1] Two comely grown-up women were in waiting on her.

" Now there were some children playing in and out of the room. One of them, who might be perhaps ten years of age, wore a white silk gown lined with yellow, and not too new. She had no resemblance to the attendants or to the rest of the children, and her beauty seemed to give

---

[1] Nuns at this time did not shave their heads, but only trimmed the hair short.

promise of a future for her. Her hair was tossed in waves like an expanded fan, and her eyes were red with weeping. The nun looked up when she saw her near, and said, 'What is the matter ? Have you been quarrelling with some of the children ?' As Genji looked at them, it occurred to him that there was a resemblance, and that the little girl was probably her daughter. 'Inuki has let go my sparrow that I had put under a basket,' said she dolefully. The waiting-woman exclaimed, 'He is always doing thoughtless things like that and plaguing the poor girl, all because he does not get scolded enough. I wonder where it has gone to ? It had at last become so delightful, and now I'm afraid the crows have discovered it.' So saying, she went out.

" This woman's hair hung down loose and was very long. She was a pleasant-looking woman. The others called her Nurse Shōnagon, and she seemed to have charge of this child. 'Come now ! be a good girl,' said the nun, 'and don't do such naughty things. You forget that my life is but for to-day or to-morrow, and you can think of nothing but your sparrow. Haven't I often told you that it was a sin [to keep birds in a cage]. You pain me greatly. Come here, child.' The little girl stood forward with a rueful expression of face, and a mist hanging round her eyebrows. The contour of her forehead, from which the hair was combed back in childish fashion, and the style of her hair itself were very lovely. 'What a charming girl she will be when she is grown up !' thought Genji, and his eyes dwelt on her with interest. She greatly resembled one to whom formerly his whole heart had been given, and at the thought his tears began to fall. The nun, stroking the little girl's head, said, 'What beautiful hair, though you think it so much trouble to have it combed! I am greatly concerned that you are so frivolous. At your age some girls are so different. When your late mother was married at the age of twelve she had an extraordinary amount of good sense. But now if you were to lose me, what would become of you ?' And she burst out weeping. Genji, at this sight, was moved unawares to sorrow for her. The little girl, child as she was, looked at her, and with downcast eyes bent her head to the ground, so that her hair fell loosely forward, showing a lustre that was very beautiful.

> *' There is no sky [weather] to dry up*
> *The dew [of my tears] at leaving behind*
> *The tender herb*
> *That knows not where shall be its abode*
> *When it has reached full growth.'*

"So the nun. 'True,' said the other waiting-woman [not the girl's nurse], and with tears answered her—

> *' So long as the first blades of grass*
> *Know not what will be their future when grown up,*
> *How can the dew*
> *Think of becoming dried ?' "*

This notice may be fitly closed by the following poem, in which Motoöri in his old age expressed his intention of returning, if time permitted, to the study of the *Genji* :—

> " *So dearly do I love them,*
> *Again I would come to see*
> *The violets on the plains of spring*
> *Which I left ungathered—*
> *Though to-day I may not pluck them.*"

The author of the *Genji Monogatari* wrote a diary called *Murasaki no Shikibu Nikki*, which has come down to us. It is not without merit, but its fame has been wholly eclipsed by that of her greater work.

CHAPTER V

"MAKURA ZŌSHI"

WITH the *Genji Monogatari* the Japanese associate the *Makura Zōshi* or "Pillow Sketches" of SEI SHŌNAGON as of equal excellence, although different in form and character. The author, like Murasaki no Shikibu, was a lady of high rank, her father, who was a poet of some fame, being descended from the Prince who compiled the *Nihongi*. Her learning and talents obtained for her the honour of being appointed Lady-in-waiting to the Empress. On the death of the latter in A.D. 1000, she retired from the world, some say to a convent, where she received to the last marks of the esteem of her former master, the Mikado Ichigo. Others, however, describe her condition as one of great poverty and misery.

The title "Pillow Sketches" is explained by some to mean that she kept the manuscript by her pillow and jotted down her thoughts and observations when going to bed and when getting up in the morning. It is more probable, however, that it is an allusion to an anecdote which she herself relates in a postscript :—

"It has become too dark for literary work, and my pen is worn out. I will bring these sketches to a close. They are a record of that which I have seen with my eyes and felt in my heart, not written that others might read them, but put together to solace the loneliness of my home life.

When I think how I tried to keep them secret, conscious of vulgar and exaggerated remarks which have escaped me, the tears flow uncontrollably.

"One day when I was in attendance on the Empress, she showed me some paper which had been given her by the Naidaijin. 'What is to be written on this?' said her Majesty. 'The Mikado has had something they call History written on his.' 'It will do nicely for pillows,' I replied. 'Then take it,' said she. So I tried to use up this immense supply by writing down strange matters of all kinds without any connection or sequence."

The *Makura Zōshi* is the first example of a style of writing which afterwards became popular in Japan under the name of Zuihitsu or "following the pen." There is no sort of arrangement. The author sets down upon the spur of the moment anything which occurs to her. Stories, descriptive enumerations of dismal, incongruous, abominable and dreary things, lists of flowers, mountains, rivers, sketches of social and domestic life, thoughts suggested by the contemplation of nature, and much more form her *farrago libelli*.

Unlike the author of the *Genji*, who loses herself in the characters which she describes, the personality of Sei Shōnagon comes out distinctly in everything which she has written. The clever, somewhat cynical, cultured woman of the world is always present to the reader. Her tastes and predilections are made known at considerable length, and she does not mind being her own Boswell, not failing to record in her "Pillow Sketches" any apt quotation or neat retort which she may have made. Subsequent writers do not acquit her, as they do Murasaki no Shikibu, of a personal share in the amorous intrigues which formed so large a part of life among the upper classes of Kiōto at this period. It may be readily gathered from her writings that she was no stranger to

> " *The politic arts*
> *To take and keep men's hearts;*
> *The letters, embassies, and spies,*
> *The frowns, and smiles, and flatteries,*
> *The quarrels, tears, and perjuries,*
> *Numberless, nameless mysteries,*"

of Cowley's poem.

The following extracts will give some idea of the general character of the work. The four seasons form the subject of the opening chapter :—

" In spring," the author says, " I love to watch the dawn grow gradually whiter and whiter, till a faint rosy tinge crowns the mountain's crest, while slender streaks of purple cloud extend themselves above."

" In summer, I love the night, not only when the moon is shining, but the dark too, when the fireflies cross each other's paths in their flight, or when the rain is falling."

" In autumn, it is the beauty of the evening which most deeply moves me, as I watch the crows seeking their roosting-place in twos and threes and fours, while the setting sun sends forth his beams gorgeously as he draws near the mountain's rim. Still more is it delightful to see the lines of wild geese pass, looking exceeding small in the distance. And when the sun has quite gone down, how moving it is to hear the chirruping of insects or the sighing of the wind ! "

" In winter, how unspeakably beautiful is the snow ! But I also love the dazzling whiteness of the hoar-frost, and the intense cold even at other times. Then it is meet quickly to fetch charcoal and kindle fires. And let not the gentle warmth of noon persuade us to allow the embers of the hearth or of the brazier to become a white heap of ashes ! "

THE EXORCIST

" What a pity it is to make a priest of a child whom one loves ! How painful it must be to have to regard as so many bits of stick the things which are in life the most desirable ! Priests have to go to bed after a meal of wretched fasting diet, and are blamed if, when young, they so much as take a sly peep into places where there are attractive girls. The life of an exorcist priest is particularly hard. What dreadful experiences he must have on his pilgrimages to Mitake, Kumano, and all the other sacred monasteries ! Even after he has gained a fame for unction and is sent for on all occasions, his very reputation is a bar to his repose. What a labour it must be to drive out the evil spirit from the sick man he is in attendance on ! And yet if he dozes a little out of sheer exhaustion, he is promptly reprimanded, and told that he does nothing but sleep. How embarrassed he must feel ! "

The exorcist is much sympathised with by the author. In another place she says—

" When the exorcist is summoned to drive out an evil spirit, he puts on a consequential air as he distributes his maces and bells to those who are present. Then he drones out his chant in tones like the note of the cicada. But suppose that the demon is not a whit disturbed, and that the spells are of no avail ? The whole household, who had joined in the prayers, begin to wonder. Still he goes on hour after hour till he is utterly weary. At last he sees that it is useless, so he lets them get up and takes

back his maces and bells with a confession of failure.
How he ruffles back his hair and scratches his head as
with many a yawn he lays himself down to sleep!"

VISIT OF THE EMPRESS TO A COURT NOBLE

"When the Empress visited the Daishin Narimasa,
her carriage went in by the East Gate, which is wide
with four pillars. Her women, however, preferred to
have their carriages go round to the North Gate, where
there were no guards. Some who had not done up their
hair thought to themselves with some disdain, "Oh, we
shall drive up to the door, so we need not be very
particular." But the palm-leaf-covered carriages stuck
fast in the narrow portal, and there was no possibility of
getting in. So the usual path of matting was laid, and
we were told to get down, to our no small annoyance
and indignation. But there was no help for it. It was
provoking to see the courtiers and servants standing
together in the guard-room to watch us pass. When
we came before her Majesty, and told her what had
happened, she only laughed at us, saying, 'Is there
nobody looking at you now? How can you be so
untidy?' 'Yes,' replied I, 'but everybody here is used
to us, and would be greatly surprised if we took special
pains about our appearance. To think that a mansion
like this should have a gate too small to admit a carriage! I shall have a good laugh at the Daishin
when I meet him.' Presently he came in bringing the
Empress's ink-stone and writing materials. 'This is too
bad of you,' said I. 'How can you live in a house with
such a narrow gate?' To which he replied with a smile,
that his house was on a scale suited to his station. 'And

yet,' said I, ' I have heard of a man who had his gate, though nothing more, made too large for his personal requirements.' 'Well, to be sure,' said the Daishin, with astonishment, 'you refer, of course, to U Teikoku [a Chinese worthy]. Who would have thought that any one but a venerable pundit knew aught of that ? I myself have occasionally strayed into the paths of learning, and fully comprehend your allusion.' ' Indeed, then,' returned I, ' your paths are none of the most sensible. There was a nice disturbance, I can tell you, when we found ourselves entrapped into walking along your matted paths.' ' I fear you must have been incommoded,' he replied. 'And it was raining, too. But I must attend the Empress.' Saying which, he made his exit.

"' What was it put Narimasa out so much ?' the Empress inquired of me later. ' Oh, nothing,' I said ; ' I was only telling him of our misadventure at his gate.'

DOMESTIC SCENE IN THE MIKADO'S PALACE

"On the sliding doors of the northern front of the Mikado's private apartments there are painted fearful pictures of creatures that live in the wild ocean, some with long arms, others with long legs. When the doors of the ante-chamber are open we can always see them. One day towards noon, while we were laughing and talking about them, saying what hideous things they are, and were engaged in setting great flower-pots of green porcelain[1] by the balustrade of the verandah, and filling them with an abundance of the most delightful

[1] Probably of the kind now known to connoisseurs as Seiji.

cherry branches five feet long, so that the blossoms overflowed to the foot of the railing, his Excellency the
Dainagon [the Empress's brother] approached. He had
on a cherry-coloured tunic, enough worn to have lost its
stiffness, and dark purple trousers. His white under-
clothing, showing at the neck, displayed a gay pattern of
a deep crimson hue. As the Mikado was then with the
Empress, he seated himself on the narrow platform
before the door and made some report to him on official
matters.

"The waiting-women, with their cherry-coloured sleeve-
less jackets hanging down loosely by their sides, some
dressed in *wistaria* [purple], some in *kerria* [yellow],
and all manner of lovely colours, showed out from the
screen of the small hatch. Just then dinner was served
in the Imperial apartments. We could hear the trampl-
ing of the attendants' feet, and the cry 'Less noise'
from one of the chamberlains. The serene aspect of
the weather was exceedingly agreeable. When the last
dishes had been served, a butler came and announced
dinner. The Mikado went away by the middle door,
attended by his Excellency the Dainagon, who subsequently returned to his former place beside the flowers.
The Empress then pushed aside the curtain, and came
forward as far as the threshold to greet him. He remarked on the beauty of the surroundings and the good
deportment of the servants, and ended by quoting the
line of poetry which says—

> ' *The days and months roll on,*
> *But the Mount of Mimoro remains for ever.*'

" I was deeply impressed, and wished in my heart that
so it might indeed continue for a thousand years.

THE ATTACK OF THE DOG OKINAMARO UPON THE CAT MIYŌBU NO OTODO

"The august Cat-in-waiting on the Mikado was a very delightful animal, and a great favourite with his Majesty, who conferred on her the fifth rank of nobility and the title of Miyōbu no Otodo, or Chief Superintendent of the Female Attendants of the Palace. One day she had gone out on to the bridge between two of the buildings of the Palace, when the nurse in charge of her called out, 'How improper! Come in at once.' But the cat paid no attention, and went on basking drowsily in the sun. So in order to frighten her, 'Where is Okinamaro?' cried the nurse. 'Okinamaro! bite Miyōbu no Otodo.' The foolish dog, thinking she was in earnest, flew at the cat, who in her fright and consternation took refuge behind the screen of the breakfast-room where his Majesty then was. The Mikado was greatly shocked and agitated. He took the cat into his august bosom, and summoning the chamberlain Tadataka, gave orders that Okinamaro should have a good thrashing and be banished to Dog Island at once. The attendants gave chase to Okinamaro amid great confusion. They soon caught him, and sent him away as they were ordered.

"Alas, poor dog! He used to swagger about so much at his ease. When on the third day of the third month he was led along with a willow wreath upon his head, and adorned with flowers of peach and cherry, did he ever think that it would come to this? At meal times he used always to be in attendance, and now, when three or four days passed without him, we missed him greatly. One day at noon there was a tremendous noise of a dog's howling. All the other dogs rushed to the spot in excitement to see what made him go on yelping so. Meanwhile a scavenger-woman of the Palace came to us running. 'Oh! how terrible!' exclaimed she. 'Two of the chamberlains are beating a dog till he is nearly dead. They say they are chastising him for having come back after he was banished.' My heart told me that it was Okinamaro who was being beaten by Tadataka and Sanefusa. I was just sending to stop them when the howling ceased. I was then told that he was dead, and that his body had been flung away outside the gate. At sundown, when we were all pitying his fate, a wretched-looking dog, trembling all over, walked in, his body fearfully and amazingly swollen. 'Can this be Okinamaro?' we said. 'No such dog has been seen about here recently.' We called to him by his name, but he took no notice. Some said it was he, others that it was not. The Empress sent for a lady who knew him well. 'Is this Okinamaro?' she said, pointing to him. 'It is like him,' replied she, 'but is too utterly loathsome to be our dog. Besides, when one called to Okinamaro by name, he came joyfully; but this animal won't come. It cannot be Okinamaro. And then Okinamaro was killed and his body thrown away. He can't possibly be alive after the beating he got from the two chamberlains.' When it got dark he was offered something to eat, but he refused it, so we made up our minds that it could not be our friend. The next morning when I went to attend the Empress at her toilet, and had served her wash-hand basin and her mirror, a dog came to the foot of one of the pillars. 'Alas!' cried the Empress, 'what a terrible beating Okinamaro seems to have got last night. I am so sorry that he is dead. I suppose he now looks something like that animal. He must have suffered miserably.' At this moment the dog lying by the pillar trembled and shook, and poured forth a flood of tears, to our intense amazement. This was Okinamaro after all, and his refusal on the previous day to come when he was called was for fear of betraying himself. The Empress was touched and delighted beyond measure. She put down her mirror and called to him, 'Okinamaro!' The dog laid himself flat on the ground and yelped loudly, at which the Empress was greatly amused. Everybody gathered round, and there was much talking and laughing. The Mikado himself, when he heard of it, came in, and smilingly expressed his amazement at the good sense shown by a dog."

The reader will be glad to hear that Okinamaro's sentence of banishment was reversed; he was well treated, and in a short time was his old self again.

But the author was not always so tender-hearted towards dogs. Among "Detestable Things" she enumerates—

A dog who barks in recognition of your lover when he comes to pay you a clandestine visit—that dog should be killed.

A few more of her enumerations may be added.

DREARY THINGS.

A nursery where the child has died.

A brazier with the fire gone out.

A coachman who is hated by his ox.

The birth of a female child in the house of a learned scholar.

A letter from one's country home with no news in it.

DETESTABLE THINGS.

Of these the author has a long list, of which the following are a few :—

A visitor who tells a long story when you are in a hurry. If he is a person you are intimate with, you can pack him off, saying that you will hear it another time. But those whom you cannot treat in this way are very detestable.

An exorcist who, when sent for in a case of sudden illness, recites his charms as if he were half asleep.

Babies that cry or dogs that bark when you want to listen.

The snoring of a man whom you are trying to conceal, and who has gone to sleep in a place where he has no business.

A carriage which creaks so loud that you cannot hear your friend speak. Also the friend who lent you such a carriage.

People who interrupt your stories to show off their own cleverness. All interrupters, young or old, are very detestable.

People who, when you are telling a story, break in with, "Oh, I know," and give quite a different version from your own.

Either at home or in the palace to be roused up to receive an unwelcome visitor, in order to avoid whom you have been pretending to be asleep.

While on friendly terms with a man, to hear him sound the praises of a woman whom he has known. This is detestable even when some time has elapsed, much more so if he is still acquainted with her.

People who mumble a prayer when they sneeze.

N.B.—Loud sneezing is detestable, except in the case of the gentlemen of the house.

Fleas are very detestable, especially when they get under your clothing and jump about.

As a contrast to "Detestable Things," a few "Things which give one a Thrill" may be added :—

To see sparrows feeding their young.

To pass by where infants are playing.

To find that your Chinese (metal) mirror is beginning to get dim.

To be asked the way by a handsome man who stops his carriage for the purpose.

Among "Things which Excite Regrets for the Past," Sei Shōnagon enumerates :—

Withered hollyhocks. (Reminding one of the festivals they have been used for.)

On a wet day to turn over the letters of a person once loved by us.

Last year's fans. (No doubt with sentimental Tanka written on them.)

Bright moonlight nights.

Here are a few "Cheerful Things" :—

Coming home from an excursion with the carriages full to overflowing, to have lots of footmen who make the oxen go and the carriages speed along.

A river boat going down stream.

Teeth nicely blackened.

To hear a well-voiced professor of magic recite his purification service on a river bank.

A drink of water when awake during the night.

When in a dull mood, to have a visitor neither so intimate as to be uninteresting, nor too great a stranger to be unreserved, who will tell us what is going on in the world—things pleasant or odious or strange, now touching on this, now on that, private matters or public—in just sufficient detail not to be tedious. This is very agreeable.

Here follow the "points" of carriage-oxen, horses, coachmen (who should be big men, of a ruddy countenance, and a consequential demeanour), footmen, pages, cats, and preachers. The last subject is treated at some length.

"A preacher," she says, "ought to be a good-looking man. It is then easier to keep your eyes fixed on his face, without which it is impossible to benefit by the discourse. Otherwise the eyes wander and you forget to listen. Ugly preachers have therefore a grave responsibility. But no more of this!" She adds, however, "If preachers were of a more suitable age I should have pleasure in giving a more favourable judgment. As matters actually stand, their sins are too fearful to think of."

If any apology is needed for the length of these extracts, it may be pleaded that they represent that which is best and at the same time most quotable in Japanese literature. They are taken almost exclusively from the first two of the twelve volumes (646 pp.) of which this entertaining miscellany consists. It is hard to realise that it was written in Japan nine hundred years ago. If we compare it with anything that Europe had to show at this period, it must be admitted that it is indeed a remarkable work. What a revelation it would be if we had the court life of Alfred's or Canute's reign depicted to us in a similar way.

Both the *Genji Monogatari* and the *Makura Zōshi* are only imperfectly intelligible even to educated Japanese, and they are little read at the present day. This is to be regretted, as modern writers would derive much benefit from making these old masterpieces their study and example.

CHAPTER VI

SOME MINOR WORKS

THE author of the *Sagoromo Monogatari* was a court
official named Daini no Sammi, the daughter of Murasaki
no Shikibu. Her work, a love-story of considerable
length, is an obvious imitation of the *Genji Monogatari*,
but much inferior both in style and matter. It is believed to have been written about A.D. 1040.

The *Sarashina Nikki*, by a daughter of Sugawara no
Takasuye, a descendant in the sixth generation of the
famous statesman Sugawara no Michizane, was completed in the reign of the Emperor Go Rei-zei (1046–
1068). It is the record of a journey from Shimōsa to
Kiōto by the Tōkaidō in 1021, and of a second journey
from Kiōto to Sarashina, in the province of Shinano,
some years later. It is written in a vein of melancholy
sentiment, and is plentifully adorned with doleful Tanka.

Nothing is known as to the date and authorship of
the *Torikayebaya Monogatari*. It is believed to have
been written subsequently to the *Sagoromo*, and would
therefore belong to the middle or end of the eleventh
century. The *Torikayebaya Monogatari* is a story of the
difficulties experienced by a nobleman in the education
of his two children, a boy and a girl. The boy is fond of
feminine pursuits and amusements, and the girl just the
reverse, much to the annoyance of their father, who used

frequently to exclaim, "Torikayebaya!" that is, "Oh! if I could only exchange them." [1] All he can do is to have the boy dressed in girl's clothes and treated accordingly, while the girl is brought up as a boy. The results are unsatisfactory from a moral point of view.

The author of the collection of stories entitled *Uji Monogatari* was a court noble named Minamoto no Takakuni, better known as Uji Dainagon, from his place of residence and rank. He died A.D. 1077, at an advanced age. Being a fat man, and greatly disliking the hot weather, he used to retire for the summer season to Uji, a village not far from Kiōto, on the bank of the river which flows out of Lake Biwa. Here he built a little tea-house on the roadside near his country-seat, where tea was offered to the passers-by. They were then invited to tell stories, which the Dainagon, sitting behind a screen, took down from their mouths. Most of the stories so collected are obviously fictitious; but, true or false, they have a special interest, inasmuch as they present a fuller and livelier picture of the lives and ideas of the middle and lower classes than most other works of this period.

As might be expected from the manner of its compilation, the *Uji Monogatari* contains a large element of folk-lore. The style is easy and unpretentious. Thirty of the sixty thin volumes of which it consists are assigned to Japanese stories, the remainder containing tales of Chinese or Indian origin. Probably not all of these were collected in the manner above described, and a certain

---

[1] The reader may think that this is a great deal to express by the one word, "Tori-kaye-ba-ya!" It is literally "Take-change-if-oh!" Note the absence of personal pronouns, to the use of which the genius of the Japanese language is averse.

proportion, it is believed, have been added by later editors.

The following outlines of a few may give some idea of the general character of this collection :—

A painter named Kawanari has an intimate friend, an architect and engineer called Hida no Takumi. The latter, having built a small square pavilion, invites his friend to enter it. The painter approaches the south door, when by some mechanical contrivance it shuts in his face. When he tries to go in by the west door, it closes and the north door opens. And so on. In revenge for the practical joke thus played on him, Kawanari paints on a screen the picture of a corpse so loathsome and repulsive, that when Hida no Takumi is made to approach it unawares he starts back in horror and rushes out into the garden.

A Buddhist monk, a renowned player of Go, is invited to visit a mysterious lady. With a screen interposed between them, they play a game which ends in the total massacre of the monk's men. The lady is never heard of again, and is presumed to have been a supernatural being.

A professor of magic, by some mistake in his ceremonies, excites the wrath of the infernal demons. They pursue him. He gets off his horse and lets it go home by itself, while he hides among the sheaves in a rice-field by the way. The demons follow the tracks of the horse's feet, and the magician escapes, having learnt from the conversation of his pursuers as they pass his hiding-place how to circumvent them when they renew their attack upon him.

A professor of magic goes to perform a ceremony of purification from evil influences. His little boy, who accompanies him, by an inward gift is able to see a number of devils, invisible to the ordinary eye, carrying away the offerings of food made to them. He afterwards becomes a great magician.

A guitar, a valued heirloom of the Mikado, disappears mysteriously. One of the courtiers who is a great musician traces it by its sound, and finds that it has been purloined by a devil. On its being explained to the devil that the guitar is a much-prized possession of the Mikado, he at once returns it.

A young woman who is urged by her parents to take a second husband, fortifies her refusal to do so by the example of a swallow which had built its nest in their house, and whose mate had been taken from it. It goes away in the autumn, and when it comes back the following summer it is still alone.

Among other fictitious Monogatari which have come down to us from this period, there may be mentioned the *Idzumi Shikibu Monogatari*, the *Ima Monogatari*, the *Tsutsumi Chiunagon Monogatari*, the *Akiyo no Naga-monogatari*, and the *Matsuho Monogatari*, which, although all useful for the study of the state of society at this time, do not present any special features of literary interest. Of many others the names only have reached us.

CHAPTER VII

"YEIGWA MONOGATARI" AND "Ō-KAGAMI"

IT was inevitable that the Japanese language, which had now reached its highest degree of perfection as an instrument for the expression of thought, should, sooner or later, be applied to some more serious purpose than the writing of poetry, stories, diaries, and other light literature. The *Yeigwa Monogatari* is notable as the first instance of its being used for history. The authorship of this work is unknown. A not very trustworthy tradition ascribes it to a celebrated poetess of this period named Akazome Yemon, but as it mentions events which occurred after her death, it cannot all be from her pen. She may, however, have left materials which were incorporated into the work of a subsequent writer. The date of its composition is also uncertain. It must be near the end of the eleventh century.

The *Yeigwa Monogatari* consists of forty books, which cover a period of about two centuries of Japanese history, ending with A.D. 1088. It is, however, not so much the general history of the country during this time as of the glorious rule (*Yeigwa Monogatari* means "A Tale of Glory") of Fujiwara no Michinaga, who was Chief Minister in the three reigns of Ichijō, Sanjō, and Go Ichijō, and who died A.D. 1027. The latter part of the work is the history of his two sons, Yorimichi and Norimichi, who succeeded to his power.

The author's style and method have been greatly influenced by his models—the more fictitious Monogatari. He (or she) betrays a preference for romantic episodes, and leans to a more or less poetical and imaginative treatment of his subject, enlivening his narrative with anecdotes, and adorning his pages freely with the ubiquitous Tanka.

The custom, common with romance writers at the present day, of placing fanciful headings to every chapter, began with this work.

The following passage illustrates the strong hold which Buddhism had upon the Japanese nation at this period. It may be premised that the Mikado Kwazan ascended the throne in 985 at the age of seventeen. He was provided with three beautiful and noble women as consorts. One of these he became passionately fond of, and when she died soon after, the shock was too great for a mind in which there already lurked hereditary germs of insanity :—

"From the beginning of the second year of Kwanwa (986) there was an uneasy feeling in the minds of the people, and many strange warnings were given. In the palace also religious abstinence was frequently practised. Moreover (at what time this began is uncertain) the people turned their minds to religion in an extraordinary degree, and nothing else was heard of but of one becoming a nun and another entering the priesthood. When the Mikado was informed of this, he bewailed the wretchedness of this transitory world. He must have thought to himself, 'Alas! how deep Kōkiden's [his favourite wife] sins must have been. Such as she was, her guilt [in some past existence] was surely great [or she would not have died so young]. Oh that I could find some means of doing away with it!' His august heart being frequently disturbed by strange and lofty thoughts like this, the result was apparent in his agitated demeanour. The Prime Minister noted this with sorrow, and the Chiunagon also, the Mikado's uncle, must in secret have been simply heart-broken. Gonkiu, a priest of the monastery of Kwazan, was continually sent for in order to expound the scriptures, and the Mikado's august heart was given up to religion in an infinite measure. His remarks about wife and child, and the priceless treasure of the sovereign rank, filled the Sachiuben Korenari with the utmost pity, and this devotion to religion gave both him and the Chiunagon great concern. 'To give up the world and enter religion,' they said, 'is an ordinary course to take, but how will it be in this case?' Certain expressions of his sentiments from time to time must have been due to nought else but an evil influence proceeding from Reizei-in [his father and predecessor on the throne, who became insane]. Meanwhile, they noted other strange, unwonted, and unconscious behaviour of the Mikado, and attended closely upon him. But on the night of the 22nd day of the sixth month of this year he suddenly disappeared. An alarm was given, and everybody, without exception, from the nobles-in-waiting down to the guards and servants of meanest rank, procured lights and sought everywhere. But no trace of the Mikado could be found. The Prime Minister with the other ministers and nobles all assembled. Every room was searched, but he was nowhere to be seen, and the night was spent by all in the utmost consternation and alarm.

"The Chiunagon, prostrating himself in grief before

the shrine of the [Shinto] gods, protectors of the palace, prayed them with tears and lamentations to reveal to him the place where his precious lord was hidden. Then he was sought for by parties despatched severally to all the Buddhist temples, but in vain. Meanwhile his consorts wept, and in their hearts thought what a terrible thing had happened. The long summer's night at length gave way to dawn, but the search was still fruitless.

"The Chiunagon and the Sachiuben Korenari went at last to Kwazan, and there they discovered him clothed as a dear little priest. They fell down before him with exclamations of grief and concern, and both followed his example and entered the priesthood."

The *Ō-Kagami* or "Great Mirror" is another historical work. It contains the history of fourteen reigns, beginning with that of Mondoku, who came to the throne A.D. 851, and ending with that of Go Ichijō, who died in A.D. 1036. The author was one Tamenari, a member of the great Fujiwara family, and an official attached to the court of the Mikado Sutoku (1124–1141). He served for some time as Director of the Empress's palace, but subsequently assumed the tonsure and retired to a hermitage on Mount Ohara, near Kiōto. Here he was joined by his two brothers, who followed his example and abandoned the world for a life of religion. Tamenari's preface to the *Ō-Kagami* shows that he was a devout Buddhist.

Whether we have regard to its matter or to its form, the *Ō-Kagami* is not a very important contribution to literature. It is in eight volumes. Volume I. contains, in sixty-four pages, meagre sketches of the lives of fourteen Mikados. The year, month, and day of birth, appointment as Crown Prince, assumption of the manly style of dressing the hair, accession to the throne and death of each sovereign, are set down baldly in a page or two. Then follow one or two sentimental or humorous anecdotes, adorned as usual with Tanka. There is little more. In the next six volumes we find biographies of the principal statesmen during the same period. This part of the work is somewhat more substantial, but there is still a marked inclination towards the anecdotal and romantic treatment of the subject. The last volume is an excursus on the origin of certain festivals at the shrines of Kamo and Hachiman.

The *Ō-Kagami* throws but little light on the times of which it professes to give the history, but it may perhaps be acceptable as an addition to the information supplied us by the drier official histories in the Chinese language.

This work, with the *Masa-Kagami*, and the *Midzu-Kagami* (to be noticed afterwards), are known as the *Mitsu-Kagami* or "Three Mirrors." Mirror, it may be explained, is a familiar metaphor for history, not only in Japan, but in China and Corea.

Before closing this chapter, one or two works in the Chinese language require to be mentioned.

The *Shōjiroku* is a sort of peerage. It was prepared A.D. 815, and contains the genealogy of 1182 noble families of Japan. It has no value as literature, but is useful for historical reference, and has one interesting feature—it shows that at this period about one-third of the Japanese nobility claimed to be descended from Chinese or Corean ancestors.

The *Yengishiki*, or "Institutes of the Period Yengi" (901–923), was completed in 927. The first two volumes contain minute directions for the celebration of the Shinto rites of worship, including the Norito or liturgies used on these occasions, which were now for the first time, so far as we know, committed to writing, although in existence for centuries previously. The remaining forty volumes give a description of the organisation of the various Government departments, the duties of the officials, &c. The *Yengishiki* is a most valuable work of reference.

The *Wamiōshō* is a Chinese-Japanese dictionary, arranged according to categories, such as Heaven, Earth, &c., and is valuable to philologists, but not otherwise. The author of this lexicon was one Minamoto no Shitagaü (911–983).

BOOK THE FOURTH

KAMAKURA PERIOD (1186–1332)

(DECLINE OF LEARNING)

BOOK THE FOURTH

KAMAKURA PERIOD (1186–1332)

(DECLINE OF LEARNING)

CHAPTER I

INTRODUCTORY

In the history of Japan, as in that of many other countries, there is observable an alternate tendency towards strong and weak central governments, which is all the more pronounced as the insular position of the country protects this natural oscillation against foreign interference. From time to time rulers of commanding abilities and resolute character made their appearance, who enlarged the sphere of authority of the State, and kept local ambitions in check. But sooner or later the central control became relaxed, and each province established a sort of Home Rule for itself, until another swing of the pendulum took place, and the reins of government were again grasped by the strong hand of a single authority.

The establishment by the Shōgun Yoritomo, after much hard fighting, of the sway of the military caste at Kamakura, near the end of the twelfth century, marked the beginning of one of these periods of vigorous centralisation. Though the Mikados were allowed to retain an outward semblance of authority, all real power, civil and military, had passed from their hands ; while, on the other hand, the local nobles saw themselves supplanted by officers appointed by the Shōguns and entirely dependent on them.

Yoritomo was succeeded by his two sons, who with their father are known to history as the "Three Shōguns." After them the Hōjō dynasty of Shikken (directors), who were simply Shōguns under a different name, took their place as the rulers of Japan. They remained in power until A.D. 1335.

The rule of a class to whose very existence a practical knowledge of war and warlike accomplishments was vital, and who necessarily neglected, if they did not despise, intellectual culture, was not conducive to the production of important literary works. Nor was this the only unfavourable condition of the time. Intercourse with China and Corea had become much interrupted. The shores of these countries were infested by Japanese pirates, in punishment for whose descents it was that Kublai Khan despatched his famous but abortive expedition against Japan. Chinese learning consequently languished. Buddhism, on the other hand, flourished greatly, as the colossal figure of Buddha (A.D. 1252) at Kamakura testifies to this day. Most of the Mikados, after a few years of reign, became monks, as did also many of the highest personages of their court, though it must be said that the adage " Cucullus non facit monachum " was in their case abundantly exemplified.

The three thousand monasteries which at this time dotted the slopes of Hiyeisan (a mountain north-east of Kiōto) were a very material embodiment of Buddhist influence. Not content with mere spiritual weapons, the inmates of these establishments were always ready, on the smallest provocation, to don their armour over their monastic frocks and troop down to the streets of Kiōto to place their swords in whatever scale of the politics of the day seemed to them most expedient. They were the terror of the Mikados, one of whom is recorded to have said : "There are three things I cannot control— the water of the Kamogawa (a river which does frequent damage to Kiōto by its floods), the fall of the dice, and the monks of Buddha."

It was, however, the Buddhist monks who were the chief maintainers of learning during this period. Some of the men of letters were ecclesiastics, and even when this was not the case, their writings are deeply imbued with Buddhist teachings and sentiments. The vanity of wealth and power, and the uncertainty of human things, form the constant refrain of their moralisings.

In comparison with the Heian period, the contributions by women to the literature of this time are insignificant, and altogether a more virile, if less refined, spirit is discernible. There are hardly any of those debonair romances which in the preceding period amused the leisure of the nobles of Kiōto. The newer literature, with its tales of combats and battles, reflects the more warlike temper of the times of which it is the product. As a Japanese writer has observed, "The Heian literature is like the Kaidō (*Pyrus spectabilis*) drooping after rain ; that of the Kamakura period resembles the plum-blossom which exhales its perfume in the snow and frost."

It is to be noted that the more important writings of this period belong to the earlier part of it.

CHAPTER II

HISTORICAL WORKS

THE authorship of the *Gempei Seisuiki* is doubtfully ascribed to one Hamuro Tokinaga, of whom we know little or nothing. He is also conjectured to have written the *Heiji Monogatari* and *Hōgen Monogatari*, but of this too there is no certainty. The precise date of its composition is likewise unknown. It must belong to the early part of the Kamakura period.

The *Gempei Seisuiki*, as its name indicates, is a history of the rise and fall of the Gen and Hei, two great noble families whose struggles for supremacy convulsed Japan during the latter half of the twelfth century. It is in forty-eight books, and embraces the period from A.D. 1161 to 1185. No doubt itself suggested by the Chinese *Yengi* or "Paraphrases of History," of which the *San-kwo-chih* is the best known, the *Gempei Seisuiki* is the first example in Japan of a large class of quasi-historical works to which there is nothing precisely similar in our literature, though a comparison with Shakespeare's historical plays will convey some idea of the relative proportions of fact and fiction which they contain. They have no original plot, and little or no introduction of imaginary personages. The writers content themselves with following the general course of real history, while adorning it with what flourish their nature prompts.

But the "flourish" means a great deal. It is not only rhetorical ornament and sententious reflections which these authors provide. They evolve from their inner consciousness speeches for statesmen and soldiers, warlike stratagems for generals, prayers for the devout, appropriate omens, dreams, incantations, and miraculous incidents in great variety, with a host of minute details of dress, of pompous processions, of hairbreadth escapes, of single combats, and the like. Tanka, original or otherwise, are supplied whenever the occasion seems to demand them.

The *Gempei Seisuiki* is a work of considerable literary pretensions, and in its own special style is only surpassed by the *Taiheiki*. The language marks a considerable advance towards the modern form of Japanese. While the works of the Heian period are very imperfectly intelligible to an ordinary educated Japanese, with the *Gempei Seisuiki* he finds little difficulty. Much of the older grammatical equipment of particles and terminations is now dispensed with, and the vocabulary shows a large increment of Chinese words, a notable proportion of which owe their introduction to Buddhist influences.

The following is part of the account of the naval engagement of Dannöura, one of the decisive battles of Japanese history. By it the strife between the great Hei (or Taira) and Gen (or Minamoto) factions was brought to an end for the time, and Yoritomo enabled to establish his authority over all Japan.

"The capture of Yashima shut out the House of Hei from Kiushiu. Unable to find a port of refuge, they drifted on to Dannöura in Nagato, Akama (Shimonoseki), Moji, and Hikushima. Here they remained afloat upon the waves, passing the time on board their ships. The Gen fleet arrived at the bay of Katsura, in the province of Awa. They had been victorious in the conflicts engaged in in various places, and had taken the palace of Yashima. They now followed the movements of the Hei ships, pursuing them by land, as the hawk urges the pheasants when the moors are burnt and no cover is left. The Gen fleet reached a place called Oitsuheitsu, twenty *chō* or more [about two miles] from where the adherents of the Hei House were stationed.

"On the 24th day of the third month of the same year [1185], Yoshitsune [the Gen general, brother of Yoritomo] and his army, in seven hundred ships or more, attacked the enemy at dawn. The House of Hei were not unprepared. With five hundred war-ships or more, they advanced to meet him, and the exchange of arrows [by way of formal defiance] took place. The Gen and Hei troops numbered together over 100,000 men, and the sound of the battle-cry raised on both sides, with the song of the turnip-headed arrows [a special kind of arrow which made a noise like a hum-ming-top] as they crossed each other's course, was startling to hear—audible, one would think, as far as the azure sky above, and re-echoing downwards to the depths of the sea.

"Noriyori [with other Gen generals] had arrived at Kiushiu with 30,000 cavalry, and had cut off the retreat in that direction. The Hei were like a caged bird that cannot escape, or a fish in a trap from which there is no exit. On the sea there were ships floating, by land were bridle-bits in ranged lines. East and west, south and north were closed, and on no side was evasion possible.

"Tomomori [a Hei general] stood forward on the bow of his ship and spoke as follows :—

"'Let us think this day our last, and let us all banish the thought of retreat. In ancient and modern times there have been examples of even famous generals and brave soldiers, when their armies were beaten and their good fortune exhausted, being captured by a traveller or taken prisoner by a wayfarer. All these arose from the endeavour to avoid a death which was inevitable. Let us each one at this time abandon our lives to destruction, and think of nothing else but to leave a name to after ages. Let us show no weakness before these fellows from the east country. What have we done that we should be grudging even of our lives ? Let us unite in the resolve to seize Yoshitsune and fling him into the sea. This should be the chief object of to-day's battle.' "

The first onset was favourable to the Hei faction, upon which :—

"Yoshitsune, observing that his troops showed signs of yielding, rinsed his mouth in the salt tide, and with closed eyes and folded palms preyed to Hachiman Daibosatsu[1] to grant him his protection. Hereupon a pair of white doves [the pigeon is sacred to Hachiman] flew thither and alit on Yoshitsune's flag. While Gen and Hei were saying, " Look there, look there," a mass of black clouds came floating from the east and hung over the scene of battle. From amidst this cloud a white flag descended, while Yoshitsune's flag, its top

---

[1] This deity has a curious history. Originally the Mikado Ōjin, he was credited with having conquered Corea while an unborn infant. Then he became the Shinto god of war, and finally was annexed by the Buddhists, who added to his name the Buddhist title of " Daibosatsu."

waving to and fro, passed away along with the clouds. The Gen joined their hands together in prayer, while the Hei's hair stood on end, and their hearts felt small within them.

"The Gen soldiers, encouraged by such favourable omens, shouted aloud in their ardour. Some embarked in boats and rowed on and on, fighting as they went. Others, marching along the dry land, and fitting arrows to their bows one after another in quick succession, engaged in a battle of archery."

This is described in a style which recalls the combats of the *Iliad*, the doings and sayings of individual heroes being related in great detail.

"The Gen were many, and encouraged by success, pressed forward to the attack; the Hei were fewer, but acquitted themselves as if that day were their last. Can the battle of Indra with the Asuras have been more terrible than this?

"The Hei ships were drawn up two or three deep. The ship of Chinese build was furnished with troops in a manner which showed that the general was on board. On the [ordinary] fighting-ships the Daijin and other fit officers of lower rank were embarked. It was the plan of the Hei, whilst the Gen were attacking the Chinese ship, that their fighting-ships should fetch a circuit round the enemy's vessels, and enclosing them, smite the Gen to a man.

"Thereupon Shigeyoshi, hitherto so faithful to the Hei cause, suddenly changed his heart, and with three hundred ships or more, manned with troops from Shikoku, rowed away, and remained a passive spectator of the battle, prepared, if the Hei proved the stronger, to shoot his arrows at the Gen; if the Gen seemed likely to gain the victory, to aim them at the Hei. How true is it that heaven may be reckoned upon, earth may be reckoned upon ; the only thing which we cannot reckon on is the heart of man."

Ultimately Shigeyoshi betrays to Yoshitsune the Hei plan of battle, with the result that the latter faction are completely overthrown.

The authorship and precise date of the *Heike Monogatari* are unknown. It was probably composed soon after the *Gempei Seisuiki,* of which it is little more than an adaptation, page after page being simply copied from the latter work. But as if its model and source had not already departed sufficiently from true history, the *Heike Monogatari,* which covers the same ground and relates the same events, adds a number of inventions of its own, under the inspiration of patriotic or pious motives, or for the sake of poetical or dramatic effect. It is said that a main object of the author was to produce a narrative which could be chanted to the accompaniment of the *biwa,* a kind of four-stringed lute. That it was so chanted by men with shaven heads called *biwa-bōzu* (biwa-bonzes) is a fact frequently referred to by later writers. In this form it became immensely popular, and even at the present day it is far better known than the *Gempei Seisuiki,* a work much superior to it in merit. Motoöri, reasoning from the premiss that everything which can be sung is poetry, classes the *Heike* accordingly. He says that even though the actual count of syllables will not come right, they can be slurred over in singing so as to make metre. The reader might expect from this to find that the *Heike* is an example of poetical prose somewhat in the style of Ossian. But there is really hardly anything to justify Motoöri's opinion. Its style, though occasionally more or less ornate, is not really more poetical than that of many books for which no such pretension is advanced. To this, however, an exception must be noticed. In a very few passages, forming altogether an utterly insignificant part of the book, there is something of that alternation of phrases of five and seven syllables which in Japan constitutes metre, and the diction and thought bear traces of an attempt to treat the subject in a poetical manner. The following is a specimen :—

A local official named Morotsune, having had a dispute with the monks of a certain temple, burnt it. The latter assembled the monks of the parent monastery, to the number of over two thousand men, and approached his official residence :—

> "*And now the sun went down.*
> *Resolved to engage battle on the morrow,*
> *That night they drew near and contained themselves.*
> *The breath of the dew-laden wind of autumn*
> *Fluttered the left sleeves of their armour.*
> *The lightning which illumined the clouds above*
> *Made the stars of their helmets to blaze.*
> *Morotsune, feeling that resistance was in vain,*
> *Fled up by night to Kiôto.*
> *The next day they advanced at the hour of the Hare* [*sunrise*]
> *And abruptly raised the battle-cry ;*
> *But within the castle not a sound was heard.*
> *A man was sent to examine,*
> *But reported that they had all decamped.*"

Even in this short passage the regularity of metre and the poetical diction are not well sustained.

It would not be necessary to dwell on this feature of the *Heike Monogatari* but for the circumstance that we have here the beginning of a kind of composition which subsequently became very popular in Japan. The *Tai-heiki* carried this "dropping into poetry" somewhat further, and the modern dramatists and novelists have bestowed on us much tediousness of this particular description.

After the battle of Dannoüra (see p. 135), the Mikado Antoku's nurse, seeing that all was over, took him into her arms (he was then a boy of eight years of age) and plunged into the sea with him. Both were drowned. The following is the *Heike Monogatari's* account of this incident :—

"Niidono was long ago prepared for this [the defeat of the Hei or Taira party]. Throwing over her head her double garment of sombre hue, and tucking up high the side of her trousers of straw-coloured silk, she placed under her arm the Sacred Seal, and girt on her loins the Sacred Sword. Then taking the sovereign to her bosom, she said, 'Although a woman, I will not allow the enemy to lay hands on me. I will accompany my sovereign. All ye who have regard for his intention make haste and follow.' So saying, she calmly placed her foot on the ship's side. The sovereign had this year reached the age of eight, but looked much older. His august countenance was so beautiful that it cast a lustre round about. His black locks hung loosely down below his back. With an astonished expression he inquired, 'Now, whither do you propose to take me, Amaze ?'[1] Niidono turned her face to her child-lord, and with tears that fell *bara-bara*, 'Do you not know, my lord,' said she, 'that although, by virtue of your keeping the Ten Commandments in a previous state of existence, you have been born into this world as the ruler of ten thousand chariots,

[1] A respectful title for women who have taken Buddhist vows.

yet having become involved in an evil destiny, your good fortune is now at an end? Be pleased to turn first to the east, and bid adieu to the shrine of the Great God of Ise. Then turn to the west, and call upon the name of Buddha, solemnly committing yourself to the charge of those who will come to meet you from the Paradise of the Western Land. This world is the region of sorrow, a remote spot small as a grain of millet. But beneath the waves there is a fair city called the Pure Land of Perfect Happiness. Thither it is that I am taking you.' With such words she soothed him. The child then tied his top-knot to the Imperial robe of the colour of a mountain-dove, and tearfully joined together his lovely little hands. First he turned to the east, and bade adieu to the shrine of the Great God of Ise and the shrine of Hachiman. Next he turned to the west, and called upon the name of Buddha. When he had done so, Niidono made bold to take him in her arms, and soothing him with the words, 'There is a city away below the waves,' sank down to the bottom one thousand fathoms deep. Alas, the pity of it!—the changeful winds of spring swiftly scattered the flowery august form. Alas, the pain of it!—the rude billows of severance buried the jewel person. His palace had been called Chōsei, to denote that it was established as his long abode; and the gate inscribed Furō, that is, the portal through which old age enters not. But ere ten years had passed he had become drift of the deep sea. In the case of such a virtuous monarch it would be wholly idle to talk of reward and retribution. It is the dragon of the region above the clouds descending and becoming a fish."

A comparison of the above with the corresponding

passage of the *Gempei Seisuiki* shows very clearly the different character of the two works. There is nothing in the latter about praying to Shinto deities or to Buddha, and no talk of a future Paradise. When the young monarch asks where his nurse is taking him, instead of the devout sentiments attributed to her by the *Heike Monogatari*, the *Gempei Seisuiki* tells us that she said, "The soldiers are shooting arrows at the august ship, and I have the honour to escort your Majesty to another one."

The honorifics characteristic of the Japanese language come in very ·oddly in some of these passages. Thus in the above the waves "respectfully" submerge the Mikado, the enemy's soldiers "respectfully" direct their arrows against the august ship, and so forth. It would be tedious to follow these peculiarities in a translation.

The authorship of the historical work called *Midzu-Kagami* ("Water-Mirror") is really unknown. It has been ascribed to Nakayama Tadachika, who was born 1131, and died 1195. Omitting the myths of the so-called "Age of the Gods," the writer begins his history with the legend of Jimmu Tennō, the first Mikado, and brings it down through fifty-four reigns to the death of Nimmiō in 850. It is of course impossible to give anything but a meagre outline of the history of this long period in three volumes of no great bulk. Its value is small. In the earlier part it is little more than an epitome of the *Nihongi*. The story is told in a plain, artless fashion, without rhetorical ornament, philosophical reflections, or the least attempt to trace the causes or connection of events. Whoever the author was, he was a devout Buddhist, to which fact is no doubt to be attributed a certain miraculous element in the latter part of the history.

The *Midzu-Kagami* is an obvious imitation of the *Ō-Kagami*. The language is comparatively free from Chinese admixture, and from the point of view of style the work is to be classed with the literature of the Heian period.

The authorship of the *Hōgen Monogatari* and *Heiji Monogatari* is attributed to Hamuro Tokinaga, who lived towards the end of the twelfth century. The former contains an account of the civil disturbances in Kiōto in the year 1157, arising out of a dispute respecting the succession to the throne ; the latter is a record of the renewal of the conflict in 1159. The result of this fighting was the downfall for a time of the power of the great Minamoto (Gen) family, and the establishment of the Taira (Hei) family in power.

CHAPTER III

CHŌMEI AND THE "HŌJŌKI"

KAMO CHŌMEI, the author of the *Hōjōki*, was a guardian of the Shinto shrine of Kamo in Kiōto. Having acquired some reputation as a musician and poet, he was appointed by the retired Mikado Go Toba to a post in the Department of Japanese Poetry. He subsequently petitioned to be allowed to succeed his father as superior guardian of Kamo, but his prayer was not granted. This he resented deeply, and shaving his head, retired to a hermitage on Ōharayama, a few miles from Kiōto.

The *Hōjōki*, written in 1212, is a record of the author's personal experiences. It is valued highly for its excellent style, which is not too close an imitation of the older classical manner, nor yet, on the other hand, overloaded with Chinese expressions. After giving an account of the great fire of Kiōto in 1177, the famine of 1181, and the earthquake of 1185, the writer of these memoirs proceeds to tell us of the mountain hermitage to which he fled in order to escape from a world so rife with direful calamities. His hut and mode of life are minutely described, with many touches which not only give indications of his own tastes and character, but reveal something of the inner spirit of the Buddhist religion. It is a tiny book on which to rest so high a reputation, containing some thirty pages only, and it is therefore possible to transcribe all the more interesting passages. *Hōjō*, it may be premised, means "ten feet square," the supposed dimensions of a hermit's cell, and actually those of Chōmei's hut. *Ki* means "notes" or "record."

"The current of a running stream flows on unceasingly, but the water is not the same : the foam floating on the pool where it lingers, now vanishes and now forms again, but is never lasting. Such are mankind and their habitations. In a splendid capital where the dwellings of the exalted and of the lowly join their roof-trees and with their tiles jostle one another, they may appear to go on without an interval from generation to generation. But we shall find, if we make inquiry, that there are in reality but few which are ancient. Some were destroyed last year to be rebuilt this year ; others, which were great houses, have been ruined, and replaced by smaller ones. The same is true of their inmates. If we have lived long in a place where we have numbers of acquaintances, we find that but one or two are left of twenty or thirty whom we knew formerly. In the morning some die, in the evening some are born. Such is life. It may be compared to foam upon the water. Whether they are born or whether they die, we know not whence they come nor whither they go. Nor in this temporary sojourning-place do we know who will benefit by the trouble we put ourselves to, or wherewithal to give pleasure to the eyes. Of a house and its master I know not which is the more subject to change. Both are like the dew on the convolvulus. The dew may fall, leaving the flower behind ; but even so, the flower fades with the morning sun. Again, the flower may wither, while the dew remains; but even so, it cannot last until evening.

"During the forty springs and summers which have passed since I first knew the heart of things, many extraordinary events have happened. In the third year of Angen (1177), on the twenty-eighth day of the fourth month, the night being unquiet by reason of a violent wind, a fire broke out in the south-eastern part of the capital, about eight o'clock, and spread in a north-westerly direction, gaining the southern gate of the Palace, the Hall of Audience, the University buildings, and the Home Office. That same night all were reduced to ashes. It was said to have had its origin in a temporary building used as a hospital. Urged by the blasts of the devious wind, it spread this way and that until it widened out like an extended fan. The distant houses were immersed in smoke, while the nearer ground was completely covered with the sparks blown on to it. The ashes, driven aloft into the sky, and illumined by the flames, formed a ruddy background against which the sparks might be seen, continually detached by the gusts, and as it were flying over a space of several hundred yards to some new quarter. Imagine the distracted state of the inhabitants! Some there were who fell down, stifled by the smoke; others, involved in flames, met with a sudden death; others, again, barely escaped with their lives, and were unable to save their property. Their seven rare things and their ten thousand treasures became mere ashes. How great were the losses! Sixteen houses of nobles were consumed, and others without number. One-third of all Kiōto was destroyed. Several thousands of men and women lost their lives, and an immense number of cattle. All the ways of man are full of vanity, but it may be deemed specially unprofitable to build ourselves dwellings in so dangerous a place as the capital, wasting our wealth, and giving ourselves much anxiety of mind.

"Again, on the 29th day of the fourth month of the fourth year of Jishō (1180), there was a great whirlwind which arose in the Kiōgoku quarter, and blew with much violence as far as Rokujō. Three or four of the city wards received its full force. In these there was not a single house, great or small, which was not destroyed by its whirling blasts. Some were simply laid flat on the ground; in others nothing was left but the posts and cross-beams. The roofs of gates were blown off and deposited at a distance of several streets. Fences were swept away, removing all distinction between a neighbour's ground and one's own. It need hardly be said that all the contents of the houses without exception rose to the sky, while the bark and shingles of the roofs were scattered abroad like autumnal leaves before the wind. The dust was blown up like smoke, so that nothing could be seen, and the din was so tremendous that one could not hear his neighbour speak. The blasts of the Buddhist Inferno of which we have been told must be something of this kind. Not only were houses destroyed, but countless numbers of people were injured, and became cripples [by exposure] while their homes were being repaired. This wind passed off in a south-westerly direction, having caused lamentation to many. Now a whirlwind is an ordinary phenomenon, but this was no mere natural occurrence; I strongly suspect that it was sent as a warning."

[Here follows an account of the miseries attendant

upon the removal of the capital to Settsu in the same year (1180).]

"It is so long ago that I do not exactly remember, but I believe it was in the period Yōwa (1181-2) that there was for two years a very wretched state of things caused by famine. Misfortunes succeeded one another. Either there was drought in spring and summer, or there were storms and floods in autumn and winter, so that no grain came to maturity. The spring ploughing was in vain, and the labour of summer planting [of the young rice] came to naught. There was no bustle of reaping in autumn, or of ingathering in winter. In all the provinces people left their lands and sought other parts, or, forgetting their homes, went to live among the hills. All kinds of prayers were begun, and even religious practices which were unusual in ordinary times revived, but to no purpose whatever. The capital, dependent as it is on the country for everything, could not remain unconcerned when nothing was produced. The inhabitants in their distress offered to sacrifice their valuables of all kinds one after another, but nobody cared to look at them. Even if buyers came forward, they made little account of gold, and much of grain. Beggars swarmed by the roadsides, and our ears were filled with the sound of their lamentations. Amid such misery we with difficulty reached the close of the first year. With the new year, men's hopes revived. But that nothing might be left to complete our misfortunes, a pestilence broke out and continued without ceasing. Everybody was dying of hunger, and as time went on, our condition became as desperate as that of the fish in the small pool of the story. At last even respectable-looking people wearing hats, and with their feet covered, might be seen begging importu-

nately from door to door. Sometimes while you wondered how such utterly wretched creatures could walk at
all, they fell down before your eyes.   By garden walls or
on the roadsides countless persons died of famine, and as
their bodies were not removed, the world was filled with
evil odours.   As they changed, there were many sights
which the eyes could not endure to see.   It was worse
on the river banks where there was not even room for
horses and vehicles to pass back and forwards.   Porters
and woodcutters too became so feeble that firewood
got scarcer and scarcer, and people who had no means
pulled down their houses and sold the materials in the
market.   It was said that a load for one man was not
enough to provide him with sustenance for a single day.
It was strange to see among this firewood pieces adorned
in places with vermilion, or silver or gold leaf.   On
inquiry, it appeared that people in their extremity went
to old temples, stole the images of Buddha, and broke
up the objects used in worship, of which these were the
fragments.   Such mournful spectacles it was my lot to
witness, born into a polluted and wicked world.

" Another very pitiable thing was that when there were
a man and woman who were strongly attached to each
other, the one whose love was the greatest and whose
devotion was the most profound always died first.   The
reason was that they put themselves last, and, whether
man or woman, gave up to the dearly loved one anything
which they might chance to have begged.   As a matter
of course, parents died before their children.   Again,
infants might be seen clinging to the breast of their
mother, not knowing that she was already dead.   A
priest of the Temple of Jisonin, grieved in his secret
heart at the numberless persons who were thus perish-

ing, consulted with a great many holy men, who by his advice, when they saw any one dead, wrote on his forehead the first of the Chinese characters for Amida [Buddha] and by this bond united him [to the Church]. The numbers of those who died in central Kiōto during the fourth and fifth months alone were 42,300. To this must be added many who died before and after ; while if we also reckon those who perished in the various outlying quarters, the number has no limit. And then the provinces ! I have heard that in recent times there was a similar famine in the reign of Sutoku, in the period Chōjō (1132–1135), but of this I do not know the circumstances. What I have described is the most lamentable state of things that I have myself witnessed."

Chōmei next describes the great earthquake at Kiōto of the year 1185, in which, when at its worst, there were twenty or thirty shocks a day, such as would be called severe in ordinary times. After ten or twenty days the shocks in one day were two to five, then one every two or three days. It was not until the third month that the earth had quite recovered its quiet.

The story of these disasters is introductory to an account of his own life, and is brought in to explain his resolve to abandon the city and to live the life of a recluse. He spent thirty years in a small cabin remote from Kiōto, but finding even this seclusion not sufficiently restful—

" Five springs and autumns," he says, " came and went to me making my bed among the clouds of Mount Ōhara. And now at sixty, when the dew does not easily evaporate,[1] I again built myself a last leaf of a dwelling, something like the shelter which a traveller

---

[1] In other words, " sad thoughts are not easily shaken off."

might erect for one night's lodging, or the cocoon spun for itself by an aged silkworm. It is not a hundredth part so commodious as the habitation of my middle-time. As my age declined with every year, at each remove my dwelling became smaller. This last one is no ordinary house. It is barely ten feet square, and only seven feet high. As it was not meant for a fixed abode, the ground about it was trodden hard and left uncultivated. The walls are of mud, and it is thatched with rushes. The joints are fastened with rings and staples, for the greater convenience of removal elsewhere if any subject of dissatisfaction should arise. How little trouble it would take to rebuild it in another place! It would barely make two cart-loads, and there would be no expense whatever beyond the cartage.

"Since I concealed my traces in the recesses of Mount Hino, I have put up a projecting roof of some three feet or more in width on the eastern side, as a place for breaking and burning brushwood. On the south I have set out a temporary shade and laid down a bamboo grating [by way of a mat]. On the west there is the domestic shrine. Within, against the north, and on the other side of a paper screen, I have installed a picture of Amida, and beside it have hung one of Fugen. Before them I have placed a copy of the *Hokkekio*.[1] Close to the eastern wall I have spread a quantity of fern, which serves me as a bed. On the south-west there is provided a hanging shelf of bamboo, on which are three or four black leather cases containing Japanese poetry, music, a Buddhist pious book, and such-like manuscripts. Besides there are a harp and a lute of the kinds known as Origoto and Tsugibiwa.

---

[1] Buddhist Scriptures.

"Such is my temporary dwelling. Now to describe its surroundings. On the south there is a water-pipe which leads to a reservoir, constructed by piling large stones one on another. A wood close by affords plenty of sticks for firewood. The Masaki creeper hides all that is beyond. The valley is thickly wooded, but is clear towards the west, which is not unfavourable to meditation.[1]

"Here in spring there may be seen the rippling blossoms of the wistaria, shedding a fragrance towards the west. In summer the Hototogisu[2] is heard, who by his reiterated cry invites to a tryst with him on that rugged path which leads to Hades. In autumn the song of the cicada fills the ears, sounding like a wail over the vanities of this earthly existence. In winter the snow excites in me a sympathetic emotion. As it grows deeper and deeper, and then by degrees melts away again, it is an apt symbol of the obstruction of sin.

"When I am too sad for prayer, or cannot fix my mind on the pages of holy writ, there is no one to prevent me from resting and being as indolent as I please, nor is there any friend in whose presence I might feel ashamed. Though I have not specially adopted silence as my rule, living alone as I do, the faculty of speech has naturally been suspended. With no definite resolve to observe the commandments, my circumstances are such that there is no temptation to break them. When at morn I approach the white waves of the lake, I feel as if I had stolen the sentiments of the novice Mansei when he gazed on the boats passing to and from Okanoya [and compared human life to the ripples left

[1] In the west is India, the native place of Buddhism.
[2] A kind of cuckoo.

in their wake]; when at evening the cassia wind rustles the leaves, I think of the estuary of Junyō and imitate the style of Gen Tōtoku. When more cheerful than usual I extol the music of the autumn wind to the accompaniment of its song among the firs, or to the sound of water join my praises of the music of the running stream. I do not pretend to anything great in music, and I sing or play all by myself, only for the comfort of my own heart, and not for the entertainment of others.

"At the foot of the mountain there is another cabin, built of brushwood, where a forester lives. He has a son who sometimes comes to see me. When I am dull I take him for a walk, and although there is a great difference in our ages, he being sixteen and I sixty, we both enjoy the same pleasures. We pluck the great rush flowers or gather cranberries. We fill our baskets with wild potatoes or collect parsley. Sometimes we go down to the rice-fields in the belt of ground at the bottom of the mountain and glean the fallen ears. In serene weather we climb to the summit and view from afar the sky over my native place. Hence we can see Kowata-yama, Fushimi, Toba, and Hatsukase. Fine scenery is not private property, and there is nothing to prevent me from enjoying it. With no toilsome journey on foot, my mind flies afar along the range of mountain peaks. I cross Mount Sumi, I pass beyond Karadori, I make a pilgrimage to Iwama, I worship at Ishiyama, or else I thread my way over the plain of Awadzu, and pay my respects to the remains of the old Semimaru [a famous musician]; I cross the river Tagami, and visit the tomb of Sarumaru Dayu [a poet].

"On our way home we break off the cherry branches, or gather the red autumn foliage; we pluck the young shoots of the bracken, or pick up nuts according to the season. Some of these are offered to Buddha, and some are taken as presents [to my companion's family].

"When on a calm night the moon shines in at my window, I think with yearning of the men of old, and at the cry of the monkeys my sleeve is wetted with tears. The fire-flies in the clumps of herbage represent to me the fishermen's cressets on the isle of Magi no Shima ; the rain at daybreak sounds to me like the leaves when fluttered by a stormy gust of wind. When I hear the copper pheasant with his cry of 'horo, horo,' I wonder whether it is my father or my mother.[1] When the stag from the mountain top approaches without shyness, I realise how far I am separated from the world.

.   .   .   .

"When I first took up my abode in this place, I thought it was only for a little while. But five years have passed and my temporary hut has become old. Under the eaves there is a deep bed of withered leaves, and moss has gathered on the earthen floor. When by chance I receive news of the capital, I hear of the deaths of many men of high rank, while of those of men of low degree it is impossible to reckon the number. I hear too of many houses being destroyed by frequent conflagrations. But this temporary cabin of mine has remained secure and undisturbed. It is small, but at night I have a bed to lie upon, in the daytime a mat on which I sit. It has all that is needed for the lodging of one person.

.   .   .   .

"Buddha has taught mankind not to allow their hearts to become enslaved by outward things. Even my love for this thatched cabin is to be reckoned a transgres-

[1] Referring to a poem in which the doctrine of transmigration is alluded to.

sion ; even my lying down to quiet rest must be a hindrance to piety. How can any one waste precious time in a continuous indulgence in useless pleasure ? One calm morning I thought long over the reasons of this, and asked of my own heart the question—'The object of leaving the world and making companions of the hills and woods is to give peace to the mind, and to enable us to carry out the practices of religion. But though your outward appearance is that of a holy man, your heart is steeped in impurity. Your dwelling is an unworthy imitation of that of Jōmyō, but in observance you fall behind even Shuri and Bandoku. Is this a natural affliction, inseparable from a mean condition, or is it due to the disorderly passions of an impure heart ?' To this my heart made no answer. A few unbidden invocations of the name of Buddha rose to my lips, and then—silence.

"Written in my hut at Toyama, the second year of Kenriaku (A.D. 1212), the last day of the third month, by me the monk Renin."[1]

Some editions add the following pious Tanka :—

> " The moon is gone—
> A cruel mountain-spur
> Where late she shone :
> Oh ! that my soul had sight
> Of the unfailing light."

Chōmei is also the author of a collection of short essays entitled *Mumiōshō* (" Anonymous Selection "), mostly relating to poetical subjects, and of the *Shiki* (" Four Seasons ") *Monogatari,* descriptive of court functions throughout the year.

---

[1] Chōmei's name as a Buddhist monk.

Several diaries and journals of travel have come down to us from the Kamakura period. The *Izayoi no Ki* is the best known of these. It was written by a lady called Abutsu, a name which indicates that she had taken Buddhist vows. She was a descendant of one of the Mikados, and the widow of a son of the Fujiwara no Sadaiye who edited the *Hiakunin-is-shiu*. The diary was composed on a journey which she took to Kamakura in 1277 to obtain justice for her son Tamesuke against an elder brother by a different mother, who had usurped one of the family estates.

The *Izayoi no Ki* is a highly sentimental journey interspersed plentifully with Tanka. The following short passage may suffice as a specimen :—

" 26th day. We crossed a river, which I believe is called the Warashina, and proceeded to the shore of Okitsu. I remembered the poem which says, 'the moonshine behind me as I took my way with tears.' At the place where we made our mid-day halt there was a queer little pillow of boxwood. I lay down quite exhausted, and finding an ink-stone there, wrote, as I lay, the following on the paper slides close to my pillow :—

> '*Twas an experience*
> *Scarce worth remembering.*
> *Tell it not to the world,*
> *O thou chance pillow !*
> *Nor say that I have bound myself.*"

Musubi-okitsu, which means " to bind oneself down," also contains the name of the place where the author was stopping. The verse is obviously composed simply for the sake of this pun, and contains no record of any actual personal experience.

"As it became dusk we passed Kiyomigaseki. The waves breaking over the rocks looked as if they were clothing them in white robes—a very pretty sight!

> *Ye ancient rocks*
> *On the shore of Kiyomi!*
> *A question let me ask of you—*
> *How many suits have you put on*
> *Of wet wave-garments?"*

["Wet garments" is a metaphorical expression for unmerited blame or punishment].

"Presently it became dark, and we put up for the night in a village in that neighbourhood which stood close by the sea. From somewhere near, there came a smoke of burning, the smell of which was very noisome. It was no doubt caused by something the fishermen were doing. It brought to my mind the words, 'the rank odours of my nightly lodging.'

"The wind was very boisterous all night long, and the waves seemed breaking in tumult over my pillow."

The next passage relates to Fujisan. It appears from it that in the author's day the smoke from this mountain was intermittent. It has long ago quite ceased to rise.

The style of the *Izayoi no Ki* is very different from that of the *Gempei Seisuiki* or *Heike Monogatari*. It is comparatively free from Chinese elements, and reads more like a work of the Heian period. The author has evidently taken the *Tosa Nikki* for her model.

Abutsu also published a volume of critical essays on poetry, called *Yo no Tsuru* ("The Crane in the Night"), and other less important writings.

The *Ben no Naiji Nikki*, also by a woman, is a diary of incidents which occurred between 1246 and 1252.

POETRY

The manufacture of Tanka at the court of Kiōto continued during this period. Several collections of verses prepared under official auspices were the result ; but, as they contain little which is characteristic, it is needless to dwell upon them. The poetry of this time deserves mention chiefly as an indication that culture was not wholly neglected during what was in the main a benighted age.

It was now that the practice began of making anthologies of Tanka consisting of one specimen each of one hundred different authors. These are called *Hiaku-nin-is-shiu*. The original collection of this kind, which contains Tanka from the seventh to the thirteenth centuries, is at this day in the hands of every Japanese schoolgirl. It was compiled about 1235 by a court noble named Sadaiye, one of the great Fujiwara clan, which at this time had almost a monopoly of Japanese poetry. It has been translated into English by Mr. F. V. Dickins.

A new metre appeared during this period, which took the place of the older Naga-uta. It is called Ima-yō or "present fashion," and consists of alternate phrases of seven and five syllables. This arrangement is more or less closely approximated to in the poetical passages which now begin to occur in prose works.

BOOKS IN CHINESE

The works written in Chinese during the Kamakura period bear witness to the general decay of learning. They are composed in a species of bad Chinese which may aptly be compared to the barbarous Latin of the Middle Ages in Europe.

The most important is the *Adzuma-Kagami* or " Mirror of the East," a history of Japan from 1180 till 1266. Invaluable as a mine of historical information, its literary worth is but small. It is one of those dry chronicles in which events are jotted down month by month and day by day without any attempt to show their connection.

BOOK THE FIFTH

NAMBOKU-CHŌ (1332–1392) AND MUROMACHI (1392–1603) PERIODS

(DARK AGE)

BOOK THE FIFTH

NAMBOKU-CHŌ (1332–1392) *AND MUROMACHI* (1392–1603) *PERIODS*

(DARK AGE)

CHAPTER I

INTRODUCTORY—"JINKŌSHŌTŌKI"— "TAIHEIKI"

TOWARDS the end of the Kamakura period the mis-government of the Hōjō regents, who were to the Shōguns what the Shōguns had been to the Mikados, was the cause of general discontent ; and when a Mikado of resolute character came to the throne, the opportunity seemed favourable for casting off the domination of the military caste. At the court of Kiōto there had always been a strong undercurrent of intrigue directed against the Shōguns' authority, and that of the regents who ruled in their name. The Mikado Go Daigo was the first who thought himself strong enough to take bolder measures. After a desperate struggle, and many vicissitudes of fortune, his enterprise was partially successful. It resulted in the establishment of two Mikados, who reigned simultaneously—one, the creature of the Shōguns, occupying the old capital of Kiōto ; while the second held his court at Yoshino and other places in the province of Yamato, and enjoyed a somewhat precarious independence. This system, known in Japanese history as the Nam-boku-chō (Southern and Northern Courts), was put an end to by the reunion of the two lines in the person of Go Komatsu (1392), after a prolonged series of intestine troubles. A new dynasty of Shōguns, the Ashikaga House, was by this time established at Muromachi, in Kiōto, a place which gave its name to the next period of Japanese history. It remained in power until 1603, when the Shōgunate, having again changed hands, was transferred a second time to the east of Japan.

The 270 years covered by these two periods were singularly barren of important literature in Japan. One or two quasi-historical works, a charming volume of essays, and a few hundred short dramatic sketches (the *Nō*) are all that deserve more than a passing notice.

" JINKŌSHŌTŌKI "

The author of the *Jinkōshōtōki* was a statesman and soldier named KITABATAKE CHIKAFUSA, who acted an important part in the civil wars which disturbed Japan during the first half of the fourteenth century.

Chikafusa was descended from a prince of the Imperial family. He was born in 1293, and held various offices in the early part of Go Daigo's reign, but on the death of a prince to whom he was attached he shaved his head and retired from public life. In 1333, when the Emperor Go Daigo returned from the island of Oki, whither he had been banished by the Kamakura Government, Chikafusa was persuaded again to take office, and distinguished himself greatly in the wars which followed. The eminent services he had rendered to the cause of the Southern Court by his sword, his pen, and his counsel, were recognised in 1351 by the highest honours which his sovereign could bestow. He died a few years later.

The *Jinkōshōtōki* is Chikafusa's principal work. His object in writing it is indicated by the title, which means "History of the True Succession of the Divine Monarchs." It was composed in order to show that the Mikados of the Southern Court, whose minister he was, were the rightful sovereigns of Japan. This explains the prominence which he gives to matters affecting the authenticity of the Mikado's claims to the throne, such as the history of the regalia, genealogies, questions of disputed succession, and the like.

It was written in the reign of Go Murakami (1339–1345). The first of the six volumes of which it consists is purely mythical. It begins literally *ab ovo* with the egg-shaped chaotic mass from which heaven and earth were developed. Then we have an account of the creation of Japan by the male and female deities Izanagi and Izanami, taken partly from the *Nihongi*, but mixed up with Chinese philosophy and Indian mythical cosmography in the strangest manner. The descent of the Mikados from the Sun-goddess, who in Japan is the daughter of the divine creator pair, is then traced with due attention through a series of deities down to Jimmu Tennō, who is reckoned the first human sovereign of Japan.

The next four volumes are a resumé, necessarily brief and meagre, of the history of Japan from Jimmu Tennō (who came to the throne, according to the ordinary Japanese chronology, in B.C. 660) down to the accession of Fushimi in A.D. 1288.

The sixth volume deals with the history of Chikafusa's

own time. It is very disappointing. Although the writer and his sons took a prominent part in the fighting and politics of their day, Chikafusa has not thought proper to give more than a short and bald account of the events in which he was a principal actor. Most of this volume is taken up with dissertations on the principles of government, which, however necessary for a comprehension of the motives and ideas of Japanese statesmen under the old regime, are not very interesting to the European reader.

By his own countrymen Chikafusa has been much lauded as an exponent of the Chinese type of political philosophy. Even modern critics bestow on him a lavish praise which to us seems hardly deserved. His writings certainly contain evidences of statesman-like capacity, as for example his condemnation of sinecures and mortmain grants to ecclesiastical foundations ; and if there is also much that we are inclined to set down as mere platitudes, it is fair to remember that Chikafusa was the first Japanese writer who attempted to apply philosophical principles to actual politics, and that what seems trite to us may have appeared novel and striking to contemporary readers.

The style of the *Jinkōshōtōki* is simple and unpretentious. Its value as literature is small in proportion to the political influence which it has exercised. Not only was the cause of which the author was a devoted champion substantially furthered by its publication, but it has also left its mark on later times. Chikafusa's patriotic sentiments and his loyalty to the *de jure* sovereign of his country had a large share, directly, or filtered down through the works of writers who derived their inspiration from him, in forming the public feeling and opinion which led to the restoration of the Mikado's power in our own day.

He is one of the few writers of this class who do not indulge in Tanka.

The following extracts will give some idea of the quality of Chikafusa's political reasonings :—

"Great Yamato is a divine country. It is only our land whose foundations were first laid by the divine ancestor. It alone has been transmitted by the Sun Goddess to a long line of her descendants. There is nothing of this kind in foreign countries. Therefore it is called the divine land."

"It is only our country which, from the time that heaven and earth were first unfolded until this very day, has preserved the succession to the throne intact in one single family. Even when, as sometimes naturally happened, it descended to a lateral branch, it was held in accordance with just principles. This shows that the august oath of the gods [to preserve the succession] is ever renewed in a way which distinguishes Japan from all other countries."

"There are matters in the way of the gods [the Shinto religion] which it is difficult to expound. Nevertheless, if we do not know the origin of things, the result is necessarily confusion. To remedy this evil I have jotted down a few observations showing how the succession from the age of the gods has been governed by reason, and have taken no pains to produce an ordinary history. This work may therefore be entitled 'History of the True Succession of Divine Monarchs.'"

"The man devotes himself to husbandry, providing

food for himself and others, and thus warding off hunger ; the woman attends to spinning, thereby clothing herself and also making others warm. These may seem mean offices, but it is on them that the structure of human society rests. They are in accordance with the seasons of heaven, and depend on the benefits drawn from earth.

"Others are skilled in deriving gain from commerce ; while others, again, prefer the practice of the mechanic arts, or have the ambition to become officials. These are what are called the ' four classes of the people.'

"Of officials there are two classes—the civil and the military. The method of the civil official is to remain at home and reason upon the right way, wherein, if he attains to lucidity, he may rise to be a Minister of State. It is the business of the soldier, on the other hand, to render service in warlike expeditions, wherein, if he gains fame, he may become a general. Therefore these two professions ought not to be neglected for a moment. It has been said, ' In times of civil disorder, arms are placed to the right and letters to the left ; in peace, letters are put to the right and arms to the left.' "

"It is the duty of every man born on the Imperial soil to yield devoted loyalty to his sovereign, even to the sacrifice of his own life. Let no one suppose for a moment that there is any credit due to him for so doing. Nevertheless, in order to stimulate the zeal of those who come after, and in loving memory of the dead, it is the business of the ruler to grant rewards in such cases [to the children]. Those who are in an inferior position should not enter into rivalry with them. Still more should those who have done no specially meritorious service abstain from inordinate ambitions. It is a truly blessed principle to observe the rut of the chariot which has preceded, at whatever risk to our own safety [that is, a conservative policy should be maintained at all hazards]."

"I have already touched in several places on the principles of statesmanship. They are based on justice and mercy, in the dispensing of which firm action is requisite. Such is the clear instruction vouchsafed to us by Tenshōdaijin [the Sun Goddess]. Firm action is displayed in various ways. Firstly, in the choice of men for official positions. Japan and China both agree that the basis of good government consists in the sovereign finding the right man and bestowing his favour on him. Secondly, in excluding private motives from the distribution of appointments to provinces and districts. This should be done on grounds of reason only. Thirdly, firm action is shown in the reward of merit and the punishment of crime. By this means encouragement is given to virtue, and wickedness is repressed. If any of these three things is neglected, we have what is called bad government."

"Sinecures and jobbery in the matter of promotions are steps towards the downfall of the State, and fatal to the permanence of the royal office."

Another work by Chikafusa is the *Gengenshiu*, in eight volumes. It contains a resumé of the myths which are articles of the Shinto faith.

Like the *Jinkōshōtōki*, the celebrated work named *Taiheiki* is a history of the attempts of the Mikado Go Daigo to shake off the domination of the " Eastern Barbarians," as the Kamakura Shōguns and their adherents were called, and of the civil wars arising out of these enterprises which distracted Japan for more than forty years.

The edition entitled *Taiheiki Sōmoku* has an introduction purporting to relate the circumstances under which this work was compiled, on the authority of a "tradition," the sources of which are unknown to us. Begun, it is said, at the instance of the Mikado Go Daigo, by a priest named Genye, it was continued by other priests at various times, until its completion in 1382. These writers, we are told, based their narratives on information obtained directly from the Shōgun Takauji, Nitta Yoshisada, Kusunoki Masashige, and other chief actors in the political events of the day. Recent investigation, however, seems to show that the author was really a priest named KOJIMA, probably belonging to one of the three thousand monasteries of Hiyeisan, who died in 1374, but of whom nothing further is known. If this be correct, either the former account is an imposture, of which there are not a few in the literary annals of Japan, or Kojima may have utilised materials collected in the manner just described. Internal evidence points to the *Taiheiki* being the work of one person who wrote some time after the events related, and who owed much more to his imagination than to direct communication with the heroes of his story.

It begins with a sketch of the history of the Shogunate from its foundation by Yoritomo in 1181, and then goes on to describe the political condition of Japan at the accession of Go Daigo in 1319. The events of this reign, which ended in 1339, are given in considerable detail, and the work is continued to the close of the reign of Go Murakami (1368).

The *Taiheiki*, as it has come down to us, contains several chapters which have little or nothing to do with the general plan of the work, and look very like interpolations by some later writer. Such are the chapters on "Rebellions in Japan," on the conquest of Yamato by Jimmu Tennō, on the Corean expedition of Jingō Kōgu, and on the Mongol invasion of Japan by Kublai Khan. The addenda in the Sōmoku edition form, of course, no part of the original work.

Taiheiki or "Record of Great Peace" is a strange name for the history of one of the most disturbed periods that Japan has ever passed through. It presents a succession of intrigues, treasons, secret conspiracies, and open warfare, with wholesale sentences of death or banishment. This was not, however, the original name of the work. It was at first called *Anki Yuraiki* or "Record of the Causes of Peace and Danger." Another name for it was *Kokuka Jiranki*, or "Record of the Cure of Civil Disturbance in the State." These last titles rather suggest a philosophical history. But the *Taiheiki* is very much the reverse of this. It is clearly the work, not of a statesman or philosopher, but of a literary man intent on producing an ornate and romantic story. So long as this end is attained, fact and fiction are to him very much alike. It is difficult to say which predominates in his narrative. He is notoriously inaccurate in such matters as numbers, dates, and genealogies; but that is nothing to the way in which he embroiders his accounts of sieges and battles with details that cannot possibly have been handed down by eye-witnesses, and to the dreams, portents, and miraculous occurrences with which his story abounds. There are also numerous speeches, apparently adapted by him to the speaker and the occasion, but which, like those in Thucydides, have nevertheless a certain historical value. The serious way in which the commentators treat the *Taiheiki's* frequent excursions into the land of romance is not a little amusing.

The style of Kojima (if he is the author) has been condemned by native critics as inflated and pedantic. It must be admitted that there is not a little truth in these charges. The *Taiheiki* supplies abundant evidence of his erudition and command of all the resources of Chinese and Japanese rhetoric. His pages at times are highly charged with Chinese words and phrases, and fairly bristle with Chinese historical allusions and quotations. In this style of writing, a " bamboo grove " means a family of princes, a " pepper court " is put for the Imperial harem, " cloud guests " stand for courtiers, the Mikado's carriage is termed the " Phœnix Car," and his face the " Dragon Countenance." A fair lady is said to put to shame Mao Ts'iang and Si She, famous beauties of Chinese antiquity. Civil war is a time when " wolf-smoke obscures the heaven, and whale-waves shake the earth." Kojima does not hesitate even to insert long episodes of Chinese and Indian history which present some resemblance to the events which he is describing, especially if they lend themselves to romantic treatment.

Still more trying to the ordinary Western reader than his ostentatious display of Chinese learning is the Buddhist theology in which Kojima was plainly well versed, and of which there is more than enough in the *Taiheiki*. Students of the history of religion, however, will find this feature of the work interesting. Kojima is a typical case which illustrates the national propensity for compromise and arrangement in matters of faith. In the *Taiheiki* he makes an attempt to reconcile three essentially conflicting systems, viz., Chinese philosophy, Shinto mythology, and Buddhism, including with the latter the older Indian myths which found their way to Japan in its company. Thus in a passage near the end of Book XVI. he describes the Yin and Yang (the negative and positive principles of nature according to the Chinese) as the origin and source of all things. These two elements by their mutual interaction evolve Izanagi and Izanami, the creator deities of the Shinto Pantheon. Their child Tenshōdaijin (the Sun Goddess) proves to be a manifestation of Buddha, one of whose services to humanity was at some far remote period to subdue the " Evil Kings of the Six Heavens " of Indian myth, and compel them to withdraw their opposition to the spread of the true doctrine (that is, Buddhism) in Japan.

Kojima, however, does not always draw his inspiration from China or from theology. Like the *Heike Monogatari*, the *Taiheiki* contains a number of highly poetical passages which owe nothing to foreign models or ideas. In metre they resemble Naga-uta, except that the order of the alternation of five and seven syllable phrases is reversed. Words of Chinese origin are not wholly excluded. One of these passages describes the enforced journey of Toshimoto, an adherent of the Mikado Go Daigo, to Kamakura, where he was executed for treason to the Shōgunate ; and another, that of the same Mikado, to an exile in the island of Oki. The names of places along the route are ingeniously woven into the narrative in such a way as to suggest reflections suitable to the circumstances. This feature of the *Taiheiki* has had an enormous influence on the work of the dramatists and novelists of the Yedo period, as is shown by the numerous direct imitations of the passages just described (known as *michiyuki* or "journeys"), and by the rhythmical swing of the alternation of seven and five syllable phrases, due to its example, which pervades so much of the subsequent popular literature.

Europeans who propose to take up the study of the *Taiheiki* will be glad to learn that there still remains a good deal of straightforward, business-like narrative, which, though not without occasional florid phrases and picturesque touches, is laudably free from recondite allusions and obscure metaphors, perplexing to the unlearned, and condemned as pedantic even by those who understand them.

The language of the *Taiheiki* is very different from that of the writings of the Heian period. Simpler forms are substituted for the older, more elaborate grammatical structure, and the vocabulary is enriched by the accession of a vast number of Chinese words, which no longer, as formerly, are only admitted to the literature after a time of probation in the colloquial speech, but are taken straight from Chinese books.

The importance of the *Taiheiki* in the history of Japanese literature is far greater than its intrinsic merits would lead us to expect. More than any other work it is the foundation of the modern literary style, and its good and bad qualities generally are reflected in the writings of a host of imitators, direct or indirect.

The events and personages which it describes are the themes of a very large share of the modern literature of Japan, and allusions to it are continually met with. Its popularity is further testified to by the fact that there sprang up at Yedo and Kiōto a distinct class of professors who earned a living by giving *Taiheiki* readings. They correspond to the biwa-bonzes who chanted the *Heike Monogatari*.

The following is an account of a battle between the Shōgun's adherents and the monks of Hiyeisan, who had for once espoused the Mikado's cause. It was fought near Karazaki, on the shore of Lake Biwa. This passage may serve as a specimen, as it was probably the model, of innumerable similar combats in Japanese literature :—

"When Kaitō saw this, 'The enemy are few,' he cried. 'We must disperse them before the rear comes up. Follow me, my lads.' With these words he drew his 3 feet 6 inch sword, and holding up his armed left sleeve as an arrow guard, rushed midmost into the whirl of the expectant foe. Three of them he laid low. Then retiring to the beach of the lake, he rallied to him his followers. Now when Kwaijitsu, a monk of Okamoto, descried him from afar, he kicked over—'*Kappa !*'—the shield which he had set up before him, and with his 2 feet 8 inch bill revolving like a water-wheel, sprang forward to attack him. Kaitō received the stroke with his armed left sleeve, while with his right he aimed a blow at the skull-piece of his adversary's helmet, meaning to split it fair in twain. But his sword glanced off obliquely to the shoulder-plate, and thence downwards to the cross-stitched rim of his *épaulière*, doing no harm. In endeavouring to repeat the blow he used such force that his left stirrup-leather broke, and he was on the point of falling from his horse. He recovered his seat, but as he was doing so Kwaijitsu thrust forward the shaft of his bill so that the point entered Kaitō's helmet from below two or three times in succession. Nor did he fail in his aim. Kaitō, stabbed through the windpipe, fell headlong from his horse. Kwaijitsu presently placed his foot on the depending tassel of Kaitō's armour, and seizing him by the hair, drew it towards him, while he cut off his head, which he then fixed on the end of his bill. 'A good beginning! I have slain a general of the military faction,' he exclaimed joyously, with a mocking laugh. Whilst he was standing thus, a boy of about fifteen or sixteen, with his hair still bound up in 'Chinese-ring' fashion, wearing a corselet of the colour of brewer's grains, his trousers tucked up high at the side, came out from among the onlookers, and drawing a small gold-mounted sword, rushed at Kwaijitsu and smote him vigorously three or four times on the skull-piece of his helmet. Kwaijitsu turned sharply, but seeing a child of twice eight years, with painted eyebrows and blackened teeth, thought that to cut down a boy of this age would be a piece of cruelty unbecoming his priestly condition. To avoid killing him he made numerous dashes, repeatedly flourishing his weapon over him. It then occurred to Kwaijitsu to knock the sword out of the boy's hands with the shaft of his bill and seize him in his arms; but while he was trying to do so, some of the party of the Hiyei cross-roads approached by a narrow path between the rice-fields, and an arrow shot by one of them transfixed the lad's heart so that he fell dead upon the spot. Upon inquiry it was found that this was Kaitō's eldest son Karawakamaru. Forbidden by his father to take part in the fight, he was discontented, and mixing with the crowd of spectators, had followed after. Though a child, he was a born soldier, and when he saw his father slain he too fell fighting on the same battlefield, leaving a name behind. Alas, the pity of it!

"When Kaitō's retainers saw this, they felt that after having their chieftain and his son killed before their eyes, and, what was still worse, their heads taken by the enemy, none of them ought to return home alive. Thirty-six of them, bridle to bridle, made an onrush, each more eager than the other to fall fighting, and make a pillow of his lord's dead body. Kwaijitsu, seeing this, laughed out, ' Ha! ha! There is no understanding you fellows,' he exclaimed. 'You ought to be thinking of taking the heads of enemies instead of guarding the heads of your own people. This is an omen of the ruin of the military power. If you want the head you can have it.' So saying, he flung the head of Kaitō into the midst of the foe, and with downward-sweeping blows in the Okamoto style, cleared a space in all directions."

The next specimen of Kojima's style is from an account of the arrest of Toshimoto, one of the Mikado Go Daigo's principal advisers, on a charge of conspiracy against the Shōgunate.

"On the 11th day of the seventh month he was arrested and taken to Rokuwara [the residence of the Shōgun's representative at Kiōto], and was despatched thence to the eastern provinces. He set out on his journey, well knowing that the law allowed no pardon for a second offence of this kind, and that whatever he might plead in his defence he would not be released. Either he would be done away with on the journey, or he would be executed at Kamakura. No other end was possible."

(Then, without any warning of type or otherwise, there follows a passage which in metre, diction, and sentiment is essentially poetry. It is not very original, however, much of it consisting of scraps of verse supplied by the author's memory from older writers.)

> " But one night more and a strange lodging would be his,
>   Far from Kadono, where in spring his steps had often wandered
>   in the snow of the fallen cherry-flowers ;
>   Far from Arashiyama, whence on an autumn eve he was wont to
>   return clad in the brocade of the red maple leaves—
>   Despondent, his mind could think of nothing but his home, bound
>   to him by the strongest ties of love,
>   And of his wife and children, whose future was dark to him.
> ' For the last time,' he thought, as he looked back on the ninefold
>   Imperial city,
>   For many a year his wonted habitation.
>   How sad his heart must have been within him
>   As he set out on this unlooked-for journey !
>   His sleeve wet in the fountain of the barrier of Osaka—
>   No barrier, alas ! to stay his sorrow—
>   He sets forth over the mountain track to Uchide [1] no hama,
>   When from the shore he cast his glance afar over the wave."

Here the author becomes so involved in ingenious punning combinations of the names of places on the route with the thread of his story that it is impossible to follow him in a translation.

The following is one of the extraneous chapters of the *Taiheiki*. It describes in a very imaginative fashion the famous Mongol invasion of Japan by Kublai Khan in the thirteenth century of our era.

" Poring over the records of ancient times, in the leisure afforded me by the three superfluous things [night, winter, and rain], I find that since the Creation there have been seven invasions of Japan by foreign countries. The

---

[1] *Uchide* means "to set forth," and *hama*, "shore."

most notable of these attacks were in the periods Bunyei (1264–1275) and Kōan (1278–1288). At this time the Great Yuan Emperor [Kublai Khan] had conquered by force of arms the four hundred provinces of China. Heaven and earth were oppressed by his power. Hard would it have been for a small country like our own to repel him, and that it was able easily and without effort to destroy the armies of Great Yuan was due to naught else but the divine blessing.

"The plan of this expedition was as follows : General Wan, the leader of the Yuan force, having estimated the area of the five metropolitan provinces of Japan at 3700 ri square, calculated that to fill this space with soldiers so as to leave no part of it unoccupied would require an army of 3,700,000 men. So he set forth from the various ports and bays with his troops embarked in a fleet of more than 70,000 great ships. Our Government, having had previous information of this design, ordered preparations to be made. The forces of Shikoku and Kiushiu were directed to assemble in all haste at Hakata, in Tsukushi ; those of the western provinces of the main island hurried to the capital ; while the men of Tōsandō and of the northern provinces occupied the port of Tsuruga, in Echizen.

"Thereupon the warships of Great Yuan, 70,000 in number, arrived together at the port of Hakata on the third day of the eighth month of the second year of Bunyei (1265). Their great vessels were lashed together, and gangways laid across from one to another. Every division was surrounded by screens of oilcloth ; their weapons were set up in regular array. From the Gotō Islands eastward as far as Hakata the sea was enclosed on all sides for 400 ri, a of and sudden became dry land.

One wondered whether a sea-serpent vapour had not been belched out and formed a mirage.

"On the Japanese side a camp was constructed extending for thirteen ri along the beach of Hakata. A high stone embankment formed its front, precipitous on the side of the enemy, but so arranged in the rear as to allow free movement for our troops. In the shelter of this, plastered walls were erected, and barracks constructed, in which several tens of thousands of men were lodged in due order. It was thought that in this way the enemy would be unable to ascertain our numbers. But on the bows of the hostile ships, beams like those used for raising water from wells were set up to a height of several hundred feet, at the ends of which platforms were placed. Men seated on these were able to look down into the Japanese camp and count every hair's end. Moreover, they chained together planks forty or fifty feet wide so as to form a sort of rafts, which, when laid on the surface of the water, provided a number of level roads over the waves, like the three great thoroughfares or the twelve main streets [of Kiōto]. By these roads the enemy's cavalry appeared in many tens of thousands, and fought so desperately that our troops relaxed their ardour, and many of them had thoughts of retreat. When the drum was beaten, and a hand-to-hand contest was already engaged, iron balls, like footballs, were let fly from things called 'cannon' [with a sound] like cartwheels rolling down a steep declivity, and accompanied by flashes like lightning. Two or three thousand of these were let go at once. Most of the Japanese troops were burnt to death, and their gates and turrets set fire to. There was no opportunity of putting out the flames.

"When the men of Upper Matsura and Lower Matsura

saw this, they felt that ordinary measures would be useless, so they made a circuit by way of another bay, and,
with only 1000 men, ventured on a night attack. But
however brave they might be, they were no more than
one hair upon a bull or one grain of rice in a granary.
Attacking with so small a force, they slew several tens of
thousands of the enemy, but in the end were all made
prisoners. They were bound with cruel cords, and their
hands nailed to the bulwarks of the line of vessels.

"No further resistance was possible. All the men of
Kiushiu fled to Shikoku and the provinces north of the
Inland Sea. The whole Japanese nation was struck with
panic, and knew not what to do. Visits to the shrines of
the Shinto gods, and public and secret services in the
Buddhist temples, bowed down the Imperial mind and
crushed the Imperial liver and gall-bladder. Imperial
messengers were despatched with offerings to all the
gods of heaven and earth, and all the Buddhist temples
of virtue to answer prayer, great and small alike, throughout the sixty provinces. On the seventh day, when the
Imperial devotions were completed, from Lake Suwa
there arose a cloud of many colours, in shape like a great
serpent, which spread away towards the west. The doors
of the Temple-treasury of Hachiman flew open, and the
skies were filled with a sound of galloping horses and of
ringing bits. In the twenty-one shrines of Yoshino the
brocade-curtained mirrors moved, the swords in the
Temple-treasury put on a sharp edge, and all the shoes
offered to the god turned towards the west. At Sumiyoshi sweat poured from below the saddles of the four
horses sacred to the deities, and the iron shields turned
of themselves and faced the enemy in a line."

(Many more similar wonders follow.)

" Now General Wan of Great Yuan, having cast off the moorings of his 70,000 ships, at the hour of the dragon on the seventeenth day of the eighth month started for Nagato and Suwō by way of Moji and Akamagaseki [Shimonoseki]. His fleet were midway on their course when the weather, which had been windless, with the clouds at rest, changed abruptly. A mass of black clouds arising from the north-east covered the sky, the wind blew fiercely, the tumultuous billows surged up to heaven, the thunder rolled and the lightning dashed against the ground so abundantly that it seemed as if great mountains were crumbling down and high heaven falling to the earth. The 70,000 warships of the foreign pirates either struck upon cragged reefs and were broken to atoms, or whirling round in the surging eddies, went down with all hands.

" Nevertheless, General Wan alone was neither driven off by the storm nor buried beneath the waves, but flew aloft and stood in the calm seclusion of the middle heaven. Here he was met by a sage named Ryo Tō-bin, who came soaring from the west. He addressed General Wan as follows : 'The gods of heaven and the gods of earth of the entire country of Japan, 3700 shrines or more, have raised this evil wind and made the angry billows surge aloft. Human power cannot cope with them. I advise you to embark at once in your one shattered ship and return to your own country.' General Wan was persuaded. He embarked in the one shattered ship which remained, braved all alone the waves of 10,000 ri of ocean, and presently arrived at the port of Mingchu [in China]."

The word rendered "cannon" is *teppō*, lit. "iron tube." It properly means a matchlock. But according to the encyclopædia called the *Sansaidzuye*, neither cannon nor

matchlocks were known to the Chinese before the sixteenth century. Matchlocks were first introduced into
Japan by Mendez Pinto and his companions in 1543, and
were not known to the Chinese until later. The inference
is that this passage, and probably the whole chapter, is a
later interpolation.

It is perhaps necessary to remind the reader that there
is a nucleus of fact hidden among all this fictitious em-
broidery. Kublai Khan did send a large fleet against
Japan about the time stated, which met with a fate
similar to that of the Spanish Armada prepared for the
conquest of England.

CHAPTER II

KENKŌ AND THE "TSURE-DZURE-GUSA"[1]

IF there are many arid wastes in Japanese literature, there are also some pleasant oases, and of these the *Tsure-dzure-gusa* is surely one of the most delightful. It is a collection of short sketches, anecdotes, and essays on all imaginable subjects, something in the manner of Selden's *Table Talk*. The author is known to us as KENKŌ-BŌSHI, *bōshi* being an honorific epithet something like our Reverend. He was a man of good family, and traced his descent through various dis-tinguished personages from the Shinto deity Kogane no Mikoto. For many years in the service of the Mikado Go Uda no In, his writings show an intimate acquaintance with the ways and customs of the Im-perial palace. On the death of his master in 1324, Kenkō became a Buddhist monk, and retired from public life, spending the remainder of his days in various secluded spots in the neighbourhood of Kiōto. The date of his death is not positively known, but there is nothing improbable in the statement that he died in 1350, in his sixty-eighth year.

Very contradictory views of his character have been taken by native writers. Some call him a profligate, unscrupulous, common priest, and quote an old scandal

[1] Translated by Rev. C. S. Eby, in the *Chrysanthemum*, vol. iii.

told in the *Taiheiki*, of his writing for Kō no Moronao the letters which he addressed to the wife of Yenya Hangwan urging his adulterous suit. But the *Taiheiki* is a very dubious authority, and there are other reasons for questioning the truth of this story. Kenkō's admirers maintain that he was a truly pious man.

Judging from his writings, there would appear to have been two personalities in Kenkō, the shrewd, polished, and somewhat cynical man of the world, and the Buddhist devotee, the former element of his character having a decided preponderance. His religion was to all appearance sincere, but was certainly not profound· Like Horace, whom he much resembles in character, he had his pious moods, but was very far indeed from being a saint. A professor of the Tendai sect of Buddhism, he has much to say, and says it well, of the uncertainty of life, the folly of ambition and money-getting, and the necessity for putting away the lusts of this wicked world and preparing betimes for eternity. But the old Adam is never far off. His unregenerate nature is not to be suppressed, and gives evidence of its existence ever and anon in passages which his devout admirers would willingly forget.

His religion was not of that robust kind which thrives amid the cares and distractions of the world, and by which ordinary life may be made " a perfumed altar-flame." He has left on record his opinion (which is indeed a commonplace of the sect to which he belonged) that true piety is impossible except in seclusion from the world. The quiet of his own hermitage having once been disturbed by the visit of a hunting party, he composed a poem complaining that the world pursued him even there, and changed his abode to a still more remote locality. But with all his precautions he never attained to Nirvana, if by that term we are to understand the holy calm of mind which is the result of long-continued meditation on divine things.

The name Kenkō, which he selected when he became a monk, is characteristic of his spiritual condition. He retained the two Chinese characters with which his lay name Kaneyoshi is written, simply altering the pronunciation to something which with a little good-will might be allowed to stand for a Buddhist priestly designation. This is much as if a man named Oliver were to enter religion as " Brother Oliverus," instead of adopting a saint's name from the calendar.

There is much self-revelation in Kenkō's writings. The personality which they portray is not a wholly lovable one. There is something wrong about the man who abhorred matrimony (not that celibacy and chastity were with him convertible terms), thought children a mistake, and declared that after forty life was not worth living. The following anecdote, which he himself relates, throws some light on his curiously mixed character :—

" Even men from whom we should not expect much feeling sometimes say a good thing. A certain wild savage of terrible appearance, meeting a neighbour, asked him, had he any children. 'Not one,' was the reply. 'Then you cannot know the Ah-ness of things, and your doings must be with a heart devoid of feeling.' This is a very fearful saying. It is no doubt true that by children men become conscious of the Ah-ness of all things. Without the path of the natural affections how should there be any sentiment in the hearts of such persons ?"

To know the Ah-ness of things (*mono no aware wo shiru*) is a phrase which is constantly recurring in Japanese literature, especially during the classical period. The learned critic Motoöri discusses it at great length in his treatise on the nature of poetry entitled *Iso no Kami Shi-shuku-gen*. It means to have a sensitive, emotional nature, the *cœur sensible* of the French, and applies more particularly to a capacity for receiving the impressions produced on man by Nature in her various moods.

Kenkō would doubtless have spurned the idea that for an accomplished gentleman, scholar, and poet like himself paternity was necessary in order to awaken the emotional sensibilities, though in the case of "such persons" as the rude peasant of his story this might very well be the case.

The followers of the various forms of religion and ethics practised in Japan have all claimed Kenkō as a teacher of their own set of doctrines. It is true that although he is in the main a Buddhist, he had, with the liberal comprehensiveness characteristic of the Japanese nation, more than a mere tolerance for other faiths. He not only showed a reverence for the Shinto deities, but was a profound student of the Confucian moral philosophy, and even of Taoism, that mass of vague speculations attributed to Laotze and his disciple Chwang-tze. But it is a mistake to regard him as a partisan of any particular creed, or as a moral teacher at all. He tells us himself in the opening sentences of the *Tsure-dzure-gusa* that it was written to while away the live-long days of tedium (*tsure-dzure*), sitting with his ink-slab before him, and jotting down all manner of trifles as they presented themselves to his mind. If one of his latest editors is correct, it was not even written for publication, but was collected after his death into its present form by some unknown person.

Kenkō was a lover of antiquity, whether in the shape of old works of art, the old customs and forms of speech which lingered (and still linger) about the Mikado's palace, or old books. He speaks in terms of special admiration of the *Genji Monogatari* and the *Makura Zōshi*, on which his own style was evidently modelled. It contrasts strongly with the idiom charged with Chinese vocables, metaphors, and allusions, which in his day had well-nigh supplanted the old Japanese of the Heian period. Kenkō, in a word, is a belated classic. He has no objection to a useful Chinese word or an apt illustration from Chinese history, but his purer taste rejects the pompous platitudes and pedantic show of learning which too often disfigure the works of imitators of Chinese models. His essays read like the conversation of a polished man of the world, and have that appearance of simplicity and ease of expression which is in reality the result of consummate art.

Those who wish to enter on the study of the older Japanese literature cannot make a better choice than the *Tsure-dzure-gusa*. It is not so difficult as the *Genji Monogatari* or the *Makura Zōshi*, and the new edition called the *Tsure-dzure-gusa Kōgi* affords every help in the way of explanation to those who have made sufficient progress in Japanese to avail themselves of it. The lover of curious books will prefer the quaint old block-printed editions of 1672 and 1688, both of which have numerous notes.

Kenkō had a high reputation as a writer of Tanka. He was one of the "Four Heavenly Kings" (a phrase borrowed from Indian mythology), as the four chief poets of his day were termed. Fortunately, most students of Japanese will say, the exercise of Kenkō's poetic talent has been diverted into other channels. The *Tsure-dzure-gusa* is not besprinkled with Tanka.

SOME EXTRACTS FROM THE "TSURE-DZURE-GUSA"

"When I was eight years of age, I asked my father, 'What sort of thing is a Buddha?' He replied, 'A Buddha is something which a man grows into.' 'How then does one become a Buddha?' said I. 'By the teachings of a Buddha.' 'But who taught the Buddha who gives us this teaching?' 'He becomes a Buddha by the teaching of another Buddha who was before him.' 'Then what sort of a Buddha was that first Buddha of all who began teaching?' My father was at an end of his answers, and replied, laughing, 'I suppose he must have flown down from the sky or sprung up from the ground.' He used to tell his friends this conversation, much to their amusement."

"However accomplished a man may be, without gallantry he is a very lonely being. Such a one reminds me of a costly wine-cup that has no bottom."

"That man is to be envied whose mind is fixed on futurity, and to whom the way of Buddha is familiar."

"What strikes men's eyes most of all in a woman is the beauty of her hair. Her quality and disposition may be gathered from the manner of her speech, even though a screen be interposed. There are occasions too when her very posture when seated leads a man's heart astray. Then, until his hopes are realised, he bears patiently what is not to be borne, regardless even of his life. It is

only love which can do this. Deep indeed are the roots
of passion, and remote its sources. It is possible to put
away from us all the other lusts of this wicked world.
But this one alone it is very hard to eradicate. Old and
young, wise and foolish, all are alike its slaves. Therefore it has been said that with a cord twined of a woman's
hair the great elephant may be firmly bound ; with a
whistle carved from a woman's shoe the deer in autumn
may without fail be lured.

"It is this beguilement which we must chastise in ourselves, it is this which we must dread, it is this against
which we must be on our guard."

"One day in the tenth month [about our September]
I took a walk over the plain of Kurisu, and exploring
a certain hill-district which lay beyond, was threading
my way along a narrow moss-grown path, when I came
upon a lonely cottage. No sound was to be heard except
the dripping of water from a pipe buried under fallen
leaves. It was, however, inhabited, as I gathered from
the chrysanthemums and red autumn leaves which be-
strewed the domestic shrine. 'Ah!' thought I, 'to
spend one's days even in such a spot !' But whilst I
stood gazing I espied in the garden beyond a great
orange-tree with branches bending to the ground. It
was strongly fenced off on every side. This [evidence
that covetous desires had penetrated even here] somewhat dispelled my dreams, and I wished from my heart
that no such tree had been."

"If we take a pen in hand, it suggests writing ; if we
take up a musical instrument, the very act of doing
so prompts us to make music ; a wine-cup suggests
drinking ; dice make us think of gambling. Our hearts
are inevitably influenced by our actions. We should

therefore be careful to abstain wholly from unedifying amusements.

"If we thoughtlessly glance at a verse of the Sacred Scriptures, what goes before and after presents itself to our minds without our effort, and this may lead to a sudden reformation of the errors of many years. If we had never read the Scriptures, how should we have known this ? Such is the virtue of association.

"If, even without any pious intentions whatever, we kneel down before the Buddha, and take in our hands the sacred book and the bell, a good work goes on of itself within us. If, even with wandering minds, we take our seat on the rope-mat, unawares we become absorbed in devout contemplation.

"At bottom, action and principle are one. If we are careful to avoid offences in our outward actions, the inner principle becomes fortified. We should therefore beware of making a profession of unbelief, and treat religion with all honour and respect."

"There are many things in this world which to me are incomprehensible. I cannot understand how any one can find pleasure in urging people to drink against their will, as is done the first thing on all occasions. The victim in his distress knits his brows, and watches an opportunity when no one is looking to spill the liquor or to steal away. But he is caught, detained, and made to drink his share as if there was nothing the matter. The nicest fellows suddenly become madmen, and give way to absurd conduct. The healthiest men, before our very eyes, become afflicted with grave illness, and lay themselves down unconscious of past and future. A sorry way indeed of celebrating a festal occasion ! Until the morrow they remain lying in a drunken state, with aching heads, and unable to eat, as if far removed from life, taking no thought for the next day, and too ill to attend to important business, public or private.

"It is not kindly or even courteous to treat people in this way. If we were told that such a custom existed in some foreign country (being unknown in Japan) we should think it most strange and unaccountable."

Here follows a description of a drunken debauch which is somewhat too graphic for transference to these pages. Kenkō goes on to say—

"In this world strong drink has much to answer for. It wastes our means and destroys our health. It has been called the chief of the hundred medicines, but in truth it is from strong drink more than aught else that all our diseases spring. It may help us to forget our miseries, but, on the other hand, the drunken man is often seen to weep at the remembrance of his past woes.

"As for the future world, strong drink is pernicious to the understanding, and burns up the root of good within us as with fire. It fosters evil, and leads to our breaking all the commandments and falling into hell. Buddha has declared that he who makes a man drink wine shall be born a hundred times with no hands."

It must not be supposed from this that Kenkō was a total abstainer, as he ought to have been if he kept his vows as a Buddhist monk. On the contrary—

"There are times when wine cannot be dispensed with. On a moonlight night, on a snowy morning, or when the flowers are in blossom and with hearts free from care we are conversing with a friend, it adds to our pleasures if the wine-cup is produced."

Kenkō goes so far as to allow that with intimate friends it is permissible occasionally to drink deeply.

"There is no greater pleasure than alone, by the light of a lamp, to open a book and make the men of the unseen world our companions."

"Nothing opens one's eyes so much as travel, no matter where."

"I love to shut myself up in a mountain temple and attend to the services to Buddha. Here there is no tedium, and one feels that his heart is being purged of its impurities."

THE SEASONS—SPRING

"It is change that in all things touches us with sympathy. Every one says, and not without some reason, that it is chiefly the autumn which inspires this feeling. But it appears to me that the aspects of nature in spring, more than at any other time, make our hearts swell with emotion. The songs of birds are especially suggestive of this season. With the increasing warmth the herbage in the hedge comes into bud, and as the spring grows deeper the hazes are diffused abroad and the flowers show themselves in all their glory. Sometimes with continual storms of wind and rain they are dispersed agitatedly, and nothing but green leaves is left. All this affects our hearts with constant trepidation.

"The flowering orange has a great fame. But it is the perfume of the plum-tree which makes us think longingly of the past. Then there are the gaily-coloured kerria and the wistaria of obscurer hues. All these have many feelings associated with them which it is impossible to leave unmarked."

"In our hours of quiet thought, who is there who has no yearnings for all that has passed away?

"When every one has retired to rest, to while away the long hours of night we put in order our little odds and ends of property. Among scraps of paper thrown away as not worth preserving, a handwriting or a sketch thrown off for amusement by one who is no more, catches the eye and brings up vividly the time when it was made. It is affecting too, after years have passed, to find a letter even from one who is still alive, and to think that it was written at such a date, on such an occasion.

"The articles their hands were familiar with remain unchanged (*they* have no hearts !) for all the long years that have elapsed. Alas ! alas ! "

"The man who writes a bad hand should not be deterred by that circumstance from scribbling letters. Otherwise he gets his friends to write for him, which is a nuisance."

"He is a fool who spends his life in the pursuit of fame or gain."

"The venerable priest Hōzen, being asked by a man whose drowsiness at prayers interfered with his religious duties, how he should remove this hindrance to devotion, replied, 'Pray earnestly enough to keep yourself awake.' This was an admirable answer.

"The same priest said, 'If you think your salvation is assured, it is assured ; if you think it is not assured, it is not assured.' This is also an admirable saying.

"Another admirable speech of his was to this effect : 'If, notwithstanding that you are perplexed by doubts, you continue your prayers, you will be saved.'"

Kenkō with some friends once attended a race-meeting, not, one would think, a fit place for a Buddhist recluse to be seen. A crowd got between their carriage and the course, shutting out their view.

"We all got down and tried to push our way forward
to the rails, but the press was too great for us to get
passage. At this juncture we observed a priest who had
climbed up a tree and seated himself in a fork to see
better. Being drowsy, he was continually dozing over,
and awaking just in time to save himself from falling.
Everybody shouted and jeered at him. 'What a fool,'
cried they, 'this fellow is to let himself fall asleep so
calmly in such a dangerous position!' Upon this a
thought flashed on me, and I exclaimed, 'Yet here are
we, spending our time in sight-seeing, forgetful that
death may overtake us at any moment. We are bigger
fools even than that priest.' The people in front of us
all looked round and said, 'Nothing can be more true.
It is indeed utter folly. Come this way, gentlemen.' So
they opened a passage and allowed us to come forward.
Now this remark of mine might have occurred to anybody. I suppose it was the unexpectedness of it at this
time which caused it to make an impression. Men are
not sticks or stones, and a word spoken at a favourable
moment sometimes finds its way to the heart."

A commentator says that "this chapter is intended to
impress us with the uncertainty of human things." The
reader may draw his own moral.

"Beware of putting off the practice of religion until
your old age. The ancient tombs are mostly those of
young people."

"When we hear a man's name we try to form to ourselves some idea of his appearance, but we invariably
find, on afterwards making his acquaintance, that we
have been quite wrong."

"I wonder if it is only I who have sometimes the feeling
that speeches which I have heard or sights that I have

seen were already seen or heard by me at some past time—when, I cannot tell."

"THINGS WHICH ARE IN BAD TASTE

Too much furniture in one's living room.

Too many pens in a stand.

Too many Buddhas in a private shrine.

Too many rocks, trees, and herbs in a garden.

Too many children in a house.

Too many words when men meet.

Too many books in a book-case there can never be, nor too much litter in a dust-heap."

"It is not only when we look at the moon or flowers with our eyes that they give us pleasure. On a spring day, though we do not leave our house; on a moonlight night, though we remain in our chamber, the mere thought of them is exceedingly cheering and delightful."

If Wordsworth had been a Japanese scholar, he might have been charged with plagiarising from this passage his

"inward eye
That is the bliss of solitude."

CHAPTER III

POETRY—THE NŌ OR LYRICAL DRAMA— KIŌGEN OR FARCE

THE manufacture of Tanka at the court of the Mikado proceeded, as usual, during these periods of Japanese history. They were duly collected into anthologies from time to time ; but as they present no features specially worthy of notice, and as they are admittedly much inferior in merit to the verse of earlier times, it is needless to dwell upon them here. A far greater interest belongs to a new development of the poetic art which now demands our attention, namely, the Nō or lyrical drama.

Like the ancient Greek tragedies and the mystery plays of the Middle Ages, the drama in Japan was in its beginnings closely associated with religion. Its immediate parent was the Kagura, a pantomimic dance, which is performed at this day to the sound of fife and drum at Shinto festivals, on a platform provided for the purpose. The antiquity of the Kagura may be inferred from the fact that when the *Kojiki* (A.D. 712) and the *Nihongi* (A.D. 720) were written, there was already a myth current which was intended as an explanation of its origin. The Sun Goddess, it is related, disgusted at the unseemly pranks of her brother Susa-no-wo, shut herself up in the rock-cave of heaven and left the world to darkness. Upon this the gods assembled in their myriads in the dry bed of the River of Heaven (the Milky Way), and among other expedients which they devised for luring her out of her retirement they caused Ame-no-Uzume (the Terrible Female of heaven) to array herself in a fantastical manner, and standing on an inverted tub, which gave out a hollow sound when she stamped on it, to perform a mimic dance which had the desired effect.

The same works give elsewhere a story which was meant to supply an explanation of another pantomime which was performed in the Mikado's palace by the Hayato or guards.

It runs as follows :—There were two brother deities, the elder of whom, Ho-no-Susori, was a hunter, and the younger, Hiko Hohodemi, a fisherman. The two brothers having quarrelled, the younger used against his brother a talisman given him by his father-in-law, the God of the Sea, by virtue of which the tide rose and submerged Ho-no-Susori. The latter then begged for pardon, and promised to be his brother's bonds-man and mime to all generations ; whereupon, by the power of another talisman, the tide retired and his life was spared. The younger brother was the ancestor of the Mikados, and the elder of the Hayato, who in memory of this were accustomed to perform a dance, in which the drowning struggles of Ho-no-Susori were imitated. The actors were naked to the waist-cloth, and smeared their hands and faces with red earth ; reminding us of the wine-lees of Thespis and his crew.

There is frequent mention in subsequent Japanese history of pantomime performances, some of which were secular, and others of a more or less sacred character.

When the dance and music of the Kagura were supplemented by a spoken dialogue, the Nō were the result. The addition of words is said to have been suggested by the chanted recitations of the *Heike Monogatari* by itinerant bonzes, and there is much in the language of the Nō to countenance this supposition. It is certain that the authors were well acquainted with it, and also with the *Gempei Seisuiki* and the *Taiheiki*.

The beginnings of the Nō date from the fourteenth century. They were at first purely religious performances, intended to propitiate the chief deities of the Shinto religion, and were acted exclusively in connection with their shrines. At Ise, the principal seat of the worship of the Sun Goddess, there were three Nō theatres, in Ōmi three, in Tamba three, and at Nara four, all devoted to the service of the respective Shinto gods worshipped in these places.

In the early part of the Muromachi period a manager of one of the Nō theatres at Nara, named Kwan-ami Kiyotsugu, attracted the notice of the ruling Shōgun, who, for the sake of his art, took him into his immediate service. It is a noteworthy circumstance, as indicating the social position of the Nō performers, that this Kwan-ami was a small daimio, holding a fief in the province of Yamato. He died in 1406. From this time forward the Nō were under the special patronage of the Shōguns, just as the Tanka found favour and official protection at the court of the Mikado. Kiyotsugu was succeeded by his eldest son Motokiyo, who died in 1455, in his eighty-first year. Their descendants enjoyed the favour of the Shōguns for a long period. Hideyoshi, who was Shōgun in all but name, was very fond of the Nō, and is said to have taken part in them as an actor. Several of the more recent date from his time. In the Yedo period the Shōguns gave great attention to Nō performances. They were made a ceremony of state, and were acted by young gentlemen of the military class educated specially for this profession. Even at the present day there are some remains of their former popularity with the Samurai. Representations are still given in Tokio, Kiōto, and other places, by the descendants or successors of the old managers who founded the art five hundred years ago, and are attended by small but select audiences composed almost entirely of ex-Daimios or military nobles and their ex-retainers. To the vulgar the Nō are completely unintelligible.

Of the two hundred and thirty-five Nō contained in the latest and most complete collection (the *Yō-kyoku Tsūge*), no fewer than ninety-three are assigned to Se-ami Moto-kiyo, the second of the line of official managers; his father, Kwan-ami Kiyotsugu, being credited with fifteen. Motokiyo's son-in-law and successor has twenty-two assigned to him, those of the remainder which are not anonymous being distributed among a dozen or so of the subsequent holders of the office. The great majority belong to the fifteenth century.

The *Yō-kyoku Tsūge* editor suggests, with great proba-bility, that although the names of Kiyotsugu, Motokiyo, and their successors are given as authors of the Nō, they were in reality only responsible for the music, the panto-mimic dance (the "business," as we might say), and the general management. He surmises that the libretto was the work of Buddhist monks, to which class almost all the literary men of this period belonged. The question of authorship is, however, of minor importance, as the characteristics of the Nō are rather those of a school of writers than of individuals.

Whoever their authors may have been, their primary object was the promotion of piety. In some cases a patriotic or martial enthusiasm is the inspiring motive, and a love of nature is discernible in almost all, but the staple material is the mass of legends associated with the Buddhist and Shinto religions. A monk or guardian of a Shinto shrine is most frequently the chief personage of the play, and the virtue of hospitality to the priestly order, the sin of taking away life, the praise of particular deities, the uncertainty of life, and the transitoriness of human things are favourite themes with them.

In the Nō, next after religion comes poetry. Not that they are exactly poems. Purely lyrical passages are not wanting, but much, both from the point of view of metre and of diction, is undeniable prose. Not a little is in an intermediate style, in which the seven and five syllable phrases succeed one another with great irregularity, and the language is alloyed with a less poetic element. The admission of Chinese words, although in moderation, also tends to lower the poetic level. It will be remembered that these are rigorously excluded from the older classical poetry.

A very striking feature of the Nō is the lavish use which they make of the poetic devices mentioned in a previous chapter.[1] Pillow-words are freely introduced, and parallelism is a common ornament. But the greatest favourite of all is the " pivot-word," which is employed in the Nō to an extent and in a manner previously unknown to

[1] See above, p. 32.

Japanese literature. This must be my excuse for dwelling on it at somewhat greater length here. "The Pivot" (I quote from Mr. Chamberlain's *Classical Poetry of the Japanese*) "is a word of two significations, which serves as a species of hinge on which two doors turn, so that while the first part of the poetical phrase has no logical end, the latter part has no logical beginning. They run into each other, and the sentence could not possibly be construed." Mr. Chamberlain adds that "to the English reader such a punning invention will doubtless seem the height of misapplied ingenuity. But, as a matter of fact, the impression produced by these linked verses is delightful in the extreme, passing as they do before the reader like a series of dissolving views, vague, graceful, and suggestive. This ornament especially characterises the old poetic dramas, and renders them a peculiarly arduous study to such as do not thoroughly appreciate its nature."

Native critics would no doubt endorse Mr. Chamberlain's favourable opinion of the pivot-word, and it is undeniable that the Japanese, who are an eminently nimble-witted race, delight in these acrobatic feats of language. But the English student will ask whether it is worth while to sacrifice sense and syntax for the sake of such inane, if sometimes pretty, antics. I venture to think that the "pivot" is a mistake in serious composition, and that the partiality for such a frivolous ornament of style manifested not only by the writers of Nō, but by the dramatists and novelists of the Yedo period, is a characteristic sign of an age of literary decadence and bad taste. Such writers as Hakuseki, Kiusō, and Motoöri disdain it utterly.

The authors of the Nō do not pique themselves on originality. They are in the habit of conveying to their own pages in the most liberal manner snatches of Tanka, texts of Buddhist scripture, or striking phrases supplied by their memory from older writers, stringing them together, however, in a way which does much credit to their ingenuity. Plagiarism, it may be remarked, is hardly recognised as an offence by the Japanese.

The Nō are not classical poems. They are too deficient in lucidity, method, coherence, and good taste to deserve this description. Still they are not without charm. *Jeux-de-mots* are not everything in them, and the reader who has the patience to unravel their intricacies of language will not go altogether unrewarded. If their vein of poetic ore is less pure than that of the *Manyōshiu* and *Kokinshiu*, it is also richer. They embrace within their scope a world of legendary lore, of quaint fancies, and of religious sentiment, to which the classical poetry of Japan is a stranger. And if we miss the perfection of form which characterises the dainty little Tanka, we have instead a luxuriance and variety which go some way to indemnify us for its absence. It is to be regretted that so promising a literary departure should have proved ultimately abortive. After the sixteenth century the Nō ceased to be written. The current of the higher Japanese thought had by this time turned away from Buddhism and everything that belongs to it, and was setting strongly towards Chinese philosophy. Though the Nō were still performed, the impulse to write new ones was apparently no longer felt.

As dramas the Nō have little value. There is no action to speak of, and dramatic propriety and effect are hardly thought of. The plot is frequently something of the following description :—

A priest appears on the scene. He announces his

name, and informs the audience that he is setting out on his travels. Presently he arrives at a temple, a battle-field, or other celebrated spot, when a ghost or deity appears, who relates to him the local legend. An exchange of edifying sentiments follows, and the supernatural personage finally reveals his identity.

The whole piece rarely occupies more than six or seven pages of print, and it usually takes less than an hour to perform. Within this narrow compass it might be expected that the unities of time, place, and action would have been observed. This is far from being the case. The action, in so far as there is any, is generally more or less coherent, but the other unities are wholly disregarded. In the *Takasago*, for example, the scene changes from Kiushiu to Harima, and again from Harima to Sumiyoshi, within seven pages, while weeks must be allowed for the journeys of the chief personage between these places.

The number of the *dramatis personæ* varies from two or three (the latter being very frequent) up to five or six. To these must be added a few musicians and the chorus. The chorus of the Nō has various functions. The chief office is to chant a narrative which serves to supplement and explain the action of the piece, as in some of Shakespeare's older plays, or to recite poetical descriptions which supply the place of the absent scenery. The chorus also indulges from time to time in sententious or sympathetic observations, or even enters into conversation with the personages on the stage.

The following description of the Nō theatre will help us to realise their character more fully. It is taken from Mr. Chamberlain's *Classical Poetry of the Japanese* :—

"The stage, which has remained unaltered in every

respect since the beginning of the fifteenth century, is a square wooden room open on all sides but one, and supported on pillars, the side of the square being about eighteen English feet. It is surmounted by a quaint roof somewhat resembling those to be seen on Buddhist temples, and is connected with the green-room by a gallery some nine feet wide. Upon this gallery part of the action occasionally takes place. Added on to the back of the square stage is a narrow space where sits the orchestra, consisting of one flute-player, two performers on instruments, which, in the absence of a more fitting name, may perhaps be called tambourines, and one beater of the drum, while the chorus, whose number is not fixed, squat on the ground to the right of the spectator. The back of the stage, the only side not open to the air, is painted with a pine-tree, in accordance with ancient usage, while, equally in conformity with established rules, three small pine-trees are planted in the court which divides the gallery from the space occupied by the less distinguished portion of the audience. The covered place for the audience runs round three sides of the stage.[1] Masks are worn by such of the actors as take the parts of females or of supernatural beings, and the dresses are gorgeous in the extreme. Scenery, however, is allowed no place on the lyric stage."

It will readily be understood that the difficulty of arriving at the meaning of such compositions as the Nō is very considerable. Mr. Mitford, no mean scholar, in his *Tales of Old Japan* pronounces them "wholly unintelligible"; though this statement must be taken with

[1] From which it is separated by a space corresponding to our pit, only open to the air.—W. G. A.

some qualification, as he gives in the same work a lucid account of the plot of several of them. But even when he has mastered their sense, the translator's difficulties are only beginning. I know of nothing in literature for which it is more impossible to give an adequate English equivalent than the intricate network of word-plays, quotations, and historical, literary, and scriptural allusions of which they consist. Mr. Chamberlain, who has done some of them into English verse, confesses that his rendering is only a paraphrase. Prose or a rough and ready blank verse has been preferred for the partial translation of the *Takasago*, which is given below. But even when freed from the temptation to introduce extraneous matter which is hardly separable from a poetical version, it is not possible to render the original as faithfully as might be desired. I have tried, however, while omitting a certain untranslatable element, at any rate to bring in nothing of my own.

"TAKASAGO"

This is one of the pieces attributed to MOTOKIYO, who died in 1455, but, as already suggested, he was probably only the director or manager of the theatre where it was produced. It is the best known, and is considered the finest of all the Nō. Its popularity was testified to no longer ago than last year (1897) by the launching, from the yard of Messrs. Armstrong & Co. at Newcastle, of a cruiser for the Japanese navy bearing the name of *Takasago*.

DRAMATIS PERSONÆ.

TOMONARI	. . .	*Guardian of the Shinto shrine of Aso, in Kiushiu.*
AN OLD MAN	.	*Really the spirit of the Sumiyoshi fir-tree.*
AN OLD WOMAN	.	*Really the spirit of the Takasago fir-tree.*
THE GOD OF SUMIYOSHI.		
CHORUS.		

CHORUS (?) [1] (*chants in nearly regular metre*).

> Now for the first time he ties the lace of his travelling
>> garb :
> His goal is distant many a long day's journey.

TOMONARI (*speaks in prose*). Now, this is I, Tomonari, guardian of the shrine of Aso, in the province of Higo, in Kiushiu. Never having seen the capital, I have now made up my mind, and am going up to the capital. Moreover, I wish to take this opportunity of viewing the bay of Takasago, in Harima.

CHORUS (?) (*chants in regular metre*). To-day he has made up his mind, and has donned his travelling raiment for a journey to a distant goal—the capital. With waves that rise along the shore, and a genial wind of spring upon the ship-path, how many days pass without a trace of him we know not, until at length he has reached the longed-for bay of Takasago, on the coast of Harima.

OLD MAN AND OLD WOMAN (*chant*). The wind of spring that blows through the fir-tree of Takasago has gone down with the sun ; the vesper bell is heard from the Temple of Onoye.

OLD WOMAN. The waves are hidden from us by the mist-enshrouded rocks.

BOTH. There is naught but the sound to mark the rise and fall of the tide.

OLD MAN. Whom can I take to be my friend? Except the fir-tree of Takasago, my ancient comrade, there is none to converse with me of the bygone days on which are ever gathering white snows [of forgetfulness]. I grow older and older, accustomed to hear nothing but the wind in the fir-tree either when I rise or go to sleep in my nest of an aged crane, where the night-long moon sheds its rays, and the spring sends down its hoar-frosts. So I make my own heart my companion, and thus give utterance to my thoughts.

BOTH. Let us sweep away the fir-needles that lie beneath the

---

[1] The distribution of the speeches is sometimes doubtful. I have made one or two changes.

tree, sleeve touching sleeve of our garments, whereon rest fallen leaves shaken down by the shore-wind asking their news of the firs.

. . . .

TOMONARI (*spoken*). While waiting for some of the villagers to appear, an old man and an old woman have come hither. I pray you, old people, permit me to ask you a question.

OLD MAN. It is I whom you address? What is it you desire to know?

TOMONARI. Which is the tree that is called the fir-tree of Takasago?

OLD MAN. This very tree whose shade we are cleansing is the fir-tree of Takasago.

TOMONARI. The phrase "growing old together" is used of the Takasago and Suminoye fir-trees. But this place and Sumiyoshi [the same as Suminoye] are in provinces distant from one another. How then can they be called the fir-trees which "grow old together"?

OLD MAN. As you have deigned to observe, it is stated in the preface to the *Kokinshiu* [1] that the fir-trees of Takasago and Suminoye make us feel as if they were growing old together. However that may be, here am I, an old man, who belong to Sumiyoshi, in the province of Settsu, while the old woman here is of this place. Be pleased to tell me, if you can, how that may be.

TOMONARI (*in verse*). Strange! I see you old couple here together. What mean you then by saying that you dwell apart, one in distant Suminoye, the other in Takasago, divided from one another by seashore, hill, and province?

OLD WOMAN (*in verse*). What an odd speech! Though many a mile of mountain and river separate them, the way of a husband and wife whose hearts respond to one another with mutual care, is not far apart.

OLD WOMAN. There is Suminoye.
OLD MAN. And here is Takasago.
TOMONARI. The fir-trees blend their hues.

[1] See above, p. 66.

OLD MAN. And the spring air——
TOMONARI. Is genial, while——

(*Here the chorus strikes in with a canticle which is chanted as the indispensable accompaniment of every regular Japanese wedding, and is one of the best known passages in Japanese literature. Figures representing the two old folks under the fir-tree with brooms in their hands are, on such occasions, set out on a sort of tray. This is a favourite subject of the Japanese artist.*)

CHORUS. On the four seas
　　　　Still are the waves ;
　　　　The world is at peace :
　　　　Soft blow the time-winds,[1]
　　　　Rustling not the branches.
　　　　In such an age
　　　　Blest are the very firs,
　　　　In that they meet
　　　　To grow old together.
　　　　Vain indeed
　　　　Are reverent upward looks ;
　　　　Vain even are words to tell
　　　　Our thanks that we were born
　　　　In such an age,
　　　　Rich with the bounty
　　　　Of our sovereign lord.

　　　　.　　　　.　　　　.　　　　.

OLD MAN. I hear the sound of the bell of Onoye, in Takasago.

CHORUS. The dawn is near,
　　　　And the hoar-frost falls
　　　　On the fir-tree twigs ;
　　　　But its leaves' dark green
　　　　Suffer no change.
　　　　Morning and evening
　　　　Beneath its shade

[1] The land and sea breezes, which blow regularly only in fine weather.

The leaves are swept away,
Yet they never fail.
True it is
That these fir-trees
Shed not all their leaves ;
Their verdure remains fresh
For ages long,
As the Masaka trailing vine ;
Even amongst evergreen trees—
The emblem of unchangeableness—
Exalted is their fame
As a symbol to the end of time—
The fame of the fir-trees that have grown old together.

TOMONARI. And ye who have made known the bygone story of these ancient firs whose branches have indeed earned fame— tell me, I pray you, by what names are ye called.

OLD MAN AND OLD WOMAN. Why conceal it longer? We are the spirits of the fir-trees of Takasago and Suminoye that have grown old together, manifested under the form of a married pair.

CHORUS. Wonderful! A miracle wrought by the fir-trees of this famous place !

OLD MAN AND OLD WOMAN. Plants and trees are without souls——

CHORUS. Yet in this august reign——

OLD MAN AND OLD WOMAN. Even for plants and trees——

CHORUS. Good is it to live
For ever and ever
In this land
Of our great sovereign,
Under his rule.
To Sumiyoshi,[1] therefore,
He would now take his way
And there wait upon [the god].
He embarks in a fisher's boat
That lies by the beach,

---

[1] Sumiyoshi means "dwell-good."

Where the waves of evening roll,
And spreading his sail
To the favouring breeze,
Puts out into the deep,
Puts out into the deep.

TOMONARI. From Takasago I set sail
In this skiff that lies by the shore,
And put forth with the tide
That goes out with the moon.
I pass under the lee
Of Awaji's shore,
I leave far behind me Naruwo,
And now I have arrived
At Suminoye.

(*The god of Sumiyoshi*[1] *appears, and enters into a poetical dialogue with the chorus.*)

CHORUS. We give thanks for this manifestation;
Ever anew we will worship
Thy spirit with sacred dance
By Sumiyoshi's pure moonlight.
. . . .

CHORUS. And now, world without end,
The extended arms of the dancing maidens
In sacerdotal robes
Will expel noxious influences;
Their hands folded to rest in their bosoms
Will embrace all good fortune;
The hymn of a thousand autumns
Will draw down blessings on the people,
And the song of ten thousand years[2]
Prolong our sovereign's life.
And all the while,

---

[1] There are in reality three gods. Doubtless only one appears on the stage.

[2] Equivalent to our "God save the Queen."

The voice of the breeze,
As it blows through the firs
That grow old together,
Will yield us delight.

Some of the Nō have more of dramatic action than the Takasago. *Nakamitsu*, a piece translated by Mr. Chamberlain, is one of these. Another example is the *Tōsen*, of which the following is a résumé :—

An inhabitant of Hakosaki, in Kiushiu, informs the audience that under an embargo placed by the Japanese Government on Chinese ships thirteen years before, he had detained a vessel from that country, and made the owner his cow-herd.

The Chinaman's two sons come to ransom their father. His master gives him leave to go, but just when they are about to sail, two sons born to him in Japan appear and propose to accompany him. Their request is refused by the master, and the father, distracted between his wish to return home with his Chinese family, and his reluctance to leave his Japanese children behind, tries to drown himself. Much appropriate sentiment ensues, which touches the heart of the master, so that he allows all five to depart together.

In *Dōjōji* a priest appears, and informs the audience that he is about to consecrate a new bell for his temple, the former one having been long ago removed. He then directs his acolyte to make the necessary preparations, enjoining on him specially to take care that no woman shall be present at the ceremony.

A dancing-girl approaches, and proposes to dance in honour of the occasion. The acolyte forgets his instructions, and allows her to do so. She takes the opportunity of seizing the bell by the suspending ring, and bringing it down over her, greatly to the consternation of the priest. He calls together his fellows and relates a legend which explains why women were not allowed to be present :—

" A man had an only daughter, who formed a union with a Yamabushi [a sort of lay-priest]. When pressed to marry her, he ran away and hid in the bell of the temple. She pursued him, and came to a river which she could not cross. But the fire of her passion was so intense that it changed her into a serpent, in which form she found no difficulty in swimming over. Coming to the temple, the serpent coiled itself round the bell, which was melted by the heat of her passion, the false lover perishing at the same time."

The priest, having told this legend, joins with his colleagues in reciting with might and main all kinds of Buddhist prayers and invocations, by which the bell is raised to its former position, and the dancing-girl forced to reveal herself in her serpent shape. Involved in flames, she plunges into the adjoining river and disappears. *Exeunt omnes.*

The Kiōgen (mad-words) are to the Nō what farce is to the regular drama. They are performed on the same stage in the intervals between the more serious pieces.

They differ from the Nō in having no chorus, and in being composed in the pure colloquial dialect of the time. They are even shorter, and of the slightest construction. The following is an example :—

" A Daimio sends his servant to the city to buy a talisman which will work miracles. The servant meets with a swindler, who sells him an object which he calls the Mallet of Daikoku (every blow of which is supposed to produce a piece of gold), telling him a charm by repeat-

ing which, as he holds the mallet, he can have anything
he pleases. The servant returns with his prize. The
Daimio asks him to produce a horse. The servant repeats
his charm, and declares that the horse is ready saddled
and bridled. The Daimio pretends to think his servant
the horse, jumps on his back, and rides him about the
stage in spite of his protestations."

Fifty of the Kiōgen have been published under the
title *Kiōgen Ki*, and there is before me a manuscript
collection which contains one hundred and fifty of these
pieces.

BOOK THE SIXTH

YEDO PERIOD (1603-1867)

BOOK THE SIXTH

YEDO PERIOD (1603-1867)

CHAPTER I

INTRODUCTORY—"TAIKŌKI"

THE student of Japanese history, in any of its branches, should note well the two dates which stand at the head of this chapter. They mark the beginning and end of that wonderful political organisation known as the Tokugawa Shōgunate. The first is the date of the establishment of his capital at Yedo by Tokugawa Iyeyasu, and the second that of the abolition of the office of Shōgun, and the resumption of sovereign authority by the Mikado after many centuries of abeyance. During this period a great wave of Chinese influence passed over the country, deeply affecting it in every conceivable way. Not only the constitution of the Government, but the laws, art, science, material civilisation, and, most of all, the thought of the nation as expressed in its philosophy and literature, bear profound traces of Chinese teaching and example. This wave has not wholly subsided even now, but it has ceased to be of importance, except, perhaps, in determining the moral standards of the nation, and 1867 is a convenient date from which to reckon the substitution of Europe for China as the source whence the Japanese draw inspiration in all these matters.

The latter half of the Muromachi period, coinciding with the second half of the sixteenth century, was a very disturbed time in Japan. The local nobles or Daimios, defying all control by the central government, engaged in continual struggles with one another for lands and power, and a lamentable condition of anarchy was the result. The first to apply a remedy to this state of things was one of their own order, Nobunaga, a man of resolute character and great military capacity. Aided by his two famous lieutenants, Hideyoshi and Iyeyasu, he succeeded in bringing most of the Daimios into subjection, and even deposed the Shōgun, although he was prevented by his descent from assuming that title himself. At his death in 1582, the reins of power passed into the hands of Hideyoshi, who completed the work which Nobunaga had begun. Under the titles of Kwambaku (Regent) or Taikō, he was practically monarch of Japan, until his death in 1598. Then Iyeyasu, after a sharp struggle, which ended in 1600 by the defeat of his opponents in the decisive battle of Sekigahara, succeeded to the supreme authority, and caused himself to be appointed Shōgun by the puppet Mikado of the day. He was the founder of the Tokugawa (his family name) dynasty of Shōguns, which lasted until our own time.

Iyeyasu was probably the greatest statesman that Japan has ever seen. By the organisation of that remarkable system of feudal government under which the nation enjoyed peace and prosperity for two and a half centuries, he solved for his day and country the problem, which will occupy politicians to the end of time, of the due apportionment of central and local authority. At no previous period of Japanese history was the power of the Central Government more effectively maintained in all essential matters, although in other respects the Daimios were allowed a large measure of independent action. Under this régime Japan increased amazingly in wealth and population, and made great progress in all the arts of civilisation.

As a consequence, the new capital of Yedo rose rapidly to importance. Under the regulation, established by Iye-yasu's grandson Iyemitsu, which compelled the Daimios to reside there for part of the year, leaving their wives and children as hostages during the remainder, its population attained to at least a million, and is believed to have been at one time considerably more.

It is not surprising that the enhanced political and commercial importance of Yedo should have brought about a displacement of the literary centre of Japan. Kiōto, especially during the early part of the Yedo period, continued to be a place of some literary activity, and Osaka became the cradle of a new form of drama, but Yedo attracted to itself all the principal learning and talent of the country. For the last two hundred years Yedo has been to Japan for literature what London is to the United Kingdom, or Paris to France.

There is another feature of the literature of the Yedo period which is traceable to the improved condition of the country. Authors now no longer addressed themselves exclusively to a cultured class, but to the people generally. The higher degree of civilisation which was rendered possible by an improved administration and a more settled government included a far more widely extended system of education than Japan had ever known before. And not only were the humbler classes better educated. They were more prosperous in every way, and were better able to purchase books as well as to read them. Books, too, were far more easily attainable than before. Printing, which in Japan dates from the eighth century, now for the first time became common.[1] Hideyoshi's armies, returning from their devastating raid upon Corea, brought with them a number of books printed with movable types, which served as models for the Japanese printers. Iyeyasu was a liberal patron of the printing-press. Since this time the production of printed books has gone on at an increasing rate, and they now form an accumulation which is truly formidable in amount.

The popularisation of literature during the Yedo period worked for evil as well as for good. Many wholesome moral and religious treatises were brought within the reach of the nation generally, and knowledge was greatly extended. But, on the other hand, the average level of taste and refinement was distinctly lowered, and notwithstanding the well-meant but spasmodic attempts of the Government to repress it, a flood of pornographic fiction not easily to be paralleled elsewhere was poured out over the country.

For the Buddhist religion the Yedo period was a time of decadence. Its continued popularity is attested by the vast number of temples which were erected everywhere, and by the hosts of monks who were maintained in idleness. But its influence was on the wane. While Confucianism became the creed of the strong, governing military caste, Buddhism attached itself to the broken

---

[1] See papers on the "Early History of Printing in Japan," by Sir Ernest Satow, in the *Japan Asiatic Society's Transactions*, vol. x. 1, and x. 2.

fortunes of the Mikados and their court. The nation generally was gradually awaking to a fuller and more vigorous life, and homilies on the instability of human things, the vanity of wealth and power, the detestableness of violence and cruelty, the duty of abstinence from the grosser pleasures, and the beauty of a life of seclusion and pious meditation, were no longer so much to their taste. The moral principles which animated politics and literature were now drawn from the more robust and manly, if more worldly, teachings of the Chinese sages. But of this more remains to be said hereafter.

Towards the end of this period there was a partial reaction in favour of the old Shinto religion. It proved to be only an eddy in the main current of the national thought, and is chiefly important politically as one of the disintegrating influences which led to the breaking up of the Tokugawa régime.

Compared with the writings of the Heian or classical period, the Yedo literature is infinitely more voluminous, and has a far wider range of subjects. It comprises history, biography, poetry, the drama, essays, sermons, a multitude of political and religious treatises, fiction of various kinds and travels, with a huge mass of *biblia abiblia*, such as dictionaries, grammars, and other philological works, bibliographies, medical works, treatises on botany, law, the art of war, commentaries on the Chinese classics (in themselves a host), expositions of Buddhist doctrine, cyclopædias, antiquarian and metaphysical works, guide-books, and so on.

But while the new literature is much richer and of a more vigorous growth than the old, there is a sad falling off in point of form. With few exceptions it is disfigured by the grossest and most glaring faults. Extravagance, false sentiment, defiance of probability whether physical or moral, pedantry, pornography, puns and other meretricious ornaments of style, intolerable platitudes, impossible adventures, and weary wastes of useless detail meet us everywhere. There is no want of ability. Plenty of genuine wit and humour is to be discovered by those who know where to look for it. True pathos is to be met with in works otherwise highly objectionable ; excellent moral advice is only too abundant; there are graphic descriptions of real life, prodigious fertility of invention, a style frequently not devoid of elegance, and generally a far wider range of thought in political and social matters than the hedonist literature of ancient Japan could boast. It is the writer "totus teres atque rotundus" whose absence is so conspicuous. Sane thought, sustained good writing, disciplined imagination and some sense of order, proportion and consistent method are sadly to seek in the profusion of written and printed matter which this period has left to us.

The Japanese language underwent considerable change at this time. To supply the needs of the new civilisation a vast increase of the vocabulary became necessary, and Chinese words were adopted so freely that they now far outnumber those of native origin. As in English, however, the latter retain their position for all the essentials of language. At the same time the simplification of the somewhat cumbrous grammatical system of the old language made still further progress.

In this period the colloquial speech, which had been gradually diverging from the written language so far as at last to necessitate separate grammars for its elucidation, began to show itself in literature. Whether its partisans will succeed in erecting it into a literary dialect remains to be seen. Up to the present their success has not been very conspicuous. It will require far more cultivation than has yet been bestowed upon it to make it equally concise and perspicuous, and to give it the same range of varied expression, as the ordinary literary language.

The "Taikōki."

One of the earliest works of the Yedo period is the *Taikōki*, a biography of the Taikō, or Regent Hideyoshi, in twenty-two books (eleven volumes). Although written only twenty-seven years after Hideyoshi's death, there had already been time for his history to acquire a certain legendary quality. The first chapter exemplifies the propensity of ignorant mankind for surrounding the birth of great men with miraculous occurrences. The *Taikōki* cannot be given a high place as literature, but it is valuable for the contemporary documents which it contains, and has supplied material for a number of later works bearing the same or similar titles. It was written in 1625 by an unknown author.

CHAPTER II

THE KANGAKUSHA (Chinese Scholars)

Towards the end of the Muromachi period, learning in Japan had reached its lowest ebb. Hideyoshi, at the height of his power and fame, was an ignorant man, as letters written by him remain to testify, and he had great difficulty in finding scholars competent to conduct the negotiations with China and Corea which arose out of his invasion of the latter country. He was, however, a friend of learning. His successor Iyeyasu (1603–1632) fully recognised the necessity of wider knowledge for building up the new social and political fabric which he created. His patronage of printing has been already mentioned. He also established schools, and devoted much attention to the collection and preservation of printed books and manuscripts. A special department was provided by him, where he employed a staff of monks in copying out the family records of the Daimios.

Among the scholars who enjoyed Iyeyasu's patronage the most eminent was FUJIWARA SEIKWA, a native of Harima, where he was born in 1560. Himself a poet, he was a descendant of Fujiwara Sadaiye, a well-known Tanka-writer of the thirteenth century. As a boy he gave great promise of talent. He received the Buddhist tonsure, but soon recognised the emptiness of Buddhism, and applied himself with great diligence to the study of the ancient Chinese literature. Finding, however, that the difficulties caused by the want of competent teachers and suitable text-books were too great for him to surmount, he made up his mind to go to China and continue his studies there. He had got as far as the province of Satsuma, and was waiting for a ship, when one of those apparently trivial incidents occurred which exercise a profound influence on the fate of a nation. He overheard a boy in the house next to the inn where he was staying read aloud from a Chinese book which was unfamiliar to him. Upon inquiry, it proved to be a commentary by Chu-Hi on the "Great Learning" of Confucius. A brief examination showed him its importance. Equally delighted and astonished, Seikwa exclaimed, "This is what I have so long been in want of." Eventually he discovered a complete set of the philosophical works of Ching Hao (1032–1085), Cheng I. (1033–1107), and Chu-Hi (1130–1200), the famous Chinese schoolmen and expositors of the doctrines of Confucius and Mencius under the Sung dynasty. He was so strongly impressed by their perusal, that he resolved to abandon his intention of proceeding to China, and to devote himself entirely to their study at home.

Seikwa subsequently made the acquaintance of Iyeyasu at the camp of Nagoya, where Hideyoshi was then preparing his famous invasion of Corea. Iyeyasu recognised his merit, and sent for him repeatedly to expound the classics ; but Seikwa, taking offence at being confounded with the rabble of ordinary monks, pretended illness, and having introduced as his substitute his pupil Hayashi Rasan, retired to a quiet village near Kiōto. Here pupils flocked to him in great numbers, many of them the sons of court nobles or Daimios ; and he also received flattering offers of appointments, all of which he declined. In 1614 he was offered a post as teacher in connection with a project of Iyeyasu's for establishing a school at Kiōto. This proposal he accepted, but some civil disorders which broke out soon after rendered this scheme abortive. Seikwa died in 1619 in his fifty-ninth year. He left nothing which deserves notice as literature ; but it is hardly possible to estimate too highly the service he performed by making known to his countrymen the philosophical literature of the Sung schoolmen. His *Kana Seiri* may be mentioned as a typical example of his writings. As its title indicates, it is an attempt to facilitate the study of the Sung philosophy in Japan.

The whole literature of the Yedo period is so thoroughly pervaded by moral principles and ideals based on this system of thought, that it is desirable to give a brief outline of it here. Those who wish to make themselves more thoroughly acquainted with it will find the means of doing so in Monseigneur de Harlez's *École Philosophique de la Chine*, and some able papers contributed by Dr. Knox and others to the *Journal of the Asiatic Society of Japan* in 1892.

Professedly an exposition of the doctrines of the ancient Chinese sages, the Sung philosophy is in reality an essentially modern system of ontology, ethics, natural philosophy, and principles of government, subjects which to the Chinese mind are inseparable.

According to Chu-Hi, the origin and cause of all things is *Taikhi* (*Taikyoku* in Japanese) or the "Great Absolute." The energy evolved by its movement produced the *Yang* (*Yō* in Japanese), and when it came to rest, the *Yin* (*In* in Japanese) was the result. The *Yang* is the active, positive, productive, male principle of nature, while the *Yin* is regarded as passive or receptive, negative and female. By the mutual action of these two principles the Kosmos was formed out of chaos, the *Yin* manifesting itself in the settling down of the impure sediment as earth, while the lighter and purer part, representing the *Yang*, ascended and formed heaven. The *Yin* and *Yang* are also the source of the five elements, water, fire, earth, metal, and wood. Each of these has its proper function, on the right discharge of which depend the regular sequence of the four seasons and phenomena generally. These processes go on eternally. There is no such thing as a creation in this system. The energy which produces all these results is called in Chinese *K'e*, in Japanese *Ki* (Breath). It follows fixed laws called *Li* (*Ri* in Japanese). The precise nature of these two last conceptions has been elucidated (or obscured) by many volumes of dissertations both in China and Japan.

Chu-Hi says little of *Ten* (Heaven). In his philosophy its place is taken by the more impersonal *Taikhi*. But in Japan, as with Confucius and Mencius, *Ten* is all-important. It is the nearest approach to a deity which the essentially impersonal habit of mind of these nations permits. *Ten* or *Tendō* (the Way of Heaven) is said "to know," "to command," "to reward," "to punish," or "to be wroth," and is looked up to with reverence and grateful emotion. But the conception falls short of that of a personal deity as we understand the phrase. There are in Japan, at any rate, no temples to *Ten*, no litanies, and no formal acts of worship.

Ethics are in the Chu-Hi system a branch of natural philosophy. Corresponding to the regular changes of the seasons in nature is right action in man (who is the crown of nature) in the relations of sovereign and subject, parent and child, elder brother and younger brother, husband and wife, friend and friend. To his sovereign or lord he is bound to be faithful, to his parents dutiful, and to his elder brother respectful. Affection should characterise the relations of husband and wife, and trust that of friend with friend. A man should also display in his conduct the five virtues of Goodness, Righteousness, Propriety, Enlightenment, and Good Faith. The same combination of ethics and natural science is implied in Confucius's doctrine when he says that the command of Heaven is called natural disposition, accordance with this natural disposition is called the path (of duty), the regulation of this path is called instruction. Man's heart is naturally good. In like manner Kiusō, a Japanese exponent of the Chu-Hi philosophy, says, " Man makes the heart of heaven and earth [nature, we would say] his own."

Principles of government are also found a place in this philosophy. If the sovereign practises the virtues above described in his own person, the people will naturally imitate his example, and good government will be the result. But the necessity of dealing out justly rewards and punishments, of encouraging sages to lead the people in the right way, and of purity in making appointments, is not lost sight of.

The Japanese have added little or nothing to Chu-Hi's philosophy. It is in its application that the national genius reveals itself, and more especially in the relative importance attached by them to the various moral obligations incumbent on man.

It is here that we must look for an answer to a question which will occur to all who take the smallest interest in the Japanese, namely " In what respect does their national character differ from that of European nations ?"

The vices and virtues are on the whole the same with them as with ourselves. It is in their " Table of Moral Precedence," as it were, that we discover some striking differences. The most noteworthy instance of this is the commanding position assigned to loyalty, which in the moral ideas of this period overshadows and dwarfs all other obligations. It means not so much the reverent submission due by all his subjects to the Mikado, although in theory this was not lost sight of, as of the Daimios to the Shōgun, and, in a still higher degree, of men of the two-sworded class to their immediate chiefs. Implicit obedience and unfaltering devotion to his feudal lord was the Samurai's most sacred duty. For his lord's sake the retainer was bound not only to lay down his own life cheerfully, but to sacrifice the lives and honour of those nearest and dearest to him. Japanese history and literature teem with instances which show the extreme lengths to which this virtue was carried, not only in theory, but in practice. It was responsible for many acts of barbarity, such as that of Nakamitsu, a favourite hero of Japanese drama and story, who slew his own innocent son, and substituted his head for that of his lord's heir, who had been guilty of a capital offence. But there was also associated with it unshrinking courage, loyal service, and disinterested self-sacrifice to a degree for which we must go to ancient Rome to find a parallel. The political system of which this virtue was the vital support is now a thing of the past. Daimios and Shōguns exist no longer. But those who know the Japan of the present day will readily recognise the same quality in the spirit of national patriotism and zeal in the discharge of public duty which honourably distinguish the descendants of the former Samurai.

Next after loyalty in the Japanese scale of virtues stands filial piety. The State being composed of families, if the family is badly managed, the State cannot be well governed. If the child is disobedient to his parents, he is not likely to prove a loyal and obedient subject when he grows to manhood. Hence the necessity, from a political point of view, of filial piety. On the extreme importance attached to this virtue both in China and Japan it is needless to dilate.

Among the chief duties of a Samurai to his lord, or of a child towards his parent, was that of revenge. The forgiveness of injuries had no place in the moral code of the Japanese of this time. No more stern obligation rested on them than to execute dire vengeance for the unmerited death or disgrace of a parent or lord. That this was not in theory only, there are many well-authenticated instances in real life to show. It applied to women as well as to men, though in their case, as in that of the lower classes of society, it was regarded more or less as a counsel of perfection. If they did rise to the occasion, all the more honour was paid them. The drama and fiction of modern Japan are full of stories of revenge (*kataki-uchi*), and this passion occupies the same place of honour with their novelists that love does in European fiction.

In presence of the obligations imposed by loyalty and filial duty, life was regarded as of no account. When we remember the humane Buddhist influences to which Japan was so long subjected, and the ancient national character reflected in the mildly sentimental Heian literature, the disregard of human life which pervades history and fiction alike during the Yedo period is not a little remarkable. It is conspicuously observable in the ethics of suicide. The moral code of this time contains no canon 'gainst self-slaughter. On the contrary, the occasions when a Japanese Samurai was bound to commit suicide were innumerable. Grave insults which it was impossible to revenge, unmerited disgrace, gross blundering, errors of judgment, or even simple failure in official matters, crimes not of a disgraceful character, all entailed the necessity of suicide, or at least made it the most honourable course to pursue. If a Samurai had occasion to remonstrate with his lord for some act of misgovernment, he frequently emphasised his appeal by suicide. The case of the forty-seven Rōnins who slew themselves in a body at the grave of their master after having executed a bloody revenge on his enemy, is known to all readers of Mr. Mitford's *Tales of Old Japan*. Another admired example is that of a governor of Nagasaki who in 1808 committed suicide in the approved manner because he was unable to detain and destroy a British man-of-war which had defied his authority. The case of the last of the Shōguns may also be quoted. On the downfall of his power in 1867 he was urged by one of his Council to save the honour of his family by a voluntary suicide. He flatly refused to do so and left the room, whereupon his faithful adviser retired to another part of the castle and solemnly performed the *hara-kiri*.[1] Of suicides, attempted suicides, or threatened suicides of men, women, and children, on the stage and in fiction, there is simply no end.

Human nature being the same everywhere, the duties

[1] Literally "belly-cut," a term which some English wag has thought fit to render by "happy despatch."

arising out of the relations of the sexes are essentially the same in Japan as in Europe. Chastity, both in men and women, is a virtue, as it is with ourselves. But in the Yedo period it was thrust into the background by the more urgent claims of loyalty and filial duty. In theory a man should have but one wife. In the case of the heads of great houses, one or even more concubines were allowed, but only with the *bonâ fide* object of having children. Vulgar licentiousness was condemned, and in the case of officials was visited with severe punishment.

The position of the wife, as of women generally, was very different in the Yedo period from what it had been in earlier times. Chinese notions of the absolute subjection and the seclusion, as far as possible, of the sex, made great progress. Women were now rarely heard of in public life, and disappear completely from the world of literature—a significant fact when we remember the feminine masterpieces of the Heian period. A woman's first duty was to be faithful and obedient to her husband. Second marriages of widows were not absolutely forbidden, but women who refused to contract such unions were highly commended, and when we meet with the word "chastity" in a Japanese book, it is generally this form of the virtue which is meant. A wife was bound to revenge her husband's murder, and in fiction at least was permitted to sacrifice her own honour with this praiseworthy object. Some European travellers and novelists speak as if an unmarried woman's maiden fame were a thing of no account in Japan. This is simple nonsense. But it can hardly be denied that more particularly in their case chastity holds a lower place in the scale of virtues than in Christian countries. According to the code of morality of novelists and dramatists, it is permissible for, and even obligatory on, a girl to allow herself to be sold into prostitution in order to support her destitute parents. Incidents of this kind are very common indeed in their pages.

The harlot figures very prominently in the literature of the Yedo period, and in Japan, as elsewhere, writers have not been wanting who have done their best to surround this calling with a halo of romance. But, as Mitford has shown, Japanese opinion on this subject is on the whole sound. There may be some difference of degree, but of the substantial identity of the feeling with which prostitution is regarded by them and by ourselves there can be no doubt. The proverb, " When you find an honest harlot and a three-cornered egg, the moon will appear on the last day of the [lunar] month," very clearly indicates the general opinion of this class.

Piety, by which must be understood a devotion to Buddhist religious practices, was not in high estimation under the Tokugawas. It is not a distinctive virtue of the Japanese character at any period of their history.

On the extreme punctiliousness and ceremony which characterised all the doings of a well-bred Japanese, of his sensitiveness on the point of honour, and of his cult of the sword as a sort of incarnation of the spirit of the Samurai, this is not the place to dilate. Nor need anything be said of the virtues of frugality, sobriety, honesty, and liberality, as they hold practically the same position in Japan as with ourselves. The duties of superiors to their inferiors, of a lord to his retainer, of a father to his son, and of a husband towards his wife, may also be taken for granted. Though less frequently insisted upon, they are by no means passed over by the Japanese moralist.

As time went on, the code of morals derived from the

teachings of the philosophers of China, and expounded and applied by their Japanese followers, gained in precision and detail. But what had originally been a wholesome and vivifying influence became a burden to the nation. It fell most heavily on the Samurai, all whose actions were governed by strict rules and punctilious etiquette, in a way which was fatal to any reasonable share of personal freedom. In short, the great fault of the later Shōgunate was over-regulation in almost every department of life. I was one day walking with the late Count Terashima, then Minister for Foreign Affairs, in one of those beautiful creations of the landscape gardener's art which abound in Tokio. He pointed to a grove of fir-trees standing by an artificial lake, which had been trimmed and trained by generations of gardeners into quaint and not unpleasing but stunted shapes. "There," he said, "is an emblem of the Japanese nation under the Bakufu [Shōgunate]. That is what Chinese learning did for us."

There is much in this type of humanity which it is hard for us Europeans to understand and appreciate. The Japanese of the ancient classical period appeal more strongly to our sympathies. Even Herodotus and Plato, far removed as they are from us in point of time, are immeasurably nearer to modern Englishmen in all their ideas, sentiments, and moral standards, than the Japanese of fifty years ago.

Fujiwara Seikwa was the forerunner of a long series of Kangakusha. His pupils became in their turn teachers, and handed on the torch of learning, which now began to burn brightly. It is difficult to give an idea of the rage for the acquisition of knowledge which possessed the Japanese people during the seventeenth century. It can only be compared to the passion for European learning of the last thirty years.

Following the example of the great founder of their dynasty, the Tokugawa Shōguns encouraged learning by every means in their power. They founded libraries and colleges, subsidised professors, and were liberal of their favours to all eminent scholars. Tsunayoshi, the fifth Tokugawa Shōgun (1680–1709), an indifferent ruler, was passionately fond of learning. He surrounded himself with scholars, and spent all his leisure time in study. He used even to deliver lectures on the Chinese classics to audiences composed of Daimios and high officials, Shinto functionaries and Buddhist priests. It was in his time that Yedo began to take prominence as a literary centre.

The Daimios, in their turn, vied with one another in attracting distinguished Kangakusha to their service, and in establishing high schools for the teaching of the classics, Chinese and Japanese history and composition. Nor were the people neglected. Nearly every temple had a *terakoya* attached to it, where the children of peasants, mechanics, and tradespeople were instructed in reading, writing, and arithmetic.

It is impossible to notice all the Kangakusha who flourished at this time, or to enumerate their most voluminous writings. They do not take high rank as literature. A word of mention is due, however, to Hayashi Rasan, also called DŌSHUN, with half-a-dozen other aliases, which it is needless to reproduce here. All the Kangakusha indulged in a profusion of aliases, much to the confusion of bibliographers and writers on Japanese literature. Dōshun (b. 1583, d. 1657) was a pupil of Seikwa. He was a devoted student, and never passed a day in his life without reading something. It is related of him that once, when obliged to flee from his house by a great conflagration, he took some books with him in his *kago*, and continued his work of annotation on the way. The list of his publications comprises one hundred and seventy separate treatises, mostly of a scholastic or moral character. There are also some memoirs useful to the historian, and one hundred and fifty volumes of miscellanies, essays, &c. He held an official position under the Shōgun's Government, by which he was employed in drafting laws, and in giving advice on knotty questions which required learning for their solution. He was the founder of a long line of official Kangakusha which lasted until the downfall of the Shōgunate in 1867.

His son, Hayashi Shunsai (1618–1680) compiled about 1652 a history of Japan entitled *Ō-dai-ichi-ran.* It is in every respect a very poor production, and is only mentioned here because a translation into French by Klaproth was published by the Oriental Translation Fund in 1835.

Passing over a number of scholars deservedly remembered with gratitude in their own country for their services to learning and good morals, we come to KAIBARA YEKKEN (1630 – 1714), who was born at Fukuoka, in Chikuzen, of the Daimios of which province his family were hereditary retainers. His father held an official appointment as physician, and Yekken himself acquired some proficiency in the art of medicine. His first teacher was his elder brother, under whose instructions he was weaned of a liking for Buddhism, and devoted himself to the study of the Chinese classics. When he grew up to manhood he went to reside in Kiōto, where he benefited by the instruction of Kinoshita Junan and other scholars. He had, however, no regular teacher. After three years spent in study he returned to his province, where he held honourable official posts under three successive Daimios until 1700, when he retired on a pension, and took up his abode in Kiōto, where he spent the remainder of his days. His wife is said to have been an accomplished woman. She accompanied him on his travels to various parts of Japan, and assisted him in his literary labours.

Yekken was a voluminous writer, and in the course of a long life (the Kangakusha were remarkable for longevity) produced over a hundred different works, comprising moral treatises, commentaries on the Chinese classics, learned dissertations on Japanese philology, botanical works, and books of travel. His sole object in writing was to benefit his countrymen ; and his style, though manly and vigorous, is wholly devoid of rhetorical ornament, and of those frivolities of language which were so freely indulged in by contemporary novelists and dramatists. He used the Kana or native phonetic script as far as possible, so as to bring his teachings down to the level of children and ignorant people. Though perhaps the most eminent scholar of his day, there is not an atom of pedantry about him. No Japanese books are more easy of comprehension than his. Their principal fault is one very common with Japanese writers of the Yedo period, namely, diffuseness and repetition.

Due allowance being made for his age and country, Yekken's writings are full of excellent morality of a plain, common-sense description. It is hardly possible to overestimate their influence, or the service which he rendered to his country by his teachings.

The following detached sentences from the *Dōjikun*, a

treatise on education, composed by him at the age of eighty, will give some idea of their quality. They have been somewhat abridged in translation.

"In the houses of the great, good persons should be chosen from the first to be attached to the child. Even the poor should be careful, so far as their circumstances will permit, that their children should associate with good people. This is the teaching of the [Chinese] sages."

"A wet-nurse should be of a gentle disposition, staid and grave of demeanour, and of few words."

"A boy's education should begin from the time when he can eat rice, speak a little, and show pleasure or anger."

"Some nurses make cowards of children by wantonly telling them frightful stories. Ghost stories and the like should not be told to children. They should not be too warmly clad, or have too much to eat."

"Cunning, chattering, lying women should not be engaged as nurses. Drunkards, self-willed or malicious persons should also be avoided."

"From their infancy, truth in word and thought should be made of the first importance. Children should be severely punished for lying or deceit. Let their parents be careful not to deceive them, for this is another way of teaching them to deceive."

"A tutor should be a man of upright life. A child should not be put to learn of a disreputable person, no matter how clever he may be."

"Better for a child to lose a year's study than consort for a day with a base companion."

"Every night the child's sayings and actions during the day should be reviewed, and if necessary, punishment administered."

"At the age of ten a boy should go to school. If he remains longer at home he is apt to be spoiled by his parents."

"Before sitting down to study, a boy should wash his hands, set a guard upon his thoughts, and compose his countenance. He should brush the dust off his desk, place his books upon it in an orderly manner, and read them in a kneeling posture. When he is reading to his teacher, he should not rest his book on a high desk, but on its case or on a low stand. It should certainly not be placed on the floor. Books should be kept clean, and when they are no longer required, the covers should be put on, and they should be put back in their place. This should be done even when the pupil is called away for some urgency. Books should not be flung about, stridden over, or used as pillows. The corners should not be turned down, or spittle used to raise the leaves. If waste paper contains texts from the classics or the names of sages, boys should be careful not to apply it to common purposes. Nor should waste paper with the names of one's parents or lord be defiled."

Yekken devotes the third volume of the *Dōjikun* to the education of girls. The two great virtues of a woman are, in his opinion, amiability and obedience. In another place he sums up the good qualities of a woman as—

"1st. A womanly disposition, as shown in modesty and submissiveness.

"2nd. Womanly language. She should be careful in the choice of words, and avoid lying and unseemly expressions. She should speak when necessary, and be silent at other times. She should not be averse to listening to others.

"3rd. Womanly apparel. She should be cleanly, avoid

undue ornament, and have a proper regard to taste and refinement.

"4th. Womanly arts. These include sewing, reeling silk, making clothes, and cooking.

"Everything impure should be kept from a girl's ears. Popular songs and the popular drama are not for them. The *Ise Monogatari* and *Genji Monogatari* are objectionable on account of their immoral tendency."

Yekken recommends parents to write out the following thirteen counsels and give them to their daughters on their marriage. I have abbreviated them a good deal.

" 1. Be respectful and obedient to your parents-in-law.

" 2. A woman has no [feudal] lord. She should reverence and obey her husband instead.

" 3. Cultivate friendly relations with your husband's relatives.

" 4. Avoid jealousy. If your husband offends, remonstrate with him gently, without hate or anger.

" 5. Generally, when your husband does wrong, it is your duty to remonstrate with him gently and affectionately.

" 6. Be of few words. Avoid abusive language and falsehood.

" 7. Be always circumspect in your behaviour. Get up early. Go to bed at midnight. Do not indulge in a siesta. Attend diligently to the work of the house. Do not become addicted to saké or tea. Avoid listening to lewd songs or music. Shinto shrines and Buddhist temples being public resorts for pleasure, should be sparingly visited before the age of forty.

" 8. Have nothing to do with fortune-tellers or

mediums, and do not offend the gods and Buddha by too familiar importunities. Attend to your human duties, and do not let your heart run astray after invisible supernatural beings.

"9. Economy in domestic matters is all-important.

"10. Keep young men at a distance. On no account have any written correspondence with them. Male domestics should not be allowed to enter the women's apartments.

"11. Avoid conspicuous colours and patterns in your dress. Choose those suitable for a somewhat older person than yourself.

"12. In everything your husband and his parents should come before your own parents.

"13. Do not attend to the tattle of female servants."

This is commonplace enough. But Yekken could rise to higher flights on occasion, as the following extract from a treatise on the philosophy of pleasure (*Raku-kun*) will show. The sentiment is of a distinctly Wordsworthian quality.

"If we make inward pleasures our chief aim, and use the ears and eyes simply as the means of procuring such delights from without, we shall not be molested by the lusts of these senses. If we open our hearts to the beauty of heaven, earth, and the ten thousand created things, they will yield us pleasure without limit, pleasure always before our eyes, night and morning, full and overflowing. The man who takes delight in such things becomes the owner of the mountains and streams, of the moon and flowers, and needs not to pay his court to others in order to enjoy them. They are not bought with treasure. Without the expenditure of a single cash he may use them to his heart's content, and yet never exhaust them.

And although he enjoys possession of them as his own, no man will wrangle with him in order to deprive him of them. The reason is that the beauty of mountain and river, moon and flowers, has from the beginning no fixed owner.

"He who knows the boundless sources of delight which are thus contained in the universe, and who finds his enjoyment therein, envies not the luxurious pleasures of the rich and great ; for such enjoyments are beyond those of wealth and honours. He who is unconscious of them cannot enjoy the delectable things in the greatest abundance which are every day before his eyes.

"Vulgar pleasures, even before they pass, become a torment to the body. If, for example, carried away by desire, we eat and drink our fill of dainty things, it is pleasant at first, but disease and suffering soon follow. In general, vulgar pleasures corrupt the heart, injure the constitution, and end in misery. The pleasures of the man of worth, on the other hand, nourish the heart and do not entice us astray. To speak in terms of outward things, the pleasures which we derive from the love of the moon or of flowers, from gazing on the hills and streams, from humming to the wind or following the flight of birds with envy, are of a mild nature. We may take delight in them all day long and do ourselves no harm. Man will not blame us, nor God remonstrate with us for indulgence in it. It is easy to be attained, even by the poor and needy, and has no ill consequences. The rich and great, absorbed in luxury and indolence, know not these pleasures; but the poor man, little affected by such hindrances, may readily procure them if he only chooses to do so."

ON GARDENING

"When you move into a house your first care ought to be to plant fruit-trees. Others may come after. Forethought for ten years consists in planting trees. In planting, fruit should come first, flowers should be your next care, and foliage last of all. Fruit is of the greatest use to man ; and fruit-trees should be planted in large numbers, particularly the orange and the lime. When their fruit has formed and ripened, it is not inferior in beauty to flowers. In planting persimmons, pears, chestnuts, and pepper, the best sorts should be selected. For flowering trees, the ordinary plum should come first. The red-blossomed plum is also good, and the cherry. It is a pity it sheds its flowers so soon. The camellia remains long in bloom, and its leaves are beautiful. It grows readily from cuttings, and blossoms early. The kaidō [*Pyrus spectabilis*], and azaleas of different kinds, are also to be commended. For foliage-trees, choose the cryptomeria, the *Thuya obtusa*, the podocarpus, and evergreen-trees generally. Bamboos should be planted on the northern side, as a protection against fire and wind. They may be cut down from time to time, and put away for use on occasion. In the front garden plant willows, cherry - trees, firs, and cryptomerias. Avoid planting too thickly ; it makes too much moisture, and in summer harbours mosquitoes, which are a plague.

"Vegetables may be planted for everyday use. They are fresher when grown at home than if bought in the market. Besides, the luxuriance of their leaves delights the eye not less than the beauty of flowers.

"Moreover it tends to edify the heart if we plant trees

and herbs in our gardens and love them. In our leisure moments we should pay some attention to looking for things easy to get, just as they may turn up, and planting them. If we strive after procuring things hard to come at, and either beg them unconscionably of our friends, or buy them at a high price, we get proud of the number of kinds we have collected, or of the superiority of the flowers. This leads to rivalry in the goodness of the flowers. Trouble ensues, and heart-burnings, which are injurious to self-discipline, yield no pleasure, and cause nothing but anxiety."

Yekken was also a poet. The following Tanka was composed by him when he felt death approaching : —

> " The past
> Seems to me
> Like a single night :
> Ah ! the dream
> Of more than eighty years !"

The most distinguished of the Kangakusha was undoubtedly ARAI HAKUSEKI. He was born in Yedo in 1657, his father being in the service of Lord Tsuchiya, a small Daimio of the province of Kadzusa. Hakuseki has fortunately left an autobiography, a very rare kind of literature in Japan, and we have therefore much fuller information regarding his life than is usual in the case of Japanese authors. It was written not for publication (the copy before me is in manuscript), but for the information of his own descendants, so that they might not have the dissatisfaction he himself had experienced of knowing little about their ancestors. This autobiography was written in 1716, after Hakuseki had retired from public life. It is entitled Ori-taku-shiba (" Burning Faggots "), in allusion to a poem of the Emperor Go Toba which speaks of the smoke of faggots at evening bringing back the memory (of a departed dear one who had been cremated ?). The early part of this work is taken up with an account of "the man who was his father," to use Hakuseki's curious phrase, a *metsuke*[1] or inspector of the Daimio's Yedo mansion. In him he has given a minute and loving description of a Japanese gentleman of the olden time. I transcribe a few sentences :—

"Ever since I came to understand the heart of things, my memory is that the daily routine of his life was always exactly the same. He never failed to get up an hour before daybreak. He then had a cold bath, and did his hair himself. In cold weather, the woman who was my mother would propose to order hot water for him, but this he would not allow, as he wished to avoid giving the servants trouble. When he was over seventy, and my mother also was advanced in years, sometimes when the cold was unendurable, a lighted brazier was brought in, and they lay down to sleep with their feet against it. Beside the fire there was placed a kettle with hot water, which my father drank when he got up. Both of them honoured the Way of Buddha. My father, when he had arranged his hair and adjusted his clothing, never neglected to make obeisance to Buddha. On the anniversaries of his father's and mother's death he and my mother prepared the rice for the offerings. This duty was never entrusted to servants. After he was dressed he waited quietly till dawn, and then went out to his official duty."

"Since I remember, there were but few black hairs on

---

[1] This is the word usually rendered "spy."

his head. He had a square-shaped face with a high forehead. His eyes were large, he had a thick growth of beard, and was short of stature. He was, however, a big-boned, powerful man. He was never known to betray anger, nor do I remember that even when he laughed he ever gave way to boisterous mirth. Much less did he ever descend to violent language when he had occasion to reprimand any one. In his conversation he used as few words as possible. His demeanour was grave. I have never seen him startled, flurried, or impatient. When he applied the *moxa*,[1] he used to say there was no use in small and few applications, and would put on five or seven great patches at the same time without showing any sign of suffering. The room he usually occupied he kept cleanly swept, had an old picture hung on the wall, and a few flowers which were in season set out in a vase. He would spend the day looking at them. He painted a little in black and white, not being fond of colours. When in good health he never troubled a servant, but did everything for himself."

As a boy Hakuseki gave many proofs of precocious intelligence. Before he was three years of age he copied out some Chinese characters in a recognisable manner. His Daimio noticed him and kept him constantly about his own person.

"In the autumn of my eighth year, Tobe [his Daimio] went to the province of Kadzusa, leaving instructions that I was to be taught writing. In the middle of the twelfth month of the winter of that year he returned, and I resumed my usual attendance on him. In the autumn

[1] A kind of tinder, applied to the skin in small patches and then burnt, as a remedy for various ailments.

of the next year, when he went again to his province, he set me a task, ordering me to write out every day in the day-time three thousand Chinese characters in the round or cursive script, and at night one thousand. When winter came on and the days became shorter, it frequently happened that the sun approached his setting before my task was finished. I would then take my desk out to a bamboo veranda which faced the west, and finish it there. Moreover, as I sometimes got intolerably sleepy over my nightly task, I arranged with the man who was told off to serve me to put two buckets of water on the aforesaid veranda. When I became very drowsy I took off my coat and poured one of the buckets of water over me. I then resumed my clothing and went on writing. The cold produced in this way for a while answered the purpose of keeping me awake. But after a time I became warm again, and the drowsiness came back, when I poured water over myself as before. With two applications of this kind I was able to get through most of my work. This was in the autumn and winter of my ninth year. . . . From my thirteenth year Tobe used me to conduct most of his correspondence."

Hakuseki was an ambitious youth, as the following saying of his shows : " If, alive, a man cannot become a Daimio, better die and be a king of Hades." In this spirit he refused an eligible offer of marriage to the daughter of a wealthy merchant, although both he and his father, who had retired on a small pension, were in great poverty. In 1682 he entered the service of Hotta, the Daimio of Furukawa, with whom he remained ten years. When he left him Hakuseki was almost destitute. His only property was a box containing three hundred cash, and three measures of rice (a week's supply). His teacher, Kinoshita Junan, of whom he always speaks with the greatest reverence, tried to procure him an appointment with the Daimio of Kaga ; but Hakuseki, being appealed to by a friend who had an aged mother in that province dependent on him for support, begged Junan to use his influence for him instead. Hakuseki had no favourable opportunity of advancement until 1693, when he was thirty - six years of age. On the recommendation of Junan, he was then engaged as Professor of Chinese by Iyenobu, subsequently (1709–1713) Shōgun, but at this time Daimio of Kōfu.

His relations with Iyenobu were throughout of the most cordial nature. He was always receiving from him presents of clothing and money. When Hakuseki lectured on the Chinese classics, Iyenobu listened with the greatest respect, refraining in summer from brushing off a mosquito, and in winter, when he had a cold in his head, turning away from the lecturer before wiping his nose with the paper of which he kept a supply in his sleeve. "You may imagine," says Hakuseki, addressing his posterity in the *Ori-taku-shiba*, "how quiet the rest of the audience were."

In 1701, by command of Iyenobu, Hakuseki composed his greatest work, the *Hankampu*, a history of the Daimios of Japan from 1600 to 1680. It is in thirty volumes and must have required immense research, yet it was written in a few months. Having received the order in the first month, he began the draft on the eleventh day of the seventh month. The manuscript was completed in the eleventh month, and a fair copy was made by Hakuseki himself and laid before Iyenobu on the nineteenth day of the second month of the following year. Hakuseki mentions these details with obvious pride in his autobiography. They are very characteristic of the extreme rapidity of composition of Japanese authors during this period. They expended no superfluous labour of the file upon their works. Yet the *Hankampu* cannot be called a carelessly written book. Not only does it contain most valuable material for the future historian of Japan, but the style is highly commended by the best native critics for its combined elegance and vigour, neither leaning too much to Chinese pedantry on the one hand, nor to Japanese purism on the other. So far as a "Western barbarian" may be allowed an opinion, this praise is not undeserved, though it is perhaps unnecessary to endorse the language of a native admirer who declares that "Hakuseki's heart is brocade, his bowels are rich embroidery, his spittle produces pearls, and his half-conscious mutterings form harmonious music." The *Hankampu* contains much genealogical and other matter which has little interest for the European reader. Even Hakuseki's countrymen at the present day will probably admit that there is more than enough of this element. Although one of the most important works of the Yedo period, I doubt whether it has been printed. The Shōguns' government was much given to *cachotterie* in matters of state, and very many of the most interesting political works of this period were only circulated privately among the official class. Two copies in my possession are both in manuscript, the form in which Hakuseki's works are usually met with. In the case of the *Hankampu* there were probably substantial reasons for refraining from publication. It was hardly possible, especially for a man of Hakuseki's fearless and uncompromising nature, to relate without offence the history of three hundred and thirty-seven noble houses down to twenty years before the time of writing.

The following extract will give some idea of the scope and character of this work :—

ITAKURA SHIGEHIDE AS A JUDGE OF CRIMINAL CASES

"It is impossible fully to set forth here the reputation of this man while he remained in office, or his fame throughout the Empire. I shall only take one principal instance.

"From the time that he received his appointment, he was in the habit, when on his way to the tribunal and before taking his place there, to pay distant worship in a corridor which faced the west. Here a tea-mill[1] was placed, and the paper slides being drawn, Shigehide seated himself behind them and heard the cases while grinding the tea with his own hand. Everybody wondered at this conduct, but no one dared to question him. Many years afterwards he was asked the reason, and replied : 'Well, the reason why I worshipped afar in a corridor which faced the west before taking my place in the tribunal was this : I was worshipping the gods of Atago. I was told that among all the many gods these were the most efficacious, and I offered a prayer to them when I thus worshipped. I said in my prayer : " In deciding the cases which are brought before Shigehide this day, may there be nothing to which his heart is unequal. If he errs and allows selfish motives to influence him, may the gods be pleased that same moment to take away his life." And I adjured them daily, in virtue of my

---

[1] A small hand-mill of stone used for reducing tea to powder before making the infusion. The whole is then drunk—leaves and all.

profound trust in them for years, not to let me live if self should get the better of me.

"'Another thing which I thought to interfere with clearness of judgment is the emotion of the heart. A really good man will not allow such emotion to arise. Shigehide [himself], however, could not reach this perfection. So in order to test my heart and ascertain whether it was calm or perturbed, the only expedient I could think of was to grind tea. When my heart was steady and calm, my hand was accordant with it. The mill then went round smoothly, and the powdered tea which fell from it was beautifully fine. I knew when the tea fell down in a fine powder that my heart was free from emotion. Not till then did I pronounce judgment.

"'The reason why I heard cases with a paper screen interposed was this : Taking men in general, a glance at their faces shows that some are ill-favoured and others prepossessing ; some are honest-looking, others knavish. There are many such varieties—more than I can tell. On looking at them we are apt to conclude that the honest-looking man's evidence is true, and that the actions of the knavish-looking fellow are all false, though they may be straightforward enough. We think that the plaint of the man of prepossessing appearance shows that he has been wronged, and that the contention of the ill-favoured man is erroneous. In all these cases the heart is moved by what we see with our eyes. Even before the witnesses utter a word, we say in our hearts, "Such a one is a knave, such a one is right, such a one is straightforward," so that when we come to hear the evidence we are apt to wrest it to our preconceived ideas. But very frequently it is seen during the trial that among prepossessing countenances some belong to men who are truly detestable, and that of ill-favoured men some are deserving of sympathy. Among the honest-looking there are knaves, and true men among the knavish-looking. Men's hearts are hard to know, and the plan of judging of them by their looks will not answer. . . . Even for those against whom there is no charge, it must be a terrible thing to appear in a court of justice. Some there are who, when they see before them the man in whose hands are life and death, are bewildered and cast down to such a degree as to be unable to plead what they might in their defence. When I reflected on this I felt that it was after all better that the judge and the prisoner should not see one another face to face. This was my reason for taking my seat with a screen interposed.'"

Next to the *Hankampu*, Hakuseki's most important work is the *Tokushi Yoron*, which was written by order of Iyenobu in 1712. It gives for the first time a general view of Japanese history for two thousand years, dwelling more particularly on periods of change and revolution, and showing the connection of events in a way which had never been previously attempted. Its historical value is considerable, but the style is not considered equal to that of his earlier work.

Iyenobu became Shōgun in 1709. From this time forward Hakuseki, although holding no definite position in the government, was his constant adviser in state affairs. His influence was given on the side of commonsense and justice. One of the first matters he was concerned in was a currency question. To meet the expenses of the installation of the new Shōgun, the Minister of Finance, Hagiwara Shigehide, proposed various schemes involving the debasing of the currency. These were vigorously opposed by Hakuseki, and with complete success, Hagiwara being deprived of office, and the currency at length (in 1714) placed on a solid foundation. A more doubtful financial measure taken by his advice restricted the export of gold and silver, and limited the number of vessels engaged in foreign commerce.

Throughout Iyenobu's reign Hakuseki was the acknowledged authority on financial matters. In 1741 an embassy arrived from Corea. He was charged with the negotiations, and acquitted himself with great credit. At this time he received the title of Chikugo no Kami, and a grant of 500 kokus of rice annually. His strong interest in foreign affairs is evidenced by a little work called *Gojiryaku*, a collection of memoranda (still in manuscript) on Loochoo, the forms of diplomatic intercourse, the movement of specie, &c.

To us Europeans the most interesting episode in Hakuseki's life is his relations with an unfortunate Italian missionary, Father Sidotti, who landed alone in the province of Satsuma in 1708, with some wild hope of being allowed to preach the Christian religion in Japan. He was at once arrested, and ultimately sent to Yedo, where, after some time had elapsed, he was handed over to Hakuseki for examination.

In the *Seiyō Kibun* ("Notes of the Western Ocean"), Hakuseki has given a history of this affair, to which he has appended such information regarding the geography and history of European countries as he was able to extract from this unhappy man. Owing chiefly to difficulties of interpretation, it is meagre in the extreme, but yet interesting as the first attempt of a Japanese writer to give an account of Europe.

Sidotti produced in Hakuseki that mixed feeling of perplexity and irritation which contact with a profound religious faith so often excites in thinkers of the positive type. The devotion to his sovereign and religious chief (for so Hakuseki thought it) which prompted him at the Pope's command to journey to so distant a country, and there for six years to undergo peril and suffering, appealed strongly to a man who had himself a stern sense of duty. Hakuseki reported to his Government that it was impossible to witness without emotion Sidotti's firm adherence to his own faith, and he also spoke with warm appreciation of his kindly disposition and scientific knowledge. "But," said he, "when this man begins to speak of religion his talk is shallow and scarce a word is intelligible. All of a sudden folly takes the place of wisdom. It is like listening to the talk of two different men."

The "folly" which Hakuseki had more particularly in view was an outline of Bible history and Christian doctrine which Sidotti had dictated to him in the fulness of his heart. In its Japanese form it is a dry and soulless husk, which affords some excuse for Hakuseki's obtuseness to its spiritual import. It should be a warning to missionaries not to attempt the teaching of religion until they have something more than a tyro's command of the language. As Hakuseki's attitude towards Christianity is essentially that of educated Japanese at the present day, I may quote some of his observations.

"The foreign word 'Deus,' which the Western man used in his discourse, is equivalent to 'Creator,' and means simply a Being who first made heaven and earth and the ten thousand things. He argued that the universe did not come into existence of itself. 'It must,' he said, 'have had a maker.' But if this were so, then who made

Deus ? How could he be born while there was yet no heaven or earth ? And if Deus could come into existence of himself, why should not heaven and earth do so likewise ? Again, there is the doctrine, that before the world existed, there was a heavenly paradise made for good men. I cannot understand how men could have any knowledge of good and evil while there was yet no heaven and earth. It is unnecessary to discuss all his notions about the beginning of the world and of mankind, of paradise and of hell, as they are all derived from Buddhism.

"What will be thought of the idea that Deus, pitying the heinous criminals who had broken the heavenly commands, and who of themselves could not give satisfaction, was three thousand years after, for their sakes, born as Jesus, and in their stead redeemed their guilt ? This sounds very childish. At the present time, the judge who is charged with the infliction of punishment may yet take a merciful view of the circumstances and grant pardon or mitigation. And in the case even of the heavenly commands, what was there to prevent Deus from pardoning an offence against them, or mitigating the punishment, more especially as he himself was the author of the prohibition which was broken."

Hakuseki discusses Noah's flood in the same spirit. The Ten Commandments, he thinks, were borrowed mainly from Buddhism, as well as the miraculous occurrences connected with the birth of Christ, and His styling Himself "Deus." The rite of baptism he refers to the same source.

The result of Hakuseki's examination was a report, in which he pointed out that the Shōgun's Government had three courses open to them : first, to send Sidotti back to his own country ; second, to retain him in imprisonment; and third, to put him to death as prescribed by law. He gave his own voice strongly in favour of the first course, but the second was the one actually adopted. Sidotti died in prison not long after.[1]

On the death of his patron in 1713, Hakuseki wished to retire from public life. But it was pointed out to him that his help was required to carry out certain measures already contemplated by the late Shōgun. He therefore consented, from public motives, to continue his counsels. Iyenobu was succeeded by his son Iyetsugu, then four years of age. A momentous question now arose which convulsed official circles in Yedo for some time. Was a child of such tender years bound to wear mourning for his father or not? Hayashi Shuntai, the hereditary official representative of Chinese learning at the Shōgun's court, declared for the negative. But he was no match for Hakuseki, who maintained the affirmative proposition, and fairly crushed his opponent under a weight of learning and argument which seems to us rather disproportionate to the occasion. In his autobiography Hakuseki tells the story of Shuntai's discomfiture with great triumph.

At Iyetsugu's death in 1716, the reins of power passed into other hands. Hakuseki was no longer consulted, and spent the remainder of his days as a recluse among his dearly loved books. He died in 1725 in his sixty-ninth year. His life shows that in Japan at this time a career was open for talent. He owed little to any one but himself. It was sheer worth, force of intellect, and a self-reliant, uncompromising character which

---

[1] The principal part of the *Seiyō Kibun*, from which the above particulars are taken, has been translated by the Rev. W. B. Wright, in the *Transactions of the Asiatic Society of Japan*, August 1881.

raised him to the unique position of influence which he held.

His works, inclusive of state papers and reports to his Government, number over three hundred. In addition to those already mentioned, there may be named *Yezo-dan Hikki* (in MS.), which treats of the productions of Yezo, the Yezo language, and the Aino revolt of 1669; *Nantōshi*, a geographical work on Loochoo; *Keizai Tenkei*, or "Principles of Finance"; *Kwahei Kō*, a work on the currency; *Gunki Kō*, on arms; *Kishin Ron*, a book on the nature of the gods; *Gwakō Benran*, a work on painting; *Ketsugoku Kō*, on knotty points of criminal law; *Dōbun Tsūkō*, on the various forms of script used in Japan; *Shuko Dzusetsu*, an antiquarian work; *Tōga*, a dictionary of Japanese words in twenty books; and *Sairan Igen*, an expansion of the historical and geographical part of the *Seiyō Kibun*.

MURO KIUSŌ was born at Yanaka, in the province of Musashi (not far from Yedo), in 1658. He was distinguished from his earliest years by a love of learning. When only thirteen he was taken into the service of the Daimio of Kaga, who was so much struck by his precocious talent that he sent him to Kiōto to study under the famous Kinoshita Junan.

In 1711, on the recommendation of his friend and fellow-pupil Hakuseki, Kiusō received a Government appointment in Yedo as Professor of Chinese. In 1713 he took up his residence in a house at Surugadai, a lofty platform which overlooks Yedo from the north, near the spot where a Christian church now stands, conspicuous to the whole city. Here he spent the remainder of his days. When Hakuseki retired from public life, Kiusō to some extent took his place as adviser to the Shōgunate. The Shōgun Yoshimune (1716–1751) esteemed him highly and consulted him continually. Kiusō died in 1734 in his seventy-seventh year.

Kiusō is best remembered by his *Shundai Zatsuwa* (1729),[1] a work of his old age. The title means " Miscellaneous Talk on Surugadai." It consists of notes taken of the discourses which he delivered in answer to " those who believed in the Old Man and came to him with questions," and covers a wide variety of subjects. It contains unsparing denunciations of Buddhism, superstition, and heresy from the faith as it is in Chu-Hi ; pantheistic philosophy, metaphysics, politics, lectures on the arts of war and poetry, literary criticisms, and so on. Kiusō propounds to the world no original ideas on these subjects. His philosophy is simply that of Chu-Hi in a Japanese garb. But in him, as in Hakuseki, the inner spirit and temper of mind which it fostered in Japan is seen at its best. Some Christian ideals are wanting. Forgiveness of one's enemies is not to be found there, nor is a chivalrous consideration for the weak and for women very conspicuous. But a noble enthusiasm for lofty ideals and high achievements with a scorn of meanness and duplicity pervades all the utterances of this Socrates of Surugadai. Loyalty to friends, devotion to duty, and a high-souled contempt for cowardice, dishonesty, and self-seeking, are their unfailing characteristics.

Kiusō, like the other seventeenth and eighteenth century expounders of Chinese philosophy, had a

---

[1] Partly translated by Dr. Knox in the *Transactions of the Asiatic Society of Japan*, 1892. But a more complete and accurate translation is desirable.

supreme contempt for Buddhism. The Kangakusha's ideal of life was essentially different. To the Buddhist the spiritual life is all-important. For its sake men should wean themselves from the things of this world, sever all family ties, and retire to hermitages or monasteries, there to spend pure and holy lives in pious meditation and religious observances. The Chinese philosophy, on the contrary, is eminently practical. It may be summed up in one word—duty. The various relations of human life being ordained by Heaven, it is man's business not to evade the obligations thus imposed on him, as the Buddhists would have him do, but to fulfil them faithfully at all costs.

Japan owes a profound debt of gratitude to the Kangakusha of this time. For their day and country they were emphatically the salt of the earth, and their writings must have helped materially to counteract the pernicious influence of a very different class of literature which now began to deluge the country, the pornographic writings of Jishō and his school.

Kiusō's style is unequal to his matter. He is frequently obscure, and is somewhat too fond of learned allusions to Chinese history and literature. In both respects he contrasts with his predecessor Yekken, and even with Hakuseki, though the latter could be erudite enough upon occasion. But his learning was probably not misplaced considering the audience whom he was addressing, while his obscurity seems due to the fact that he moved in an intellectual sphere so far above his contemporaries that he found the Japanese language of his time an inadequate vehicle to convey his thoughts.

The following extract from the *Shundai Zatsuwa* will give some idea of Kiusō's philosophic vein :—

THE MORNING-GLORY (or *Convolvulus*)

" ' *Oh for the heart*
Of the morning-glory!
Which, though its bloom is for a single hour,
Is the same as that of the fir-tree
Which lives a thousand years.'—MATSUNAGA.

" To my mind there is a profound meaning in this verse. Many poems, some of ancient date, have been composed on the morning-glory, for the most part alluding to its short-lived bloom, and associating it with the melancholy sentiment of autumn. It is thus made an emblem of this transitory world. Such verses have no deeper meaning. The lines of Haku Kyo-i [in Chinese, Peh Kü-yih]—

' *After a thousand years at last the fir decays:*
The hibiscus-flower glories in its one day's life'—

have the stamp of official approval, and are reckoned elegant. But there is here a forced endeavour to make glory and decay the same, and to assimilate robust life with early death. This may sound fine in the ears of the vulgar, but it is after all a very superficial view. Such ideas go no further than to reproduce the drivel of Gautama [Buddha], or to lick the spittle of Chwang-chow [a Taoist philosopher]. This cannot be the meaning of Matsunaga's ' heart differing not from that of the fir-tree.' What do you say, gentlemen ? To this old man's mind it says, ' He that in the morning has found the Way may die content at night.' To blossom in the early morn, to await the sun's rays and then to fade, is the nature which the morning-glory has received from heaven. There are in the world fir-trees which live a thousand years, but the morning-glory, though endowed with so brief a span of existence, never forgets itself for a moment or is envious of others. Morning after morning the flowers unfold, enchantingly beautiful; and having exhausted that natural virtue which has been allotted to them, they wither. Herein they show their faithfulness to duty. Why should it be regarded as vain and unprofitable? The fir does just the same, but the morning-glory, being short-lived, illustrates this principle in a more striking manner. Not that in the mind of the fir-tree there is any idea of a thousand years, or in that of the morning-glory the thought of a single day. Each simply fulfils its allotted nature. The view of the thousand years of the fir-tree as robust vigour, and of the one day of the morning-glory as vain and transitory, belongs simply to the man who looks on them from without. It is absurd to suppose that in the mind of the fir-tree or convolvulus there is any such thought.

"All things without sense are the same. But man, endowed with feeling, and described as the soul of the universe, becomes entangled by his own craftiness, and so long as he does not learn the Way, falls short of this perfection. This is why it is necessary for him to learn the Way. To learn the Way must not be taken to be anything of a special kind, such as the spiritual vision of the Buddhists or the like. The Way is the original right principle of things. It is something which vulgar men and women know and practise as well as others. But as they do not truly know it, they do not thoroughly practise it. They learn it, but do not fully comprehend it; they practise it, but not with conspicuous success. They may go on striving to the end of their days, but they will never enter into its full meaning. Now to learn the Way is nothing more than to acquire a true knowledge of this principle, and to practise it effectively until you have the restful feeling of a fish in water, and take the same pleasure in it that a bird does in the groves. It should be made one's very life at all times, never being departed from for a moment. If, so long as we live, we follow the Way, when we die these bodies of ours and the Way come to an end together, and a long peace ensues. Living for a day, let us fulfil the Way for that day and die ; living for a month, let us fulfil the Way for that month and die ; living for a year, let us fulfil the Way for that year and die. If we do so, there will be left not an atom of regret, even if we die in the evening after having learnt the Way in the morning.

"Looking at the matter in this light, why should the morning-glory resent that it must fade when the sun's rays fall upon it ? Though its life is but for a day, it has bloomed to the full extent of its endowment, and there is nothing left. It is widely different from the thousand years of the fir-tree in length of time, but they are both alike in that they exhaust the command of Heaven [fulfil their destiny] and are satisfied. This is what is meant by the expression 'a heart differing not from that of the fir-tree.' Doubtless Matsunaga wished that his heart should become even like it, and therefore wrote this poem of the morning-glory."

In the following passage, which contains echoes of Taoist doctrines, Kiusō approaches very nearly to the idea of a personal Deity :—

"The *Saden* [an ancient Chinese book] says, 'God [1] is uniformly intelligent and just.' It is his very nature to

[1] Or "the Gods." The Chinese and Japanese languages rarely distinguish between singular and plural. The concluding part of this extract, however, shows that Kiusō was thinking of a single Deity.

be so. Now while all men know that he is just, they do not know that he is intelligent. Yet there is nothing of so keen an intelligence as God. How is this? Man hears with his ears, and beyond their reach he hears nothing though he were as quick of hearing as Shikō; he sees with his eyes, and beyond their range he can see nothing, were he as sharp-sighted as Rirō; with his heart he reflects, and, however swift his intuitions may be, still this must involve delay. God borrows not the help of ears or eyes; nor does he waste time in reflection. With him sensation is immediate, and is followed by immediate responsive action. This, be it observed, is his nature, and flows not from two or three, but from a single reality.

"But although there is in heaven and earth a something infinitely quick of hearing and infinitely sharp of sight, independent of conditions of time or space, present as if actually on the spot, passing to and fro without any interval, embodying itself in all things which are, and filling the universe, it has neither form nor voice, and is therefore not cognisable by our senses. It is, however, sensible to the Real and the True. As it feels, so it responds. If there is no truth or reality, there can be no response. If it did not feel, it would not respond. The response is therefore a proof of its existence. That which responds not, of course does not exist. What a wonderful property for heaven and earth to possess!

"In the words of a stanza composed by priest Saigiō when he made a pilgrimage to the shrines of Ise—

' *What it is*
That dwelleth here
I know not;
Yet my heart is full of gratitude,
And the tears trickle down.' "

"Think not that God is something distant, but seek for him in your own hearts ; for the heart is the abode of God."

"To forsake all evil and follow good is the beginning of the practice of our philosophy."

"The Way of the Sages is not sundered from matters of everyday life."

"That which in Heaven begets all things is in man that which makes him love his neighbour. So doubt not that Heaven loves goodness of heart and hates its opposite."

"Has not bravery itself its root in goodness of heart, and does it not proceed from sympathy ? It is only when it arises from goodness that bravery is genuine."

"Once when I was in Kaga I heard a man say, 'All faults whether great or small may be excused in the eyes of the world upon repentance and amendment, and leave behind no stain of deep-seated baseness. But there are two faults which are inexcusable, even when repented of—theft, and the abandonment by a Samurai of a post which he is bound to defend with his life."

"Avarice and cowardice are the same. If a man is stingy of his money, he will also grudge his life."

"To the Samurai first of all comes righteousness, next life, then silver and gold."

Kiusō's righteousness and our righteousness are appreciably though not essentially different. The former approaches the Roman ideal more than the Christian. He uses the word to describe the conduct of the forty-seven Rōnins, who, having avenged an insult to their master which led to his death, by the murder of the offender, then committed *hara-kiri* together. This incident occurred in Kiusō's own lifetime. He consecrated their memory in a booklet in the Chinese language entitled *Gi-jin-roku*, which, although not in itself a very important contribution to history, has been the parent of a whole literature. A later writer gives a list of one hundred and one works relating to this subject, including fiction and the drama. Mr. Mitford has told the story in his *Tales of Old Japan*. It is highly characteristic of the Yedo period of Japanese history.

It is not creditable to the Japanese Government of this time, that although Kiusō presented the *Shundai Zatsuwa* to his patron the Shōgun in 1729, it was allowed to remain unpublished until 1750, although all the while a flood of pornographic literature was being poured out over the country without let or hindrance.

The modern literary language of Japan owes much to the Kangakusha, more especially to those of the seventeenth and early eighteenth centuries. The older Japanese of the *Taiheiki* was wholly inadequate for the expression of the host of new ideas which were the offspring of the revival of learning and the reorganisation of the State. The social changes and the marked advance in civilisation and the arts which accompanied this movement required a new vocabulary. Just as we resorted to Latin and Greek to meet a similar want, the Kangakusha enriched their language by the adoption of large numbers of Chinese words. This process was carried to great excess in later times. But writers like Hakuseki and Kiusō were no pedants. They were practical men who were accustomed to use their pens for practical purposes, and who wrote to make themselves understood, not to display their cleverness or learning.

In their hands the Japanese language not only gained much in fulness of vocabulary, but acquired a clearness and directness unattainable with the more cumbrous forms of the older language. Needless to say, pillow-words, pivot-words, and all such frivolous excrescences of style were utterly disdained by them.

CHAPTER III

THE SEVENTEENTH CENTURY

POPULAR LITERATURE—SAIKAKU—CHILDREN'S STORIES —CHIKAMATSU, AND THE POPULAR DRAMA

CONCURRENT with the movement described in the preceding chapter, another and very different development of literature was going on in Japan. It was threefold, comprising fiction, the drama, and a new kind of poetry known as Haikai. But while the Kangakusha wrote mainly for the Samurai class, the writers of romances, plays, and Haikai addressed themselves for the first time in Japanese history to the people. Their public consisted more especially of the populace of the three great cities of Yedo, Kiōto, and Ōsaka. In Japan as in China, the traders occupy a very low place both morally and socially. Of the four classes into which the population is divided, the Samurai, including men of learning, soldiers, and officials of all grades, stand at the top. Next to them are the peasants, the artisans come third, and the merchants last of all. It cannot be denied that there was much justice in this classification. Under the Tokugawa régime the city populations enjoyed great material prosperity. But their moral standards were not high. Naturally quick-witted, and educated up to a point which may fairly be described by our own slang phrase,

" the three R's," they had little real culture or refinement. The many-headed beast had, however, learned to read, and demanded an intellectual pabulum suited to its tastes. A want had been created which required to be supplied. The result was a popular literature of which some account must now be given.

The seventeenth century has not much to show in the way of fiction. One of the earliest romances of this time was the *Mokuzu Monogatari*, a highly melodramatic tale of love, jealousy, and revenge, the leading feature of which is of such a nature as to debar more particular description.

The *Usuyuki Monogatari* and the *Hannosuke no Sōshi* (1660) both relate the same story. A man while visiting the temple of Kiyomidzu, in Kiōto, meets a woman named Usuyuki (thin-snow). They love and are united, but the woman dies soon after, and the man shaves his head and retires to a monastery.

IBARA SAIKAKU was the founder of a new school of popular writing in Japan. He revived a class of composition which had been sadly neglected since the days of Murasaki no Shikibu and Sei Shōnagon, and gave to the world a large number of volumes consisting of tales, novels, and sketches of contemporary life and manners. The latter are extremely lifelike and humorous. Saikaku was a resident of Ōsaka, where he followed the profession of composer of Haikai. The world has very willingly forgotten his poetry. Nor have the short dramatic pieces which he wrote for the Ōsaka stage fared much better with posterity. He was a man of no learning. Bakin says that he had not a single Chinese character in his belly,[1] and his books, most of which have very little story, are mainly descriptions of the man-

---

[1] The seat of knowledge, according to the Chinese and Japanese.

ners and customs of the great lupanars which then, as now, formed a prominent feature of the principal cities of Japan. The very titles of some of them are too gross for quotation. The immoral tendency of his works was denounced even in his own day by a hostile critic under the suggestive title *Saikaku no Jigoku Meguri* (" Saikaku in Hell "), and led to their suppression by the Government. It is only recently that a new edition has been permitted to appear, the reason for this tolerance being perhaps the circumstanee that the fugitive humour of fast life in the seventeenth century has become in a great measure unintelligible to modern readers.

Saikaku has written one decent book, a collection of gossipy stories about his fellow-writers of Haikai. It is entitled *Saikaku Nagori no Tomo*, and was published posthumously in 1699. He died in 1693, in his fifty-second year.

For various reasons it is impossible to give a really characteristic specimen of Saikaku's writings. The following is a story of the Enoch Arden class, with a Japanese ending. It is one of a series of tales woven into a work entitled *Fudokoro no Suzuri* or " Bosom Ink-slab," a fanciful title for what we might call *Notes of Travel* (1687). This work is less objectionable than most of his productions :—

" Listening to the cries of the plovers that frequent the Isle of Awaji, one may perceive the sadness of the things of this world.

" Our junk anchored for the night in a harbour called Yashima. A wretched place it was. With what eyes could the poet have regarded it who called it 'the flowery Yashima' ? Even though it was spring, there were no cherry-flowers ; so, with feelings suited to an autumn eve, I approached a mat-roofed shed which stood near the beach. There were some women assembled here enjoying themselves over a cup of tea. Usually it would have been a case of commonplace ill-natured daughter-in-law gossip ; but judging from their excited manners that something unusual was going on, I inquired what was the subject of their important-seeming conversation. It appeared that a fisherman of this shore, by name Hokugan Kiuroku, was in the habit of hiring himself annually for the sardine fishery off the east coast. He usually went down there in company with many others, but the previous autumn nobody else came forward, and so he wilfully went alone. Time passed and nothing was heard of him. Being an illiterate man, he naturally held little communication with the world, and thus became a cause of anxiety to his relations. That autumn there were many storms, and great numbers of fishing-vessels were lost. All his family, when they listened to the noise of the wind, lamented, 'Ah ! Kiuroku is no more of this world.' Others talked as if they had actually witnessed his end. There was a rumour that two hundred and fifty men had perished in a body in the outer sea, and all congratulated themselves that owing to a presentiment of ill-luck they had this year stayed at home. His wife hearing this, even in the depth of her misery and sorrow, felt her condition still more profoundly wretched. Morning and evening she could think of nothing else, to such a degree that she was on the point of throwing away her life. Thus she gave proof of a gentle, womanly heart. Moreover, Kiuroku, in his capacity of *iri-muko*,[1] had been on excellent terms with his wife, and had done his duty faithfully

[1] Adopted heir and son-in-law.

towards her parents, so that when she remembered his position, his loss was a source of great grief to her.

"Winter arrived, spring came and went, nearly a year passed with no news of him. There could be no longer any doubt that he was dead. The day on which he said good-bye and left his native village was chosen for the anniversary of his death. Priests said the proper masses, his personal effects were restored to his true parents, and, as is the way of the world, he began gradually to be forgotten.

"Now his wife was still young. People thought it a pity she should remain a widow, and urged her to take a second husband for the relief of her parents' cares, as was the custom. But she could by no means be persuaded to give her consent. She resolved by-and-by to shave her head, to abandon the world, and with profound 'incense-and-flowers' purpose of heart to devote herself to her husband's memory. Everybody did his best to dissuade her, saying first of all how undutiful it would be towards her parents. In short, they insisted with such success that a lucky day was chosen for her nuptials. The man selected for her husband was a fisherman of the same village, named Iso no Mokubei, a far better match than Kiuroku, and satisfactory in every respect. The parents rejoiced, the friends exulted, and though it was a second marriage, even in this fishing hamlet everything was done in a style equal to that of the ceremony of breeching a boy. The women had on their boxwood hair-combs ; saké was circulated freely. But there are jealous people everywhere, and the company were disturbed from time to time by pebbles flung against the door. As the night went on, this too ceased. The bride and bridegroom retired to their chamber, and placing their wooden pillows side by side, began a confidential talk, in which Kiuroku was naturally forgotten. The wedding company, fatigued with their enjoyment of the previous night, slept soundly late into the next morning. When the door was opened, there was Kiuroku in his travelling garb. He walked in with an air of being at home, his heart full of love for the wife he had not seen for so long. He entered the disordered sleeping-chamber, which was lighted up by a ray of sunshine from the southern window. A feeling of pride came over him when he caught a glimpse of his wife's hair, which was more beautiful than ever. 'The prettiest woman in this village,' he thought to himself. But observing her companion, his dream was shattered. The woman, too, waking from her joy, burst into tears, and Mokubei came out, looking much embarrassed. With a strange expression on his countenance, 'What is this?' asked Kiuroku. Mokubei explained what had happened, laying the blame of this terrible misadventure on fate. What made things worse was the presence of so many people, and the fact that Mokubei had for a long time been on bad terms with Kiuroku. But Kiuroku, showing him a more friendly cheer than usual, collected himself and related the story of his sufferings when cast away on the remote sea. When he had done he calmly stabbed his wife, cut down Mokubei, and with the same sword put an end to himself. What a heroic winding-up of the matter for a mere rustic!"

CHILDREN'S TALES

To the fiction of the seventeenth century belong a number of children's tales,[1] which retain their popularity

---

[1] Most of these have been translated by Mr. Mitford in his *Tales of Old Japan*.

even at the present day, unless they have been swept away of late years by the advancing tide of European civilisation. Though they bear a general resemblance to such stories as *Cinderella*, and appear in various forms, I am inclined to think that they are not really folk-lore, but had definite authors, whose names have long been forgotten. The *Nedzumi no Yomeiri* ("Rat's Wedding") dates from before 1661, while of the *Saru-kani Kassen* ("Battle of the Ape and the Crab") and the *Shitakiri Suzume* ("Tongue-cut Sparrow") we have "new editions" which bear the date of Hōyei (1704–1711). Others are *Momotaro* ("Little Peachling"), *Hana Sakaye Jiji* ("The Old Man who made Trees to Blossom"), *Usagi no Kataki-uchi* ("The Hare's Revenge"), and *Urashima Tarō* (a version of the legend told above, p. 39).

The novelist Bakin, a very competent authority on folk-lore, was much interested in these tales, and has been at the pains to ransack Chinese and Japanese literature for anything which might be thought to suggest the incidents related in them.[1]

THE POPULAR DRAMA—CHIKAMATSU

It would not be quite correct to say that the popular drama owed nothing to the Nō. But it certainly followed a different and independent line of development. Its literary progenitor is the *Taiheiki*, which, it may be remembered, was chanted or recited in public by men who made this their profession. The *Taiheiki* was followed by more or less dramatic stories, which were recited by a single person seated before a desk, to the accompaniment of taps of a fan to mark the time or to give emphasis. To this was subsequently added the music of the sami-

[1] See his *Yenseki Zasshi*, vol. iv.

sen, a three-stringed guitar recently introduced from Loochoo. A favourite story for this purpose was the *Jōruri jiu-ni dan Sōshi*, written towards the end of the Muromachi period. It relates the loves of the famous Yoshitsune with a heroine whose name, Jōruri, is now used as a synonym for a whole class of dramatic compositions.

Towards the middle of the seventeenth century we hear of Jōruri-Katari (chanters of Jōruri) at Yedo, for whom two authors named Oka Seibei and Yonomiya Yajirō are said to have written a number of pieces, some of which, known as *Kompira-bon*, are still in existence. They relate the adventures of a hero named Kompira, nine feet two inches high, with a face so red that nothing could be redder, whose doughty deeds in quelling demons and slaying savage beasts are still the delight of the Japanese schoolboy.

The first Kabuki Shibai, or popular theatre, as distinguished from the Nō Shibai, and from the Ayatsuri Shibai, or marionette theatre, is said to have been established at Kiōto early in the seventeenth century. We are told that a priestess of the great temple of Kidzuki in Idzumo, named O Kuni, having made the acquaintance of one Nagoya Sanzaburō, ran away with him to Kiōto. There they got together a number of dancing-girls and gave performances on the bank of the river Kamo, where the Theatre Street stands at the present day. O Kuni as a priestess would naturally be acquainted with the pantomimic dances performed in honour of the Shinto gods, and was doubtless herself a trained dancer and mime. Owing to certain abuses, the employment of women as actors was put a stop to by the authorities. Their place was taken by boys, but this also was eventually prohibited.

A marionette theatre was next established. In 1661 it was transferred to Ōsaka, where it was famous in subsequent dramatic history as the Takemoto Za. The marionette theatre is still popular in Japan. The puppets are elaborate contrivances, fitted with machinery for rolling the eyeballs, raising the eyebrows, opening and closing the mouth, moving the fingers so as to grasp and flirt a fan, and so on. The popularity of the Takemoto Za procured it several rivals, the most celebrated of which was the Toyotake Za.

The fame of the Takemoto Za was chiefly owing to the genius of CHIKAMATSU MONZAYEMON, who is unquestionably the most prominent figure in the history of the Japanese drama. The birthplace of this remarkable man has been as much disputed as that of Homer. The most probable statement is that he was a Samurai of Hagi, in Chōshiu, where he was born in 1653. It is said that in his boyhood he became a priest. He himself tells us that he was a retainer of more than one noble house in Kiōto. For some reason his services ceased, and he became a Rōnin. The Rōnin, that is, a Samurai who has been dismissed for misconduct, or whose indocile temper has found the severe discipline of the *Yashiki* irksome beyond endurance, is a very familiar personage during the Yedo period of Japanese history, not only in fiction, but in real life. Countless deeds of desperate courage and many atrocious crimes are related of them, among which may be mentioned the well-known revenge of the forty-seven Rōnins and their subsequent suicide, and the murderous attacks on the British Legation in 1861 and 1862. In the early days of foreign intercourse with Japan, Rōnin was a word of fear to all quiet, law-abiding people. It is significant that the principal playwright as well as the most eminent novelist (Bakin) of this period should both belong to the ranks of these *hommes déclassés*.

After leaving the service of the Kiōto nobles, Chikamatsu wrote a number of stories and pieces of no great merit for dramatic performance at Kiōto. One of these, formerly attributed to Saikaku, is the *Kaijin Yashima*, which bears traces of a study of the older Nō drama and Kiōgen. Its subject is an episode in the life of Yoshitsune. Chikamatsu's earliest dated work was written in 1685. In 1690 he took up his residence in Ōsaka, when his connection with the Takemoto marionette theatre began. From this time until his death in 1724, he produced in rapid succession a number of dramas which, whatever their faults, leave no doubt of his possessing a fertile and inventive genius.

On a superficial examination of one of Chikamatsu's plays, a European reader might fail to recognise the fact that it is a drama at all, and take it for a romance with rather more than the usual proportion of dialogue. All the Jōruri contain a large narrative element of a more or less poetical character. This part of the play is chanted to music by a chorus seated on a platform overlooking the stage on the spectator's right, where also the persons sit who declaim the speeches of the puppet actors. It is the narrative part which is more especially designated by the term Jōruri. The chorus which recites it is the true successor of the Jōruri-Katari or dramatic reciters above mentioned, and is the nucleus of the whole, the dialogue being at first merely subsidiary. It not only supplies a thread of story to connect the scenes represented by the puppets on the stage, but aids the imagination of the audience by describing expressions of countenance, scenery, and much more that the resources of a theatre, and especially of a marionette theatre, fail to convey.

On closer examination, however, it becomes apparent that Chikamatsu's works are not really romances, but stage-plays. They have a well-marked movement of plot from the opening scene up to the final catastrophe ; they abound in dramatic situations, and many of the scenes are obviously designed with a view to spectacular effect. These things were new in Japan, and to Chikamatsu therefore belongs the credit of being the creator of the Japanese drama.

Chikamatsu's plays are classified by the Japanese as Jidai-Mono or historical plays, and Sewa-Mono or dramas of life and manners. With the exception of a few in three acts, they are all plays of five acts; but whether the choice of this consecrated number had anything to do with the fact that the Dutch were in the habit of visiting the theatres of Kiōto and Ōsaka on their periodical journeys to Yedo to pay their respects to the Shōgun, I have not been able to ascertain. Nor is it possible to verify a suspicion that the arrangements of the Japanese popular theatre, with its capacious pit and galleries, and a stage well furnished with scenery, trap-doors, turn-tables (as in ancient Greece), and other appliances, may owe something to hints given by these visitors. In these respects the Japanese popular theatre is certainly far in advance of any other in Asia, and more particularly of the Nō Shibai above described.

Chikamatsu was a voluminous writer. The modern edition of his selected works comprises fifty-one plays, and runs to more than two thousand closely printed pages. He is credited with the authorship of as many more. Each is of about the same length as one of

Shakespeare's plays, so that they constitute a truly formidable bulk of literary matter. The novelist Kiōden tells us that a three-act piece of his called *Naga-machi onna Hara-kiri* ("The Woman's *Hara-kiri*," a gruesome title) was written in a single night, and the statement, whether true or not, bears testimony to the opinion entertained by his countrymen of his facility of composition. His works deal with all manner of subjects. They show that he was well acquainted with the Shinto and Buddhist religions, and that he possessed a wide and varied knowledge of the history and institutions of Japan and China.

Of Chikamatsu's merits as a dramatist and poet it behoves a European writer to speak with some degree of reserve, more especially as it is impossible to read more than a tithe of his works. The admiration of his own countrymen for him is unbounded, some of them going so far as to compare him with Shakespeare. It is certainly possible to trace resemblances. Both in Shakespeare and Chikamatsu, comedy frequently treads on the heels of tragedy ; in both, prose is intermixed with poetry, and an exalted style of diction suited to monarchs and nobles alternates with the speech of the common people ; both divided their attention between historical and other dramas ; both possessed the fullest command of the resources of their respective languages, and both are tainted with a grosser element which is rejected by the more refined taste of later times. It may be added that neither Shakespeare nor Chikamatsu is classical in the sense in which we apply that term to Sophocles and Racine. Chikamatsu in particular is very far removed indeed from the classical type.

But few such comparisons have any value, and it is

really idle to compare Shakespeare with a writer whose portraiture of character is rudimentary, whose incidents are outrageously extravagant and improbable, whose philosophy of life is wholly wanting in originality or depth, and who is constantly introducing scenes brutal and revolting to a degree inconceivable to the Western mind. Of this last blemish his audiences must share the responsibility. Nothing seems to have given greater pleasure to these smug, unwarlike shopmen and mechanics with their womankind (no Samurai with any self-respect ever entered a theatre) than sanguinary combats, and scenes of torture, suicide, and murder. They loved to have their blood curdled, and their flesh made to creep, and Chikamatsu, like other writers of his day, took care to supply this demand in no stinted measure. Defects like these are only partially compensated for by a certain barbaric vigour and luxuriance which undoubtedly distinguishes his works. That such a writer should hold the position of the prince of Japanese dramatists only shows by what an imperfect standard this art is judged in Japan.

It is difficult for a Western reader to understand the esteem in which Chikamatsu is held by his countrymen as a poet. In that part of his plays which is chanted to music by the chorus we may, it is true, find metre, rhythmical cadence, fit language, and play of fancy, but all in a very modest degree. The metrical form adopted by him is the usual alternation of seven and five syllable phrases, which is even less substantial than our ordinary blank verse, or the irregular, unrhymed lines favoured by Southey. Nor does he adhere strictly even to this. Longer or shorter lines are introduced from time to time for no other apparent reason than the author's convenience. The rhythmical quality of his poetry is unmistakable ; but, for reasons already pointed out, the Japanese language does not lend itself to any but the simplest harmonies of this kind. A more serious blemish is the abundant use of pivot-words and other meretricious ornaments, which are fatal to coherent sense, and destructive to grammar. The general result is seldom such as to satisfy a European taste.

It will nevertheless, I think, be found that Chikamatsu's poetry, with all its faults, occupies an important place in the history of Japanese literature. The writers of Nō had done something to extend the domain of the poetic art beyond the narrow limits prescribed by tradition : Chikamatsu continued their work, and took possession of, if he failed to reclaim, large tracts of subject-matter which had been neglected by his predecessors. The older poetry may be compared to a trim garden of a few yards square : Chikamatsu's Jōruri resembles a wide clearing in a forest where the products of a rude agriculture are seen growing among tree-stumps and jungle.

Chikamatsu's most famous play is one which is entitled *Kokusenya Kassen* (1715), or the " Battles of Kokusenya." Kokusenya (called Coxinga by older European writers on Japan) was a famous pirate, the son of a Chinese by a Japanese mother, who played a considerable part in the wars of the last days of the Ming dynasty in China. As this is considered the masterpiece of the greatest of Japanese dramatists, it seems desirable to give an analysis of it here.

ACT I

The scene opens at the court of Nanking. The last of the Ming Emperors is seen surrounded by his ministers.

An envoy from the King of Tartary appears, bringing rich presents, which are piled up in the courtyard. He makes a speech in which, on behalf of his master, he asks for Kwasei, the favourite concubine of the Emperor, so that he may make her his queen, and thus cement friendship between the two powers.

The Emperor and his court are much disturbed by this proposal, as Kwasei was just then expected to give birth to an heir to the Ming throne. A traitorous minister named Ri Toten urges its acceptance. General Go Sankei rushes forward and protests indignantly, ordering the Tartar King's presents to be taken away. The Tartar envoy replies with spirit, and is about to fling out of the Imperial presence, when Ri Toten strives to pacify him. To enforce his appeal, he digs out his own left eye with a dagger, and hands it on an ivory slab to the envoy, who receives it with respect, and accepts it in satisfaction for Go Sankei's insult to his sovereign and himself. The envoy takes his departure.

The next scene is in the apartment of the Emperor's younger sister. The Emperor appears, accompanied by two hundred youthful inmates of his harem, half of whom bear branches of flowering plum and half of cherry. They draw up on each side of the stage. The Emperor tells his sister of Ri Toten's noble self-sacrifice, and again urges the latter's suit for the hand of the Princess, which had previously been rejected by her, suggesting that her answer should depend on the result of a battle between the plum and cherry squadrons of ladies. The Princess agrees to this, and puts herself at the head of the plum party, who, acting in collusion with the Emperor, allow themselves to be defeated.

Go Sankei now rushes in, clad in full armour, and with his lance drives off both squadrons. He remonstrates with the Emperor for setting an example in the palace which, if followed by the people, would lead to disastrous civil tumults, charges Ri Toten with treachery, and by an elaborate analysis of the Chinese written character for Ming, the name of the dynasty, proves that Ri Toten's digging out his eye was merely a private signal to the Tartar envoy that the time was ripe for the execution of their treacherous schemes. The Emperor scoffs at this learned sophistry, and kicks Go Sankei on the forehead with his Imperial foot.

From all sides there now comes a sound of conchs, drums, and battle shouts. The Tartars have arrived, and are surrounding the palace. Their general rides into the courtyard. He tells the Emperor that the Tartar King's love for Kwasei was all a pretence, and that his real object was the destruction of the unborn heir to the Ming throne. He avows Ri Toten's treacherous complicity, and announces to Go Sankei his intention of carrying off the Emperor and Kwasei as prisoners, and of making them serve as menials in his master's kitchen.

Go Sankei's wife, Riuka, now appears with an infant in her arms. She flies with the Princess by a postern gate, leaving her child behind. Go Sankei makes a sally, and with one hundred men drives off several millions of the enemy. In his absence Ri Toten's younger brother, Ri Kaihō, murders the Emperor, cuts off his head, and binds Kwasei. Go Sankei returns, cleaves Ri Kaihō in two, releases Kwasei, and reverently sets up the Emperor's headless trunk, which he adorns with the hereditary regalia. While he is hesitating whether to save the

Emperor's body or the pregnant consort Kwasei, the enemy renew their attack. Having beaten them off, he resolves to save the unborn heir to the throne, and to abandon the corpse.

Meanwhile his own infant child begins to cry for his natural nourishment. "What a nuisance!" he exclaims. But on second thoughts he reflects that the child is his own heir, and that it would be on the whole better to save him. So he binds him firmly to the shaft of his spear and retreats to the seashore with Kwasei, pursued by the enemy. Kwasei is killed by a bullet, and Go Sankei, by an improvised Cesarean operation (*coram populo !*), rescues her living child, a beautiful boy, which he wraps in his dead mother's sleeve. "But stay! if the enemy find that the child is gone, they will spare no pains to discover it." So he stabs his own child, who, it may be remembered, was all this time lashed to the shaft of his spear, and substitutes it for the infant Prince. *Exit* Go Sankei.

Enter Go Sankei's wife with the Princess. They hide among the reeds by the seashore. A Tartar officer named Godatsu follows in pursuit. He takes a small boat and searches all the creeks near them. Riuka (Go Sankei's wife) catches his oar and overturns his boat. He goes to the bottom, and Riuka gets into the boat with the Princess. Godatsu comes up from below all dripping, and a combat ensues, in which Godatsu has his head cut off by Riuka. Then, as in her bedraggled and blood-stained condition she is no fit company for a princess, she shoves off the boat containing the latter, which is carried away by the wind and tide, and remains behind on the shore. The chorus describes the situation in poetical imagery.

ACT II

The scene changes to Hirado, in Japan. Kokusenya, with his wife, is gathering shellfish on the seashore, when a small boat approaches. It proves to contain the Princess, who had drifted over from China. Kokusenya's wife, a low, vulgar woman, who provides the comic element of the play, is overcome with laughter at the Chinese which the Princess and her husband talk. Jealousy then gets the upper hand, but this gives way to respect when she learns the rank of the stranger.

Kokusenya, who is the son of a trusted minister of the Ming Emperors, makes up his mind to restore that dynasty, and proceeds with his father and mother to China, leaving the Princess in his wife's charge. On arriving there, they resolve to seek the assistance of Kanki, a Chinese magnate who had married a sister of Kokusenya. While travelling through a forest on their way to his castle, Kokusenya bearing his aged mother on his back, they fall in with a tiger. Disdaining to use his sword against the beast, Kokusenya gains the mastery over him after a struggle, which, doubtless, gave much gratification to the "groundlings" of the Ōsaka theatre. A hunting party arrives; their leader claims the tiger for Ri Toten, the traitorous one-eyed minister of the first act. Kokusenya replies in a style of inimitable braggadocio. With the tiger's assistance he subdues the huntsmen, and forms of them the nucleus of an army with which to conquer the Tartar invaders. Kokusenya's first care is to cut off the pig-tails of his recruits, and to give them new names, in which Japanese terminations are stuck on to names indicative of their foreign origin. One of

these names is Igirisu (English)-bei. We may well wonder
what an Englishman was doing *dans cette galère*.

ACT III

Kokusenya, at the head of his newly recruited force,
arrives before Kanki's castle, but he is absent, and they
are refused admittance. The old mother, however, is
permitted to enter in the guise of a prisoner bound with
cords. Kanki returns. The old woman begs him
earnestly to espouse her son Kokusenya's cause. He
forthwith draws his sword and tries to kill his wife, but
is prevented. He then explains that he has not suddenly
gone mad, but that if he joined Kokusenya people would
say he was influenced by women, so it was necessary to
remove his wife as a preliminary to granting her request.
His wife being still alive, this was impossible.

News of this refusal being conveyed to Kokusenya,
he bounds over the moat and parapet of the castle,[1] and
presents himself before Kanki. After mutual Homeric
defiance they prepare to fight, when Kanki's wife ex-
poses her breast, showing that in order to remove all
obstacle to the plans of her husband and brother, she
has given herself a death-wound. The two then frater-
nise, and a quantity of warlike gear is produced, in
which Kokusenya is clad, his mother looking on with
great admiration. She then commits suicide, enjoining
on her son and Kanki to show no weakness in fighting against the Tartars, but to regard them as the
enemies of mother and wife. She dies with a smile
on her face, gazing at the gallant appearance of Kokusenya in the new armour supplied him by Kanki.

[1] Incidents like this remind us that it was a marionette theatre for which
Chikamatsu wrote. Puppets can do many things impossible to human actors.

ACT IV

We now return to Go Sankei, who, at the end of the first act, had retired to a secluded place among the hills with the heir to the Ming throne. Here follows a Rip van Winkle episode, at the end of which Go Sankei finds that the young Prince has become a boy of seven, whose voice sounds to him "like the first song of the nightingale heard in some secluded valley where snow still lies." Kokusenya's father now appears upon the scene, accompanied by Kokusenya's wife and the Princess, who have come over from Japan. Whilst they are giving mutual explanations the enemy come in chase; but the gods having been prayed to, a cloud issues from a cave and forms a bridge, over which they cross an abyss to the mountain on the other side. The enemy attempt to follow, but the bridge is blown away by a puff of wind. The five hundred foes tumble to the bottom and are crushed to pieces.

ACT V

Kanki, Kokusenya, and Go Sankei hold a grand council of war, at which the most impossible nonsense is talked. A letter arrives from Kokusenya's father, stating that finding life at his age, seventy-three, not worth living, he is about to find death in the enemy's ranks. The three, full of determination to save him, rush off to Nanking, now the Tartar King's stronghold.

The scene changes to Nanking. Kokusenya's father appears before the gate and challenges Ri Toten to single combat. The Tartar King is seen on the battlements. By his order the old man is seized and brought into the city. Kokusenya and his party appear before the walls. Ri Toten tells Kokusenya that he must choose between his father committing *hara-kiri* or their both going back to Japan. Consternation of Kokusenya and his party. Speech by Kokusenya's father, reminding him of his mother's dying injunctions, and adjuring him not to think of his fate. Kokusenya is about to spring at the Tartar King, but is deterred by Ri Toten putting his sword to the old man's throat. Go Sankei now throws himself at the feet of the Tartar King, offering to give up Kokusenya if the lives of the other two were spared. No sooner has the Tartar King granted this request than Go Sankei springs at him, knocks him over, and binds him. Kokusenya also rushes forward, releases his father, and seizes Ri Toten. The Tartar King has five hundred blows of a bamboo administered to him, and is sent off a prisoner to Japan. Ri Toten's head is wrenched off there and then, and the play ends amid general rejoicing.

A summary of this kind gives too much prominence to the defects of this most famous of Japanese dramas. Its manner is better than its matter. There is a copious flow of sonorous and often picturesque language, of exalted sentiment, and sententious oratory, which divert the reader's (and still more the audience's) attention from the improbabilities of the story. The personages do and say many absurd things ; yet they speak and bear themselves in a manner not altogether unworthy of tragic heroes. It may be added that even in his maddest moods Chikamatsu never neglects dramatic force of situation, and that he has a turn for impressive dialogue which ought not to be ignored. Dulness is not among the numerous faults of the *Kokusenya Kassen*.

The European reader is not likely to relish the more

poetical passages of this drama, with their pivot-words and closely woven allusive phrases. Yet possibly there is more in them than we are willing to acknowledge. The Japanese find them the choicest part of the work, and they might not unreasonably deny to foreigners the right to sit in judgment upon the finer raptures of their national muse. As a poet Chikamatsu may readily be allowed one merit: if Japan ever produces epic, dramatic, or long narrative poems of importance, he will have done much to prepare the way.

The popularity of the *Kokusenya Kassen* with the audiences of Ōsaka was so great as to call for two continuations in the same style, and it is still one of the stock pieces of the Japanese theatre.

KABUKI THEATRE

Meanwhile a somewhat different development of the dramatic art was taking place—chiefly at Yedo. Kabuki theatres, which had men for actors, had been established there before the middle of the seventeenth century. The pieces produced in these theatres were at first the composition of the actors engaged in them, but towards the beginning of the eighteenth century[1] we hear of definite authors whose works were published under the title of Kyaku-bon. Native critics agree that the Kyaku-bon contain little that is of value as literature. In form they approach the European drama far more nearly than do the Jōruri. The dialogue is here all-important, the chorus, with its narratives and poetical descriptions, taking a subordinate position or being altogether wanting.

---

[1] The first of the series of great actors bearing the name of Ichikawa Danjurō made his *début* on the stage in 1673. The present holder of that name is the ninth of the line.

CHAPTER IV

POETRY OF THE SEVENTEENTH CENTURY— HAIKAI, HAIBUN, KIŌKA

HAIKAI

IT might naturally be supposed that in the Tanka of thirty-one syllables poetry had reached its extreme limit of brevity and conciseness. But a still further step remained to be taken in this direction. In the sixteenth century a kind of poem known as Haikai, which consists of seventeen syllables only, made its appearance. The Haikai is a Tanka minus the concluding fourteen syllables, and is made up of three phrases of five, seven, and five syllables respectively, as in the following :—

> " *Furu ike ya !*
> *Kawadzu tobi-komu,*
> *Midzu no oto.*"

It differs from Tanka, however, in more than metre, being much less choice in diction and matter than the older kind of poetry. It admits words of Chinese derivation and colloquial expressions, and often deals with subjects which the more fastidious Tanka refuses to meddle with.

The earliest professor of this accomplishment was Yamazaki Sō-kan, a Buddhist priest (1445–1534). The verses of his which I have met with have mostly a comic character. Here is one :—

> " *Even in the rain, come forth,*
> *O midnight moon !*
> *But first put on your hat.*"

A halo is called in Japanese *kasa*, which also means a broad hat or umbrella.

Another early Haikai writer was Arakida Moritake (1472–1549). The following is from his pen :—

> " *Thought I, the fallen flowers*
> *Are returning to their branch ;*
> *But lo ! they were butterflies.*"

Coming down to the Yedo period, the first name of note in this department of literature is that of Matsunaga Teitoku (1562–1645). A well-known Haikai of his is the following :—

> " *For all men*
> *'Tis the seed of siesta—*
> *The autumn moon.*"

In other words : The autumn moon is so beautiful that people sit up half the night to gaze on it, and have therefore to make up for their want of sleep by a siesta on the following day.

If it were not, however, for the fame of MATSURA BASHŌ (1643–1694) and his disciples, it would hardly be necessary to notice this kind of composition at all. He imported a more serious element, and greatly refined and improved the Haikai, until it became a formidable rival to the Tanka. The latter had in these days become too exclusive for the popular taste. The Fujiwara family, who were its special patrons, practisers, and critics, maintained the traditional canons of the art in all their rigidity, and the nation was glad of a new and more unconfined field for its poetical talent. To write tolerable Tanka required a technical training, for which the many had neither time nor opportunity, but there was nothing to prevent any one with ordinary cleverness and a smattering of education from composing Haikai. Saikaku, an unlearned man, is said to have produced twenty thousand stanzas of this kind of poetry during one day's visit to the shrine of Sumiyoshi, and to have received on that account the cognomen of "the twenty-thousand old man." The story is an obvious exaggeration, but it shows what an easy thing Haikai writing was thought to be.

Bashō belonged to a Samurai family, hereditary retainers of the Daimio of Tsu, in the province of Ise. He acquitted himself with credit in an official capacity connected with water-works in Yedo, but for some reason threw up his appointment and entered the Buddhist priesthood. He built himself a cottage in the Fukagawa district of Yedo, and planted a banana-tree beside the window. It grew up and flourished, and from it he took the name of Bashō (banana), by which he is known to posterity. He was a diligent student of the Zen Buddhist doctrines and of Taoism, and was also an artist. From time to time he took long excursions to the remotest parts of Japan, leaving behind him traces of his presence, which remain to this day, in the shape of stones inscribed with poems of his composition. On one of these journeys he took suddenly ill, and died at Ōsaka in the fifty-first year of his age.

Shōtei Kinsui relates the following incident which happened on one of Bashō's tours. It illustrates the favour in which Haikai was held even by the lowest classes of the people :—

Once, when on his travels, Bashō passed through a certain rural district, making Haikai as he went along. It was full moon. The whole sky was flooded with light, so that it was clearer than noonday. It was so bright that Bashō did not think of seeking an inn, but continued his journey. In a certain village he came upon a party of men who had brought out saké and something to eat with it into the open air, and were enjoying the moonlight. Bashō stood still to watch them. Presently they fell to composing Haikai. Bashō was greatly pleased to see that this elegant accomplishment was practised even in so remote a place, and continued looking on, when a silly fellow of the party noticed him and said, " There is a priest who looks like a pilgrim. He may be a begging priest, but, never mind, let us invite him to join us." They all thought this would be great fun. Bashō could not refuse, so he joined their circle, taking the lowest seat. The silly fellow then said to him, " Everybody here is bound to compose something about the full moon. You must compose something too." Bashō apologised. He said he was a humble individual, belonging to a country place. How should he presume to contribute to the entertainment of the honourable company ? He begged, therefore, that they would kindly excuse him. " No ! no !" said they, " we can't excuse you. Good or bad, you must compose one verse at least." They urged him until at last he consented. Bashō smiled, folded his arms, and turning to the clerk of the party, said, " Well, I will give you one :—

" '*Twas the new moon*——' "

" The new moon ! What a fool this priest is !" cried
one. " The poem should be about the full moon." " Let
him go on," said another ; "it will be all the more fun."
So they gathered round, and mocked and laughed at
him. Bashō paid no attention, but went on—

> "'*Twas the new moon !*
> *Since then I waited—*
> *And lo ! to-night !*
> [*I have my reward*]."

The whole party were amazed. They took their seats
again and said, " Sir, you can be no common priest to
write such a remarkable verse. May we ask your name ?"
Bashō smilingly replied, " My name is Bashō, and I am
travelling about on a pilgrimage for the sake of practising the art of Haikai." The rustics, in great excitement,
apologised for their rudeness to an eminent man "whose
fragrant name was known to all the world." They sent
for their friends who were interested in Haikai, and
began their *al fresco* feast anew in his honour.

It has been objected that Haikai, even in the hands of
an acknowledged master like Bashō, is too narrow in its
compass to have any value as literature. The Kangakusha Dazai Shuntai calls it a *tsutanaki mono* (a stupid
sort of thing), and Shōtei Kinsui admits that in the eyes
of "the superior man" this is doubtless so. Its popularity, however, is undeniable. The name of Bashō was
known to the very cow-herds. He had ten disciples, and
they in their turn had pupils whose name is legion.
Monthly conferences of Haikai amateurs were held
regularly both in the capital and the provinces, and there
were professors who contrived to make a living by
practising this art.

It would be absurd to put forward any serious claim on behalf of Haikai to an important position in literature. Yet, granted the form, it is difficult to see how more could be made of it than Bashō has done. It is not only the metre which distinguishes these tiny effusions from prose. There is in them a perfection of apt phrase, which often enshrines minute but genuine pearls of true sentiment or pretty fancy. Specks even of wisdom and piety may sometimes be discerned upon close scrutiny. Suggestiveness is their most distinctive quality, as may be seen by the following :—

> " *A cloud of flowers!*
> *Is the bell Uyeno*
> *Or Asakusa ?* "

To the English reader this will appear bald, and even meaningless. But to an inhabitant of Yedo it conveys more than meets the ear. It carries him away to his favourite pleasure resort of Mukōjima, with its long lines of cherry-trees ranged by the bank of the river Sumida, and the famous temples of Uyeno and Asakusa in the vicinity. He will have no difficulty in expanding it into something of this kind : " The cherry-flowers in Mukōjima are blossoming in such profusion as to form a cloud which shuts out the prospect. Whether the bell which is sounding from the distance is that of the temple of Uyeno or of Asakusa I am unable to determine."

But *brevis esse laborat, obscurus fit*. A very large proportion of Bashō's Haikai are so obscurely allusive as to transcend the comprehension of the uninitiated foreigner. The following are some of the more lucid. The same quality of suggestiveness pervades them all.

> " An ancient pond!
> With a sound from the water
> Of the frog as it plunges in."

> " I come weary,
> In search of an inn—
> Ah! these wistaria flowers! "

> " Ah! the waving lespedeza,
> Which spills not a drop
> Of the clear dew!"

> "'Tis the first snow—
> Just enough to bend
> The gladiolus leaves!"

> " Of Miidera
> The gate I would knock at—
> The moon of to-day."

That is to say, How beautiful the scenery about the temple of Miidera must look on a fine moonlight night like this! I would that I were there to see it.

> " On a withered branch
> A crow is sitting
> This autumn eve."

> " The cry of the cicada
> Gives no sign
> That presently it will die."

The following are by other writers :—

> "'Tis the cuckoo—
> Listen well!
> How much soever gods ye be."

> "'Tis the first snow,
> Yet some one is indoors—
> Who can it be?"

> " The club-shaker's
> Rising and falling in the water
> Until it becomes a musquito."

The water-grub, which subsequently becomes a mosquito, moves about by the rapid vibration of its tail. Hence the name "club-shaker." To the Japanese it is an emblem of the mischievous boy who is destined to develop into a wicked man.

> "*O ye fallen leaves!*
> *There are far more of you*
> *Than ever I saw growing on the trees!*"

> "*Alas! the width of this musquito-net*
> *Which meets my eye when I wake*
> *And when I lie down.*"

The following characteristic specimen of this kind of poetry is quoted in Mr. B. H. Chamberlain's *Handbook of Colloquial Japanese* :—

> "*Asagao ni*
> *Tsurube torarete,*
> *Morai-mizu !*"

Literally, "Having had my well-bucket taken away by the convolvuli,—gift-water !" The meaning, as Mr. Chamberlain not unnecessarily explains, is this: "The poetess Chiyo, having gone to her well one morning to draw water, found that some tendrils of the convolvulus had twined themselves around the rope. As a poetess and a woman of taste, she could not bring herself to disturb the dainty blossoms. So, leaving her own well to the convolvuli, she went and begged water of a neighbour. A pretty little vignette surely, and expressed in five words."

HAIBUN

The Haibun is a kind of prose composition which may be conveniently mentioned here, as it is a sort of satellite of the Haikai, and aims at the same conciseness and suggestiveness. The most noted writer of Haibun is YOKOI YAYU (1703–1783), a high official of Nagoya, in Owari. He is the author of the much admired apologue which follows :—

"An earthen vessel, whether it be square or round, strives to adapt to its own form the thing which it contains : a bag does not insist on preserving its own shape, but conforms itself to that which is put into it. Full, it reaches above men's shoulders ; empty, it is folded up and hidden in the bosom. How the cloth bag which knows the freedom of fulness and emptiness must laugh at the world contained within the jar !

> O thou bag
> Of moon and flowers
> Whose form is ever changing!"

In other words : How much better it is to yield our hearts to the manifold influences of external nature, like the moon and flowers, which are always changing their aspect with the weather and the season, than, self-concentrated, to try to make everything conform to one's own narrow standard !

KIŌKA

Kiōka (literally "mad poetry") is a comic and vulgar variety of Tanka. There is here an absolute freedom both in respect to language and choice of subject. The Kiōka must be funny, that is all. In this kind of poetry, of which an immense quantity was produced during the Yedo period, the punning propensity of the Japanese has been allowed full scope. *Share* (pronounced "sharry") reigns there supreme. *Share* is one of those numerous

Japanese words for which there is no exact English equivalent. It may be translated " wit," but in order to express its full meaning a spice of what is comprehended under the terms gaiety, esprit, playful fancy, stylishness, must be added. Japanese wit, like that of other countries, has an element which defies analysis or classification. But the *jeu-de-mots* predominates. *Share* infests not only the Kiōka, but the drama and fiction, to an extent well-nigh intolerable to European tastes. Dr. Florenz, Professor of Philology in the Imperial University of Tokio, has treated this subject with truly German conscientiousness and erudition in a paper read before the German Asiatic Society of Japan in July 1892. Following a native investigator named Tsuchiko Kaneshiro, he classifies *share* under two heads with divisions and subdivisions, making in all twenty different kinds. Our old enemy the pivot-word is here, also the pillow-word, and several varieties of the ordinary pun, with various fearfully complicated acrobatic contortions of speech which I shall not attempt to describe. Even the reader who has a competent knowledge of the language requires a special study to understand and appreciate them. He follows these far-eastern waggeries with a halting step, and frequently finds himself in the position of the Scotchman who was heard suddenly to burst into laughter at a joke which had been made half-an-hour before. Nothing testifies more strikingly to the nimbleness of the Japanese apprehension than their delight in these "Taschenspielerkunstchen des sprachlichen Ausdrucks" (linguistic prestidigitations), as Dr. Florenz has aptly called them, whether in conversation or in books. It may be doubted whether such an excessive fondness for mere verbal wit does not amount to a disease, and whether it has not constituted a serious obstacle to the development of higher qualities in their literature.

In quite recent times a popular kind of lyrical poetry has come into fashion which somewhat resembles the ancient Naga-uta in form. The following may serve as a specimen :—

> " *Vain has been the dream*
> *In which I thought that we met ;*
> *Awake, I find myself again*
> *In the darkness*
> *Of the wretched reality.*
> *Whether I try to hope*
> *Or give way to gloomy thought,*
> *Truly for my heart*
> *There is no relief.*
>
> *If this is such a miserable world that I may not meet thee,*
> *Oh ! let me take up my abode*
> *Deep in the far mountains,*
> *And deeper still*
> *In their furthest depths,*
> *Where, careless of men's gaze,*
> *I may think of my love."*

CHAPTER V

EIGHTEENTH CENTURY

KANGAKUSHA—FICTION—JISHŌ AND KISEKI—JITSUROKU-MONO—WASŌBIŌYE—POPULAR DRAMA

KANGAKUSHA

THE pursuit of Chinese studies reached its height in the eighteenth century. In its early years Hakuseki, Kiusō, and other distinguished men of letters still lived and wrote. They had numerous successors, who continued to bring out volume after volume of commentaries on the Chinese classics, works on government, the art of war, history, finance and political economy, ethics, metaphysics and religion, under which the shelves of Japanese libraries are groaning at this day. But, as the *Heike Monogatari* says, "that which flourishes must also decay." After the philosophers came the sophists. Japan had little more to learn from the Chu-Hi philosophy, and the renewed study of the ancient Chinese literature which it had promoted. The impulse derived from these sources had spent its force, though it continued to be indirectly felt in other departments of literature than the writings of the Kangakusha.

In the eighteenth century the Chu-Hi philosophy was no longer so universally recognised as the unquestioned standard of doctrine. Even in the preceding century there had been heretics, vigorously denounced by Kiusō, who followed the teachings of Wang Yangming,[1] a Chinese thinker who "endeavoured to substitute an idealistic intuitionalism for the scientific philosophy of Chu-Hi." Another heretic was Itō Jinsai (1627–1705), who was one of the founders of a new sect known as the Kogakusha, which set aside Chu-Hi's exposition of the Chinese classics, and sought to base a system of philosophy on the direct study of the works of Confucius. His son Tōgai (1670–1736), a distinguished scholar, followed in the same track as well as the still more eminent Ogiu Sorai (1666–1728). Tōgai was the author of *Yuken Shōroku* and *Hyōsoku-dan*, collections of miscellaneous writings in the Japanese language ; and Sorai is remembered for his *Seidan* ("Talk on Government") and *Narubeshi*, both of which are in Japanese. Dazai Shuntai, also a heretical philosopher, was the author of a work on finance called *Keizairoku*, and of a volume of desultory essays, in a plain, straightforward style, entitled *Dokugo* ("Soliloquy"), which is much esteemed. All these were voluminous writers in the Chinese language.

Meanwhile the Chu-Hi or orthodox school of philosophy was not without its champions, and a war of contending sects arose whose wrangles disturbed Japan until the end of the century. The intolerance of all classes of Kangakusha for Buddhism, and the aversion and contempt of the Wagakusha (or students of the native learning and religion) for Chinese scholars and Buddhists alike, helped to increase the turmoil and confusion. Towards the end

---

[1] See *Transactions of the Asiatic Society of Japan*, vol. xx. p. 12 ; also Dr. Knox's translation of Nakai Tojiu's *Okina Mondo*, in vol. ii. of the *Chrysanthemum*.

of the century this state of things became so unbearable that the reigning Shōgun, Iyenari, was driven to apply a partial remedy. He prohibited all philosophical teaching whatever other than that of Chu-Hi and his adherents.

The Kangakusha, by their excesses and extravagances, were themselves responsible for the decay of their influence. Their admiration for things Chinese passed all reasonable bounds. Sorai, for example, spoke of himself as an "Eastern barbarian," and Chinese standards were blindly accepted as unquestionable rules of conduct both in private and public matters.

In the world of literature the most noticeable result of the Kangakusha craze (for such it ultimately became) was the neglect of Japanese composition. For all serious writings Chinese was preferred, and it was only for their lighter and more carelessly written works that these scholars condescended to use their own language. The native style was for a long time left mainly to the writers of fiction.

JISHŌ AND KISEKI

At the beginning of the eighteenth century there was at Kiōto a bookseller and publisher whose place of business was known as the Hachimonjiya or "Figure-of-eight-house." The principal of this establishment was also an author, and in that capacity signed himself JISHŌ (spontaneous laughter). Associated with him was a writer who styled himself KISEKI. Kiseki was a broken-down tradesman of Kiōto, the heir of a long line of shopkeepers who had amassed wealth by the sale of a kind of sweetmeat or cake. Such part of their substance as had descended to him he wasted in riotous living, and was at last compelled to resort to authorship for a subsistence. At first Kiseki allowed his works to be published in Jishō's name ; but as their popularity became established, he insisted on his own name also appearing on the title-page. Ultimately author and publisher quarrelled, and Kiseki opened an independent establishment, where a good number of his works were brought out. Some go so far as to say that Jishō never wrote anything, but that the books which bear his signature were in all cases really the work of Kiseki or other needy authors, whom he paid for their services. Whatever may have been the relations between them, the two names Jishō and Kiseki are constantly associated by the Japanese, just as we speak of Erckmann-Chatrian or Besant and Rice.

Kiseki died about 1736, in his seventieth year, and Jishō in 1745, at an advanced age. In a preface to his last published work, the latter commends to the favour of the public his son Kishō and his grandson Zuishō, who were authors of writings of a similar character to those for which the Hachimonjiya had acquired its reputation. One of these, printed in 1746, contains a catalogue of one hundred and three publications of this notorious press. The names of a considerable proportion are sufficiently indicative of their character. They are pornographic novels, tales, or sketches. Even when the title is a harmless one, the reader after a few pages is pretty sure to find himself introduced to one of the Kuruwa or brothel-quarters of Kiōto or elsewhere, and the manners and customs of these places furnish a large part of the subject-matter.

There is a reason, if not an excuse, for the prevailing choice of this unsavoury topic by Japanese writers of fiction during the Yedo period. There was no social intercourse to speak of between men and women of the better class. Whenever reasons of economy did not stand in the way, the women lived a very secluded life, seeing no men but their near relations. Their marriages were arranged for them, and romantic attachments were extremely exceptional. The manners and customs of the respectable classes of society were therefore not a promising field for the writer of fiction. He preferred the freer atmosphere of the Kuruwa, to which pretty gardens and handsome buildings, with the showy education and gay costumes of their inmates, lent a superficial appearance of elegance and refinement. The element of romance in the lives of these women was perhaps small, but it existed, and it was far more natural to credit them with romantic adventures and passions than their more immaculate sisters. And if the novelist's description of these places as the home of wit and jollity, and the natural resort of all young men of spirit and fashion, had a tendency to corrupt public morals, it is also to be remembered that the class of readers whom he addressed were not particular in these matters. It was a case of *populus vult corrumpi, et corrumpitur*.

The most famous of the Hachimonjiya publications is a work entitled *Keisei Kintanki* (1711). Jishō's name appears on the title-page, but it is probably one of those which were really written by Kiseki. It is not a novel, but a debate on a subject of which I must renounce the attempt to give an idea. In so far as mere words go, there are more objectionable works, but the whole attitude of the author is profoundly immoral. What is specially unpardonable is his irreverent use of terms borrowed from the Buddhist religious vocabulary, and the scandalous way in which here and elsewhere the great names of Japanese history are dragged by him through the mire. Its humour, however, is undeniable.

A somewhat less objectionable work is the *Oyaji Katagi* or "Types of Elderly Men," by Jishō and Kiseki. It is a series of racy, lifelike sketches of "The Gourmand," "The Devotee," "The Valetudinarian," "The Patron of Wrestlers," with others which need not be specified.

This was followed by a number of similar works, such as *Musuko Katagi* ("Types of Youths"), *Tedai Katagi* ("Types of Merchants' Assistants"), *Musume Katagi* ("Types of Girlhood"). The last-named work has a preface, which makes what I have no doubt is a sincere profession of the most unexceptionable moral aims.

The *Kokusenya Minchō Taiheiki*, by Kiseki, is a version, with variations, of Chikamatsu's well-known play. The practice of novelising dramas is more common in Japan than the reverse process. As has been already explained, there is far less difference between these two forms of composition than in European literature.

The *Fūriu Gumpai Uchiwa* is a romance of the olden time, related in the Hachimonjiya manner. Other romances are the *Shōnin Gumpai Uchiwa* (Kiseki, N. D.), *Fūriu Saikai Suzuri,* and *Fūriu Tōkai Suzuri.*

It is not easy to discover in the works of these writers passages which are suitable for quotation in these pages. The following is an outline of a story from the *Zen-aku Mimochi Ōgi,* or "Good and Evil Conduct Fan," a series of moral tales, signed by Jishō and Kiseki:—

"PIETY HAS ITS REWARD"

There was once an ink-maker of Nara, named Kuro-suke (Blackie), tolerably well off, but not rich. He was a very pious man, and went every day to the shrine of Kasuga, near that city, to pay his devotions. One day, as he went to make his usual morning prayer, he met a white-haired man in the garb of a Shinto priest, who told him that on his way home he would find a reward of his piety at the great Torii (Shinto archway) leading to the shrine. He accordingly found there a purse of fifty gold kobans. He took it home, intending to advertise it, and so give the loser an opportunity of making a claim. Meanwhile Kurosuke heard a sound of great lamentation which proceeded from the house of a neighbour. It appeared, on inquiry, that the father of the family had gone security for a friend who had absconded, leaving him liable for a sum of one hundred rios. It was totally impossible for him to raise this amount. The creditor offered to take thirty, but even this sum was far beyond his means. His daughter (the experienced reader of Japanese novels knows what is coming) then offered to let herself be sold to a Kuruwa in order to provide the needful money, and an establishment of this kind, far away in Chikuzen, was selected, so as to lessen the family disgrace as much as possible. It was the lamentation at her approaching departure which had drawn Kurosuke's attention. He concluded that with the gift of the gods he could not do better than release this unhappy household from their difficulty. So he paid the thirty rios, and returning home, deposited the balance of the money in the domestic shrine and went about his business. Now his wife, of whom he had made a confidante, was a foolish woman. She took it into her head that her husband had stolen the money. Full of this idea, she must needs let their landlord know of her suspicions. And so from one to another the matter became public property. Kurosuke was arrested, and although he told the true story over and over again, nobody believed him. The authorities directed that he should be detained in custody until the loser of the money should appear to corroborate his statement. At last the original owner came forward. She was a young widow from a distance, who had meant it for the erection of a stone lantern in front of the shrine, in memory of her deceased husband, and on her relating the circumstances of its loss, Kurosuke was at once released. He obtained the magistrate's permission to divorce his wife for her treacherous conduct, and married the widow. They adopted the young girl who had been saved from a life of shame, and were happy and prosperous ever after, leaving children and grandchildren who handed down their name. This true story is told to this day as an example of the saying that " piety has its reward."

The Hachimonjiya continued its activity until the end of the eighteenth century. Meanwhile other houses had sprung up, first at Kiōto and subsequently at Yedo, to supply the public demand for literature of this kind. Their publications, known as *share-bon*, or witty books, were of so outrageous a character that the Government at last (in 1791) interfered, and visited both authors and publishers with severe but not unmerited punishment. *Non ragioniam di lor*.

With all their faults, Jishō and Kiseki must be pronounced the truest representatives for their time of the characteristic qualities of the Japanese national genius. They fill an important place in the history of Japanese literature, continuing the tradition of Saikaku by their graphic and humorous descriptions of real life and manners, while they far excelled him in culture and literary ability. They have been called realistic writers by some native critics, and when we think of the extravagant and unreal romances so much in vogue at a later period, they must be admitted to have considerable claim to the title. But in fidelity to the facts of everyday life and actual human nature, unsophisticated by superfine Chinese ethical notions, they fall short of some of their successors. Their works are by no means uniform in this respect, and some of them contain a large element of romance.

"JITSUROKU-MONO"

In the *Heike Monogatari* and *Taiheiki* we have seen examples of what may be called "history paraphrased." The authors of similar works in the eighteenth century went a step further. They treated real personages and events with still greater freedom, and thus produced what, notwithstanding the name *Jitsuroku-mono* ("True Record"), was in reality closely akin to the historical novel. Their favourite themes are battles and vendettas, warlike exploits, and the disorders which from time to time disturbed the peace of the Daimios' Governments. Their style is for the most part plain and unadorned, but not without a certain naïve charm, and their works are still popular, although the authors' names have long been forgotten.

Among the principal works of this kind may be mentioned the *Ōkubo Musashi Yoroi*, *Onna Taiheiki*, *Mikawa Go Fudoki*, *Taikōki*, and the *Ōka Seidan*. The *Taikōki*, written in the early years of this century, relates the history of the famous soldier and statesman Hideyoshi in a highly imaginative fashion and at enormous length. It is to be distinguished from the earlier *Taikōki* already noticed, and from subsequent works with the same or similar titles.

An even more popular work was the *Ōka Seidan*, which purports to be a collection of *causes célèbres* tried by a judge named Ōka Echizen no Kami, famous for his impartiality and acumen. He was Machibugiō or civil governor of Yedo, a post which carried with it high judicial powers, under the Shōgun Yoshimune, in the early part of the eighteenth century.

The *Ōka Seidan* consists of forty-three stories, some of which are founded on fact, though the hand of the romancist is readily distinguishable in all. It may be cordially recommended to European students for its simple, unpretentious style, which is entirely free from the irritating tricks of the writers of superfine Japanese.

The most interesting of the stories related in this bulky volume is the first. It is an account of an attempt by a scoundrelly young Buddhist priest, named Tenichi Bō, to pass himself off on the Shōgun[1] as a son of his by a woman whom he had known in his youth. In order to carry out this design, he and his accomplices commit some forty murders and other crimes. By means which recall the devices of a famous claimant of our own day, they persuade the merchants of Ōsaka and Kiōto to advance them large sums of money wherewith to furnish Tenichi Bō with an outfit suitable to his supposed station. He then proceeds to Yedo with a train of several hundred followers, and takes up his residence there in a handsome *yashiki*, built specially for his reception from the funds supplied by his deluded adherents. The Shōgun is strongly inclined to recognise him; but Judge Ōka, at the imminent risk of receiving an invitation to commit

---

[1] Arai Hakuseki's patron, Yoshimune.

hara-kiri, urges caution. He ultimately succeeds in tracing out, by his detectives, the whole history of Tenichi Bō's criminal career, and the story ends dramatically with the arrest, exposure, and execution of the chief culprits. It is true in all its more important features.

The *Jitsuroku-mono* were suppressed by the Shōgun's Government in 1804, as containing matter injurious to the fame of Iyeyasu, the deified founder of the dynasty, and his lieutenants. At the same time all mention of real personages belonging to the military caste who lived after 1573 was prohibited in works of fiction. The *Jitsuroku-mono* continued, however, to be read in manuscripts, which formed a substantial part of the stock of the circulating libraries.

"WASŌBIŌYE" (1774)

Wasōbiōye is a sort of Japanese Gulliver. The hero drifts out to sea from the port of Nagasaki in a fishing-boat, and reaches the Land of Perennial Youth and Life, the Land of Endless Plenty, the Land of Shams, and finally the Land of Giants, meeting with numerous adventures, which are related with no little humour. This work has not been treated as a very important contribution to Japanese literature. Mr. Chamberlain, who has translated the best part of it for the *Transactions of the Asiatic Society of Japan*,[1] speaks of it as of no particular importance or celebrity, and the native writers of literary history take no notice of it whatever. It appears to me that it is deserving of a more favourable judgment, and I confess that I prefer it to the more celebrated work suggested by it, namely, the *Musōbiōye* of Bakin. I tran-

[1] Vol. vii. (1879).

scribe from Mr. Chamberlain's version a passage which will give some idea of its character :—

"Now you must know that, as in this country there were no such phenomena as death and disease, none of the people knew what death or disease felt like, though they were much given to speculating on the subject. Some few volumes of the Buddhist Scriptures that had been brought over in ancient times from India and China, described heaven in such glowing terms that they were filled with quite a desperate admiration for death, and distaste for their own never-ending existence, so much so that when, as a rare exception, any of their countrymen chanced to die, he was envied in the same manner as in Japan would be envied one who should have obtained immortality. They studied the 'art of death' as it were the art of magic, retiring to mountain districts and secluded valleys, where they subjected themselves to all manner of ascetic privations, which, however, rarely obtained for them the desired effect. In the matter of food, all such articles as ginseng, wild potatoes, eels, wild duck, &c., which increase the action of the kidneys, and strengthen the spleen and stomach, were feared and avoided as being poisonously life-giving; whereas what people of rank and consideration highly prized and delighted in were such viands as were likely to cause the eater's death. Thus mermaids were unusually cheap and plentiful—plentiful as cuttle-fish on the coast of Idzumi—and you might see slices of them piled up on dishes, as well as whole ones hanging from the eaves of every cook-shop. But nobody who was anybody would touch with the tips of his fingers a fish so apt to poison you to life, and it was accordingly left to the lowest of the populace. The globe-fish was much esteemed, commanding a high price, and a favourite dish to set before the most honoured guests was a broth made of this fish powdered over with soot. These would not, of course, in this Land of Perennial Youth and Life, actually kill a man. But still the poison would have a certain slight effect, making him feel giddy for half-an-hour or so, and giving him sensations as pleasurable as that experienced by us Japanese after drinking rice-beer. 'Ah,' he would exclaim, ' this is what death must feel like !' and he would clap his hands and dance and sing, and believe himself to have attained the very acme of felicity. If, in trying to say something flattering about a friend's child, a caller were to remark on its apparent healthiness, both father and mother would remember his words with uneasiness ; whereas, if he should say, ' The little thing doesn't look as if it would live long,' he would give the parents the greatest pleasure, and they would reply, ' Ah, if only what you say may come true !'"

POPULAR DRAMA

The eighteenth century was the flourishing period of the Japanese popular drama. Nearly everything of note in this department of literature belongs to it. Chikamatsu, it is true, began his career somewhat earlier, but all his principal works date after 1700. Since the beginning of the nineteenth century, on the other hand, the writing of Jōruri has almost altogether ceased.

Chikamatsu was succeeded by TAKEDA IDZUMO, who wrote about the middle of the century. Most, however, of the plays commonly attributed to him were composed in collaboration with other writers, some being the work of as many as five or six authors. It seems to have been the usual practice at this time for playwrights to work together in this way. A committee having been formed, the proceedings began by the president giving out a subject. At a subsequent meeting each member offered his suggestions as to its treatment, and the work of composition went on in concert, nothing being accepted until it met with the general approval.

One of the best known works of Idzumo is a historical play of five acts, founded on the fortunes of Sugawara Michizane, a celebrated statesman of the ninth century, who was deified after his death as Temman Tenjin, and is now worshipped as the god presiding over penmanship. It is entitled *Sugawara denjiu tenarai no Kagami* or "Mirror (that is, History) of the Transmission of the Art of Calligraphy by Sugawara" (1746). The names of four authors appear on the title-page.

A still more famous drama by Idzumo and two collaborators is the *Chiushingura*[1] (1748) or "Magazine of Faithful Retainers." Chikamatsu's five-act arrangement was at this time no longer adhered to, and the *Chiushingura* is in eleven acts or scenes. It is a version of the favourite story of the forty-seven Rōnins. There are no fewer than forty or fifty plays on this subject, some of them, however, being mere adaptations of previous works.

In their general character, Idzumo's plays greatly resemble those of his predecessor. There is the same overcrowding of exciting incidents, the same mixture of comedy and tragedy, and the same desire to shock the audience with brutal murders and other enormities enacted on the stage, and to pander to their lewder tastes. But although it is heresy to say so, I confess to a preference to Idzumo over his more famous master.

---

[1] Translated into English by Mr. F. V. Dickins, under the title *Chiushingura ; or the Loyal League : a Japanese Romance.*

The improbabilities are not quite so startling, the personages are several degrees nearer to ordinary humanity, and their sentiments are somewhat less unnatural and less stilted in their expression. The poetical element is, perhaps, thinner, but that, to the European reader at least, is a doubtful disadvantage.

Idzumo died in 1756. He was followed as playwright for the Takemoto theatre by Chikamatsu Hanni, who did his best to attract audiences by startling novelties and spectacular effect. He reduced the share given to poetical narrative, and depended more on dialogue. But in his hands the Jōruri declined sensibly. The public got tired of it, the Takemoto Za went into bankruptcy, and after the end of the century this kind of drama became practically extinct.

CHAPTER VI

EIGHTEENTH CENTURY (*Continued*)

WAGAKUSHA (STUDENTS OF JAPANESE ANTIQUITY)

THE Kangakusha's extravagant admiration for everything Chinese, and their persistent and largely successful
endeavours to mould the thoughts and institutions of
Japan upon Chinese models, were followed by an inevitable reaction in favour of a more genuinely national
development. This movement, which has been fully
described by Sir E. Satow in the *Transactions of the
Asiatic Society of Japan* (1875), forms one of the most
interesting features of recent Japanese literature.

It began with the renewed study of the old literary
monuments of Japan, which for centuries had been so
much neglected that the very language in which they are
written was no longer understood. Iyeyasu's patronage
of literature, and his measures for the preservation of old
books, have been already referred to. One of his grand-
sons, the famous Mitsukuni (1622–1700), Daimio of Mito,
inherited his great ancestor's love of learning. He appropriated a considerable part of his revenue to the cost of
collecting a vast library of books of all kinds, and to the
maintenance of scholars whom he employed in the compilation of works of research. The chief outcome of
their labours was the well-known *Dai Nihonshi*, a history

of Japan in the Chinese language, which is recognised at the present day as the standard work of its class.

One of Mitsukuni's services to literature was the publication in 1678 of an anthology of masterpieces in the Wabun or pure Japanese style, under the title *Fusō-jiu-yo-shiu*, given to it by the reigning Mikado, to whom it was dedicated. It is a fine specimen of the block-printing of the time.

A priest named KEICHIU (1640–1701) was the chief pioneer of the revived study of the old literature. He was by birth a Samurai, but out of a love for learning abandoned the world for the quiet of a Buddhist monastery. His fame as a scholar reached the ears of Mitsukuni, who invited him in the most courteous manner to come to Yedo and be enrolled in his company of learned men. Keichiu declined this offer, upon which the Prince sent one of his staff to prosecute his studies under Keichiu's guidance. The latter, not to be outdone in courtesy, compiled and dedicated to Mitsukuni a treatise on the *Manyōshiu*, in twenty volumes, entitled *Manyō Daishōki*. The task of preparing a similar work had already been vainly assigned to another of the Prince's protégés, a learned but lazy Wagakusha called Shimo-kawabe Chōriu. The *Daishōki* is now superseded, but it was in its day a work of the highest importance for the study of the old Japanese. Mitsukuni evinced his satisfaction by sending the author a present of one thousand ounces of silver and thirty rolls of silk.

Another book of Keichiu's was the *Kokon Yozaishō*, which means literally " A Selection of Spare Timber, Old and New." It is a miscellaneous collection of material prepared by him in the course of his researches for the *Daishōki*, but not used in that work. He also contributed to the interpretation of the *Ise Monogatari* and the *Genji Monogatari*, and wrote a number of other erudite treatises which are still valued by scholars. Like most of the Wagakusha, he was a poet, and has left both Tanka and Naga-uta, which in metre, diction, and sentiment are little more than echoes of the *Manyōshiu*. They are adorned with the same devices of pillow and pivot words, and are in short the old wine in the old bottles. The following simple effusion is in its way not unpleasing :—

THE FIRST DAY OF SPRING

" *Bending its magic bow,*[1]
The spring hath come :
The eternal heavens,
Likewise the ore-yielding earth,
Are dim with haze ;
The snow begins to melt
On the mountain's rim,
And the ice dissolves
From the surface of the pond ;
The nightingale's tender note
Sounds (oh ! how lovely !)
From amid the first blossoms
Of the plum branch.
Now from the memory fade
Our regrets for the bygone year.
How many days must pass
Before we can go forth into the meadows
And pluck the young pot-herbs ?[2]
When will the willow
Flame into bud ?

---

[1] *Haru* in Japanese means "to bend" and also "spring." Hence this conjunction. There is no intention of personifying spring as an archer. A small bow forms part of a magician's outfit in Japan.

[2] An old custom in early spring.

When will the cherry-flowers open?
Such are the expectant thoughts
That on this day
Crowd into all men's minds."

About the same time Kitamura Kigin, a scholar employed by the Shōgun's Government, performed a useful service by editing and annotating most of the classical works of the Heian period. His editions of the *Genji Monogatari* and *Makura Zōshi* are still much esteemed by students. Kigin also wrote Tanka and Haikai.

Kada Adzuma-maro (1669–1736), the son of the guardian of a Shinto shrine, was Keichiu's successor as a student of Japanese antiquity and the old classical literature. He presented to the Government a memorial, in which he protested vigorously against the exclusive study of Chinese, and urged the establishment of a school for the cultivation of the Japanese language and literature at Kiōto. This project received the approval of the Shōgun's Government, but was never carried out. Kada was succeeded by his nephew and adopted son, Kada Arima-maro (1706–1751). Arima-maro took up his residence in Yedo, where he continued his uncle's teachings with some success.

Among the elder Kada's pupils the most distinguished was MABUCHI (1697–1769). Like his master, Mabuchi came of a family of guardians of Shinto shrines. In 1738 he removed to Yedo, where he spent the remainder of his life. He formed there a school which produced many famous men, and soon rivalled the Kangakusha in popularity and influence. Motoöri, who was one of his pupils, describes him as "the parent of the study of antiquity."

"It was he," he adds, "with whom began that style of

learning which consists in devoting oneself to the examination of the ancient language and thought with a mind wholly detached from Chinese prepossessions. Before the time of this master the study of poetry was confined to the *Kokinshiu* and later collections. The *Manyōshiu* was thought obscure and incomprehensible. Nobody dreamed of judging between the good and bad, of distinguishing the old from the more recent poems, or of mastering their language so as to use it as his own. But now, thanks to the teachings of this master, we have appropriated the ancient language. It has become possible to compose poetry in the style of the *Manyōshiu*, and even to write prose after the manner of antiquity. The men of this day fancy that this is due to their own exertions, but in reality they owe everything to Mabuchi. It is now universally acknowledged that in studying ancient books like the *Kojiki* and *Nihongi*, it is necessary to avoid being misled by Chinese notions, and having first thoroughly mastered the old language, to guide ourselves by its meaning. This is the very spirit of Mabuchi's teaching of the *Manyōshiu*."

Mabuchi was a purist in style, and aimed at the exclusion from his writings of words of Chinese derivation as far as this was possible. He has left numerous commentaries and other works of research, indispensable even now to the student of the older Japanese language. Among them may be mentioned treatises on pillow-words (*Kanjikō*), on poetry, and on prose composition, and commentaries on the *Manyōshiu*, on the Norito (*Norito Kō*), the *Genji Monogatari*, and other classical books. He was also a writer of Tanka and Naga-uta.

The greatest of the Wagakusha, and one of the most

remarkable men whom Japan has produced, was MOTO-ŌRI NORINAGA. He belonged to a family which had been originally Samurai, and was born in 1730 at Matsuzaka, in the province of Ise. There can be no doubt that the proximity of his native place to the famous shrines sacred from antiquity to the worship of the Sun Goddess and the Goddess of Food, had a considerable influence on his career. Stories are told of his youth, of his omnivorous appetite for knowledge, his precocious talent, and his boyish ambitions, which it is needless to repeat here. At the age of twenty-one he was sent to Kiōto by his widowed mother to study medicine. There he became acquainted with the works of Keichiu, which he read with avidity. In 1757 he returned to Matsuzaka and set up in practice as a physician. Soon afterwards his attention was drawn to Mabuchi's writings. In 1761 he had a personal meeting with that great scholar. This, their only interview, was followed by a long-continued and voluminous correspondence.

Motoöri's life was from this time forward a very busy one. In addition to his medical practice, which was in a flourishing condition, he was engaged in collecting material for his great commentary on the *Kojiki*, and in giving instructions to hundreds of pupils whom the fame of his learning had attracted to him. Eventually he was taken into the service of the Daimio of Kishiu, who was a great admirer of his writings. Late in life Motoöri resigned his official position and removed to Kiōto, where he gave lectures which were attended by audiences drawn from the highest classes of society in that city. He died there in 1801, in the seventy-second year of his age. By his own desire he was buried at his native place on a hill over the temple of Miōrakuji, a fir and cherry tree were planted by his grave, and a stone set up inscribed simply with his name.

Motoöri was a prolific writer. He brought out fifty-five distinct works in over one hundred and eighty volumes. His fame as a scholar and writer rests chiefly on his *Kojiki-den*, a commentary on the *Kojiki*, the sacred book of the Shinto religion.[1] Before his time the study of the *Kojiki* had been much neglected, the very language in which it is written being well-nigh unintelligible even to educated Japanese. In this monumental work, which fills no fewer than forty-four good-sized volumes, he brought to bear on the elucidation of a very difficult text a vast store of erudite knowledge, derived from a long study of the *Manyōshiu* and other books of the old literature. It occupied him for many years. Begun in 1764, it was not completed until 1796, and the final volumes were not issued from the press till long after his death.

The *Kojiki-den* is not only valuable for its prodigious learning; it was a vigorous blow aimed at the supremacy of the Chinese school of ethics and philosophy. No opportunity is lost of girding at everything Chinese, and of exalting the old Japanese customs, religion, and language, in a spirit of ardent and undiscriminating patriotism. The *Kojiki-den* had no small share in producing the reaction against Chinese ideas and institutions which has become so pronounced a characteristic of modern Japan.

The *Reki-chō Shoshi-kai-in* is an edition, with notes, of the speeches and proclamations of some of the early Mikados which have been preserved to us in a historical work entitled *Shoku Nihongi*.

Other works of Motoöri's are his edition of the *Kokin-*

---

[1] See above, p. 18.

shiu already noticed; the *Iso no Kami Shishukugen*, a treatise on poetry; the *Gio-jin Gai-gen*, an attack on the Chinese philosophy; the *Tama no Ogushi*, a valuable critical and exegetical work on the *Genji Monogatari;* the *Kenkiōjin* ("The Madman Fettered"), a controversial work written in reply to hostile criticisms of the sacred Shinto books; the *Kuzuhana*, composed in answer to a similar attack by a scholar named Ichikawa Tatsumaro; the *Uiyama bumi*, a treatise on methods of study, and the *Tama-arare* ("Hail of Pearls"), a lively and amusing critique of common errors in writing Japanese.

The *Saki-take no ben* is a refutation of various erroneous notions current with regard to the gods of Ise and their worship. The "abominable heresy" of some Kangakusha who would euhemerise the Sun Goddess into an ordinary mortal empress, and make the Takama no Hara (or Plain of High Heaven) the name of the place where her capital stood, is duly anathematised. "What doubt can there be that Amaterasu no Ohomi Kami [the Sun Goddess] is the great ancestress of the Mikados, and that she is no other than the Sun of Heaven which illumines this world? These things are in their nature infinite, not to be measured, and mysterious."

The *Tamagatsuma* (in fifteen volumes, published posthumously in 1812), may be called "Motoöri's Note-book." It is a collection of jottings of a very miscellaneous character, comprising notes on Shinto ceremonial, on the old literature, on grammar and spelling, on poetry, on ancient customs, on the iniquity of Chinese principles and institutions, &c., &c. It is a mine of instruction to all students of Japanese antiquity, but has little except perhaps a few autobiographical memoranda which will interest others.

Another miscellaneous work, the *Suzunoya no Bunshiu*, also contains some interesting personal reminiscences. I should like to transcribe from it a delicately drawn description of how the author spent a very hot day in the society of some congenial friends. It is unfortunately too long for quotation.

Before Motoöri's time there was no Japanese grammar, one or two dictionaries of the Teniwoha or particles being hardly an exception. Although he did not produce a systematic grammar of the Japanese language, Motoöri did much to throw light upon its structure. The *Tama-arare*, already referred to, contains many useful grammatical hints. In the *Moji-goye no Kana-dzukai* (1771) he enunciated the principles of the correct spelling of Japanese words, and in the *Kanji Sanonkō* (1785) he dealt with the various modes of spelling and pronouncing words of Chinese origin. His principal grammatical work, however, is the *Kotoba no Tama no wo* (1779), in which he set forth and illustrated at great length certain rules of Japanese syntax. Conciseness was not one of Motoöri's merits. The seven volumes of which this work consists have been compressed without material loss into seven pages of English. His grammatical researches were continued by his son, Haruniwa, in whose well-known work, the *Kotoba no Yachimata*, the inflexional system of the Japanese verb and adjective was for the first time formulated, and by his adopted son, Ōhira, who was the author of a treatise on causative and passive verbs. European writers on Japanese grammar owe much to the researches of Motoöri and his followers.

Carlyle's idea that the qualities which go to make a man of literary genius fit the same person for being a

statesman is a favourite one with the Japanese. We
have seen that Hakuseki and Kiusō were constantly consulted upon official matters by the Shōgun's Government.
Motoöri was invited by the Daimio of Kishiu to place
on record his views on the government of a Daimio's
domain, and did so in a little work in two volumes
entitled *Tama Kushige* ("The Precious Casket"). In this
treatise he unbends from the severe purism of his other
works, and sets an example of a simple, practical style
well suited to the subjects discussed, and level to the
meanest understanding. His position is that of a cautious
reformer. He saw that one of the greatest abuses of the
day was the excessive number of officials and retainers
of all kinds, and urged earnestly that it should be
diminished ; gradually, however, so as to avoid injury
to vested interests. The oppressed condition of the
peasantry had his warmest sympathy. He thought that
the *ikki* or agrarian risings, which had become common,
were a disgrace to the Daimios in whose jurisdiction they
occurred, rather than to the ignorant men who took part
in them. The *hara-kiri* is another subject on which he
had a strong opinion. In his view this form of suicide
had become far too common. It was not for the public
advantage, he considered, that honest and capable men
should do away with themselves because they were
responsible for some trifling official miscarriage, as was
too often the case. He was in favour of prohibiting
all *hara-kiri* without a formal order from the culprit's
superior.

It is not by writing of this kind, however, that Motoöri's
political influence is to be measured. His works helped
materially to enfranchise the Japanese nation from their
moral and intellectual servitude to China, and to produce

a spirit of self-reliance and patriotism which at a subsequent period became translated into political action.
Though he was himself loyal to the Shōgunate, he contributed indirectly, but most effectively, to the national
movement which in 1867 brought about its downfall,
and restored the descendant of the Sun Goddess to the
sovereign position which was the logical result of the
principles advocated in his works.

Motoöri's efforts on behalf of the Shinto religion produced little tangible result. It was too late to call back
the deities of the old pantheon from the Hades to which
the neglect of the nation had consigned them. In his
own lifetime nothing was done, and although a half-
hearted, perfunctory attempt to re-establish the ancient
faith was made in 1868, the efforts of its supporters
were soon relaxed. The Buddhist priests ceased to be
the guardians of the Shinto shrines, and a so-called
Shinto form of burial was introduced, but little more
was effected that was not soon afterwards allowed to
fall into abeyance. At the present day this religion is
practically extinct.

All the Wagakusha considered themselves bound to
compose poetry in the old style. Motoöri acquitted himself of this obligation more creditably than most of his
fellows. The following Tanka is much admired :—

> " If one should ask you
> What is the heart
> Of Island Yamato—
> It is the mountain cherry blossom
> Which exhales its perfume in the morning sun."

In other words, "The Japanese are instinctively and
naturally noble and virtuous—not like the Chinese, who

require a clumsy and artificial system of ethical philosophy for the cultivation of their moral natures."

Motoöri's anti-foreign and patriotic prejudices go far to explain his antipathy for the Kangakusha with their extravagant admiration for everything Chinese. But there was a deeper cause for his dislike to their philosophy. As already stated, the Chinese nation has a strong bias against the conception of the power which rules the universe as a personal being. The *Ten* (Heaven) of Confucius and Mencius, and the *Tao* (Way) of Laotze,[1] not to speak of the *Taikhi* and other metaphysical conceptions of the Sung schoolmen, all fall short of this idea. The main bent of the Japanese mind is in the same direction. But there is evidence in both countries of a contrary current of thought. Here, too, there are men born with a craving which refuses to be satisfied with abstractions in the place of a personal God (or gods) to whom they can look up as the Creator and Ruler of the universe, and as exercising a providential care over mankind. Motoöri was one of these. He professed not even to understand what the Sung schoolmen meant by their *Taikhi* and their *Yin* and *Yang*, and stoutly maintained that these were mere fictions. But whatever may be the case with philosophical notions, no man can evolve a God from his own inner consciousness. He must accept the God or gods which he finds already acknowledged, whether by his own or by other people's fathers. Motoöri's intensely patriotic temper compelled him to seek at home for the satisfaction of his inborn religious instincts. He turned naturally to Shinto. But in his time Shinto had fallen on evil days. It had suffered

[1] The late General Alexander, in his work on *Laotze*, translates *Tao* by " God." He explains his reasons for doing so in the preface.

grievously from the encroachments of Buddhism. Buddhist priests had assumed the guardianship of the great majority of the shrines of the national cult, and had adulterated its ceremonies and doctrines with much that was alien. The native gods were not abolished—they had still some hold on the popular mind ; but they were degraded to the position of temporary manifestations of Buddha. As one of Motoöri's pupils said, they were made domestics in the Buddhist household.

This state of things was a great grief to Motoöri. It drove him back from the present to the old unadulterated Shinto taught in the *Kojiki*, *Nihongi*, and *Norito*. Here he found the satisfaction to his mind and heart which he had failed to find elsewhere. Himself convinced of the excellence of the old national religion, he made it the business of his life to propagate it among his fellow-countrymen, and to denounce the abominable depravity of those who neglected it in favour of sophistical heresies imported from abroad.

Hence arose a controversy which is not without interest to ourselves as an episode in the unending conflict between science and religion. Both parties to the struggle fought under grievous difficulties. Not only could the Kangakusha offer nothing to satisfy the heart-need of a personal Deity, but they were sorely hampered by the imperfections of their philosophy, and by a belief in divination, ghosts, and spiritual beings, which they did not perceive to be inconsistent with it. Motoöri and his followers, on the other hand, were weighted by an antiquated mythology which presented many glaring absurdities even when viewed in the dim light of Chinese philosophy. The Wagakusha were also embarrassed by the absence from Shinto of anything like a code of morals. They were therefore driven either to deny the necessity of anything of the kind, or to put forward as derived from Shinto a system of ethical teaching which was really borrowed from China.

It may not be out of place here to describe in as few words as possible the old Shinto of the seventh and eighth centuries, which Motoöri aimed at restoring. It was essentially a nature-worship, upon which was grafted a cult of ancestors. It tells us nothing of a future state of rewards and punishments, and contains the merest traces of moral teaching. The *Norito*, quoted in an earlier chapter, in enumerating the offences from which the nation was purged twice a year by the Mikado or his representatives, makes no mention of any one of the sins of the decalogue. What then remains ? A mythical history of the creation of the world, and of the doings of a number of gods and goddesses, the chief of whom, namely, the Sun Goddess, was the ancestress of the human rulers of Japan, while from the subordinate deities were sprung the principal noble families who formed their court. Add to this a ceremonial comprising liturgies in honour of these deities and we have the Shinto religion.

The mythological record begins with the bare names of a number of gods who seem to have been provided merely in order to form a genealogy for Izanagi and Izanami, the male and female creator deities of Japan. The creation is thus described :—

Izanagi and Izanami, at the bidding of the other deities, took into their hands the " Jewel-spear of Heaven," and standing on the " Floating-bridge of Heaven," stirred with it the chaotic mass below. The brine which dripped from its point curdled and became an island. The divine pair descended thither and proceeded to procreate the islands of Japan. They also became the parents of a multitude of other deities, such as the Mountain Gods, the Wind God, the Goddess of Food, the Gods of the Sea, Rivers, and Moors, with many others whose attributes are obscure and whose worship is forgotten. The last god to be produced was the Fire God, in giving birth to whom Izanami died. She went to the Land of Yomi or Hades, whither Izanagi followed her, but was obliged to retreat hastily to the upper world hotly pursued by the thunder gods and the Ugly Female of Hades. In his flight he made use of various expedients to delay his pursuers, which recall similar devices in European folk-lore. After his return to earth, Izanagi bathed in the sea in order to wash away the pollutions which he had contracted during his stay in Hades, and in doing so generated various deities, among which were the Sun Goddess, produced from his left eye, and the Moon God, produced from his right eye. A third deity, named Susa no wo, was at the same time born from his nose. Izanagi conferred on these three the dominion of the Plain of Heaven, of Night, and of the Sea respectively. Susa no wo was a boisterous and rowdy deity, whose mischievous and unseemly pranks so disgusted the Sun Goddess that she hid herself in the rock-cave of heaven and left the world to darkness. The other gods had much ado to persuade her to emerge from her seclusion, inventing for the purpose dances and other expedients which are evidently meant to represent the ceremonies in use at Shinto shrines in the times of the *Kojiki* and *Nihongi*. Susa no wo was then tried by a council of gods, and sentenced to a fine, and banishment to this lower world.

A grandson of the Sun Goddess became the first ruler

of Japan. From him was descended, after a few generations, Jimmu Tennō, the first human sovereign of Japan, and the founder, according to tradition, of the present dynasty of Mikados.

There is food for reflection in the fact that it was possible for a man of high intelligence and vast learning like Motoöri, not unacquainted with the philosophy and religions of India and China, to accept these childish fables as the basis of his faith. Yet not only was he himself a sincere believer. He had a large and zealous body of followers, drawn from the highest and most enlightened classes of his fellow-countrymen. Truly it would almost seem as if, in the words of the Japanese proverb, "Iwashi no atama mo shinjin-gara," that is to say, "It is the quality of faith that is important, were its object only the head of a sardine."

The following passage from the *Tamagatsuma* will help us to define more precisely Motoöri's attitude towards the Chinese school of thinkers. It is headed

"Chinese Opinion

"In China all good and bad fortune of men, all order and disorder in the State—everything, in short, which happens in this world—is ascribed to the action of Ten (Heaven). Using such terms as the Way of Ten, the Command of Ten, and the Principle of Ten, they regard it as a thing to be honoured and feared above all. China, however, is a country where the true way generally has not been handed down. There they do not know that all things are the doing of the gods, and therefore resort rashly to such inventions. Now Heaven is nothing more than the region where the gods of Heaven dwell. It is a thing destitute of sense, and it is unreasonable to talk of its 'command' and the like. To fear and honour Ten, and not fear and honour the gods, is like yielding an idle honour and awe to the Imperial Palace, and showing no reverence or honour to its sovereign. Foreign countries, however, not having attained to the knowledge that everything is the doing of the gods, may be pardoned for believing this Doctrine of the Way of Ten or the Principle of Ten. But what is to be thought of those who, in this imperial country, where a knowledge of the true way has been handed down, do not take the trouble to examine it, but, simply accepting the erroneous doctrines of foreign lands, imagine that that which they call Ten is a thing of peerless excellence, and in all matters can talk of nothing but its principle? Take again their pedantic and wearisome *Taikhi* [the Great Limit], *Mu Ki* [the Limitless], *Yin* and *Yang* [Positive and Negative Principles of Nature], *Ch'ien* and *K'un* [Celestial and Terrestrial Principles], *Pakwa* [Eight Diagrams of the Book of Changes], and *Wu-hing* [Five Elements], which are pure inventions of the Chinese, and for which there is in reality no sound reason. What consummate folly it is for those who would interpret our sacred books to rely implicitly on principles of this kind. In recent times even those who try to divest themselves of Chinese prejudices in their interpretations fail to understand the falseness of their doctrines of the Principle of Ten, and of the Positive and Negative Powers of Nature, and do not succeed in bursting the barrier because they do not put thoroughly away from them their Chinese notions, nor resolutely rouse themselves from their deluding dreams. Moreover, the refusal of some to identify Ama-terasu no Ohomi Kami [the Sun Goddess] as the Sun of Heaven is owing to their being steeped in Chinese narrow-minded reasonings, and so become blind to the wondrous and profound principle of the true way."

Towards Buddhism his antagonism is less pronounced. He acknowledges elements of good in it, and for Laotze he confesses to a certain measure of sympathy, prompted no doubt by the circumstance that the doctrines of this philosopher are irreconcilable with the teachings of the Sung schoolmen. On the question of the immortality of the soul he formally declines to give an opinion.

Motoöri's religion is frankly anthropomorphic, as indeed it could hardly fail to be if he attached any credence to the statements in the *Kojiki*. He says in so many words that the Shinto deities had hands and legs. When pressed with the obvious inconsistencies which are involved in this belief, Motoöri has nothing better to say than they are "a proof of the authenticity of the record, for who would have gone out of his way to invent a story so ridiculous and improbable, if it were not true. [*Credo quia impossibile.*] The acts of the gods are not to be explained by ordinary principles. Man's intelligence is limited, and there are many things which transcend it."

Not the least of Motoöri's achievements was his creation of a new literary dialect. It is true that his style was more or less modelled on that of his teacher Mabuchi. But the latter was content to use the pure Japanese language, or Wabun, as it is called, just as he found it. Stiff and antiquated, it was by no means an apt instrument for the expression of modern ideas. In Motoöri's hands it became flexible, picturesque, and expressive. All foreign students have felt the charm of his lucid and flowing style. But it is marred by one terrible fault, prolixity. This is partly inseparable from Motoöri's purism, which leads him to reject many useful and thoroughly naturalised Chinese words in favour of Japanese forms of expression, however circuitous, and is partly owing to an inveterate habit which he has of repeating himself, especially when an opportunity offers of denouncing Chinese proclivities or of magnifying the merits of Shinto.

Motoöri's Wabun has had many imitators, and it has exercised a perceptible influence on some departments of the more recent Japanese literature.

CHAPTER VII

NINETEENTH CENTURY

Hirata—Kangakusha—Shingaku Sermons— Buddhist Literature

The eminent theologian Hirata Atsutane[1] (1776–1843) was born in Kubota, a town of the remote province of Dewa. His parents belonged to the Samurai class, and he traced his genealogy on the father's side through the Mikado Kwammu, up to the Sun Goddess herself. In his youth he followed the usual course of instruction in the Chinese classics, and had also made fair progress in the study of medicine, when, at the age of nineteen, he suddenly made up his mind to run away from home. He left a paper behind in which he informed his parents of this resolution, and set out for Yedo with one rio in his pocket. On arriving in the capital he applied for help neither to the officials of his province nor to private friends, but sought an upright and virtuous teacher under whose guidance he might devote himself to learning. For four or five years he lived from hand to mouth, having sometimes to resort to manual labour for a livelihood. In 1800 he was adopted by a Samurai of the Matsuyama Daimiate,

[1] For a full account of Hirata and his theology, I would again refer the reader to Sir E. Satow's "Revival of Pure Shinto," in the *Transactions of the Asiatic Society of Japan*, 1875.

and his position thus became assured. The following year he first became acquainted with Motoöri's writings. This led him to give himself up entirely to the study of Japanese antiquity.

His first published work, a criticism of a treatise by the famous Kangakusha, Dazai Shuntai, was written two years later. In 1804 he began to take pupils, and from this time forward not a year passed without some publication by him. He also practised as a physician. In 1808 he was sent on a mission to instruct certain Shinto official guardians in the principles of the old faith, and acquitted himself with credit of this duty. In 1811 he retired to Suruga, where he composed the *Seibun*, which was the most important work he had yet written. In 1822 the Abbot of Uyeno (an Imperial prince) asked for a copy of his works, and sent him a handsome present in return. This led subsequently to his visiting Kiōto, and having his work brought to the notice of the Mikado and his court. Some of his later writings gave offence to the Shōgun's Government, and in 1841 he was ordered to return to his native province and to publish nothing more. He at once started from Yedo and proceeded to Akita. The arrival of the distinguished scholar caused no little excitement in that remote place. His contemporary relations were mostly dead, but he was welcomed by numerous nephews and other younger branches of the family. The social duties thus imposed upon him, together with the demands upon his skill as a physician, soon wore out his strength. He died two years later at the age of sixty-seven.

That in view of their own interests the Shōgun's Government were perfectly right to put a stop to Hirata's career is not to be doubted. The attention drawn by his writings to the divine descent of the Mikados, and their unquestioned and unquestionable claim to be considered the *de jure* sovereigns of Japan, was tending slowly but surely to sap the authority of the *de facto* rulers. It was, however, a little late in the day for them to interfere. Nothing could undo the work of nearly forty years of assiduous propagation of his views both through the press and by *vivâ voce* lectures to his hundreds of disciples. His published works amount to several hundred volumes. It is impossible to notice more than a very few of them here.

The *Kishin Shinron* (1805), or "New Treatise on the Gods," is a characteristic specimen of Hirata's writings. He here combats the rationalistic theories of the Kangakusha by proving, or attempting to prove, that the ancient Chinese believed in a real God called Shangti or Tien,[1] who dwells in heaven, and guides the affairs of this world, but whom the Sung schoolmen endeavoured to explain away as a mere allegory, attributing all phenomena to the action of principles without life which they called *Yin* and *Yang* (Positive and Negative Principles of Nature). "But how," argues Hirata, "can there be action without life ? Certainly the existence of activity presupposes a living God from whom it proceeds."

"In this connection," Hirata goes on to say, "I will relate a story. Of late some people have introduced the learning of a country called Holland. It has found a good number of students here in Great Yedo. It may be true, as I am told, that the men of this country are fond of examining profoundly the principles of things. Among other inventions they have a machine called 'electer,' which they say is constructed by an application

[1] In Japanese *Ten.*

of the principles of thunder and lightning. I saw this machine some years ago. [Here follows a description of the electric machine and its operation.] The friend who showed it to me said, 'Thunder and lightning are caused truly by this same principle. Why, then, should we fear them? The reason why some people dread them so much is that they do not understand their principle. This is very foolish.' 'Verily,' replied I, 'this is an admirably constructed machine. Whether the actual thunder and lightning are really of the same nature is a matter on which I am unable to form an opinion. But supposing that to be the case, is not the production of lightning [the electric spark] by it dependent upon you and me and our friend, one holding one thing, another another, while the third turns a handle? Well, then, the same principle applies to the real thunder and lightning of the universe. It cannot be produced without the action of something corresponding to you and me. Moreover, this machine, made by the skill of man, is merely a small engine, entirely subject to our control, and so there is no need to fear it. But the real thunder rages among the clouds, turning them to confusion, or, leaving them, comes down to earth and indiscriminately splits trees or grinds rocks to powder. It may be thought a thing of no feeling, yet there are frequent instances in history of evil things and wicked men having been destroyed by it.'"

Mutatis mutandis, is not this precisely the position taken up by Paley in his well-known apologue of the watch?

The conversation ended in a hot discussion, in which both parties lost their tempers. Hirata saw no prospect of convincing his opponent, and returned home.

Good and evil, according to Hirata, flow from the

action of two classes of deities, each of whom has his or her own particular function. But deities are, after all, like men. None are wholly bad or wholly good. A benevolent deity, if angered, may send a curse, and an evil deity, on the other hand, may occasionally dispense blessings. Moreover, an action of the gods which is indifferent in itself may be good or bad, according to the object affected. The hot sun, which delights the cicada, scorches the worm.

The efficacy of prayer and the nature of sacrifices are next discussed.

To the question, " Is a pious Shinto believer to worship Buddha ? " Hirata replies in the affirmative. He quotes a verse of Motoöri's to the effect that " Shaka and Confucius are also Kami [gods], and their way is a branch of the way of the Kami." That this is really the case is proved, he says, by the Buddhist miracles which have been worked in Japan as in other countries. Moreover, everything which takes place in this world being ordered by the Kami, Buddhism too must be in accordance with their will. Hirata, in short, wants to turn the tables on the Buddhists, and, in revenge for their giving the Shinto deities a subordinate place in their theological system, proposes to make Buddha a sort of inferior Kami.

Hirata believed in the immortality of the soul, and takes pains to prove that Confucius did so also. " If the dead are non-existent," he argues, "what meaning can there be in the worship of ancestors, and how shall we account for the undoubted fact that dead men send curses upon those who have injured them while alive ? "

The *Koshi Seibun*, which with its dependent works the *Koshi-chō* and *Koshi-den* constitute Hirata's chief claim to a reputation for learning, was begun in 1812. It is an attempt to harmonise the myths of the *Kojiki*, *Nihongi*, and other ancient books in a continuous and consistent narrative, written in the archaic dialect of the *Kojiki*. As these old stories differ very considerably among themselves, Hirata was naturally obliged to do them violence in order to make them agree, and scholars will prefer to go to his originals rather than accept his version of them. A higher value attaches to the *Koshi-chō* (eleven volumes, 1819), in which he gives an account of the authorities for the text of the *Seibun;* but his greatest contribution to our knowledge of Japanese antiquity is the *Koshi-den*, a commentary on the *Seibun*, in twenty-eight volumes, begun in 1812, but never completed. It covers only 143 sections of the 165 of which the *Seibun* consists. The *Koshi-den* stands next after Motoöri's *Kojiki-den* as a monument of Japanese old-world learning. It is indispensable to the student of Shinto.

The *Tamadasuki* (ten volumes) was composed originally in 1811, in a colloquial style, and rewritten in the literary dialect in 1824. It is a sort of breviary containing a set of prayers addressed to the very numerous deities of Shinto, intended, however, not for temple but for individual use. The prayers are accompanied by a considerable and very heterogeneous mass of commentary.

The *Kodō Tai-i*, or "Summary of the Ancient Way" (two volumes, 1811), states the principles of the Shinto religion in easy language and in a brief and intelligible form. It is very clearly printed, and forms an excellent introduction to the study of Shinto in its native language.

Hirata also published summaries of Chinese learning,

of Buddhism, of the art of medicine (chiefly from the point of view of its divine origin), of the art of poetry, and of the vulgar Shinto, with other works far too numerous even to mention.

A professed disciple of Motoöri, Hirata was more exclusively a theologian than his master. All his works were intended either directly or indirectly to promote a belief in Shinto, which in his hands assumed a far more definite and tangible character than it had ever done before. Consciously or unconsciously, he added to it several new features, such as the doctrine of the immortality of the soul, and a moral code purloined from the stores of the detested Kangakusha. Thus he says : "Devotion to the memory of ancestors is the mainspring of all virtue. No one who discharges his duty to them will ever be disrespectful to the gods or to his living parents. Such a man will also be faithful to his prince, loyal to his friends, and kind and gentle with his wife and children. For the essence of this devotion is in truth filial piety. These truths are confirmed [!] by the books of the Chinese, who say that the 'loyal subject issues from the gate of the pious son,' and again, 'filial piety is the basis of all good actions.'"

Hirata's writings have no high value from a purely literary point of view. The native History of Literature dismisses him in a few contemptuous sentences. His literary style is more useful than elegant. It is formed on the Wabun of Motoöri ; but he is much less of a purist than his master, and does not reject useful words simply because they come from China. His style has gained thereby in vigour and conciseness, but it falls far behind that of Motoöri in distinction and charm.

A certain number of his less important works are in the

colloquial dialect. They consist of lectures taken down by his students just as they were delivered. Two little works on Buddhism, named *Godōben* and *Shutsujō Shōgo*, belong to this class. In them Hirata has undertaken the easy task of ridiculing popular Buddhism in Japan. They are racy and entertaining diatribes, but, it must be added, are disgraced by scurrilous abuse quite unworthy of the would-be founder of a new form of religion.

KANGAKUSHA

There is not much to be said of the Kangakusha who wrote in the Japanese language during the nineteenth century. Among them, ŌHASHI JUNZŌ (1816–1862) has left a certain reputation as one of the most determined opponents of the policy which led to the opening of Japan to foreign trade in 1859. His chief work, the *Heki-ja-shō-ron*, which is a violent and ignorant attack upon the moral and philosophical ideas of Europe, was written to promote this object. It was published in 1857. The character of its contents may be gathered from the headings, " Europe knows not philosophy," " Europe knows not heaven," " Europe knows not benevolence and righteousness," " Europe knows not versatile talent." He also wrote a history of the Tartar invasion of Japan, entitled *Genkō Kiriaku* (1853).

Junzō did not confine himself to attacking European learning in his writings. He took part in the anti-foreign agitation which culminated in the murder of Andō Tsushima no Kami in February 1862. He was arrested, thrown into prison, and examined under torture, but succeeded in satisfying his judges that he was not directly implicated in this crime. Exhausted by his sufferings, he died five days after his release from prison.

SHINGAKU (HEART-LEARNING) SERMONS

As Buddhism absorbed Shinto, and as Hirata, on behalf of the latter religion, proposed to admit Buddha and his saints to a humble place in the native assemblage of deities, so the Shingaku movement was an attempt to utilise both religions in the interests of Chinese philosophy and ethics. The preachers of this school professed to combine the teachings of all three faiths, and they spoke with something more than tolerance of Buddhism and Shinto ; but they were at heart rationalists, to whom much in the popular presentation of both these religions must have appeared utterly unworthy of credence. They tried, however, to smooth over matters by introducing the proviso that everything in them which is irreconcilable with reason is to be regarded as *hōben*. This *hōben* is a word of great virtue. It is quite inoffensive, and embraces everything which, though not strictly in accordance with fact, tends to edification. It is alike applicable to the parables of the Gospels, the lives of the saints, and even to the Neapolitan miracle of the liquefaction of the blood of St. Januarius. To the tolerant minds of the Shingaku preachers the use of any weapon which was likely to be useful in that struggle between the powers of light and darkness which goes on in Japan, as elsewhere, was not only permissible, but laudable, and even imperative. That it might have been taken from the armoury of the enemy was with them a very minor consideration.

Practically, the maxims of Confucius and Mencius are the sources of the Shingaku doctrines. The preachers usually take their texts from the writings of one of these two sages. They address themselves to the ignorant, and more especially to women and children, and their language is the ordinary colloquial speech of Kiōto and Ōsaka. Works of this kind are much despised in Japan by the learned, who look upon the language of ordinary life as quite unfitted for literature. These discourses, however, are not without merit ; the style is homely, but vigorous and direct, and they are admirably suited to arouse the minds of the ignorant to some sense of the cardinal truths which underlie all systems of morality.

The best are the collections entitled *Kiuō Dōwa*, *Shingaku Dōwa*, and *Teshima Dōwa*. Of these the *Kiuō Dōwa* is undoubtedly the most amusing. Indeed, it may safely be said that few more entertaining sermons are to be found anywhere. But the reader must not be squeamish. For although of unexceptionable morality, and addressed *virginibus puerisque*, the stories and illustrations with which this and others of these collections abound are frequently of a very Rabelaisian character. The *Shingaku Dōwa* is somewhat more scrupulous in this respect, and reaches a higher level in every other way except that it is unfortunately less amusing.

Three sermons from the *Kiuō Dōwa* have been translated by Mr. Mitford in his *Tales of Old Japan*. One of these, comprising the original text, notes, a romanised version, and an English translation, was published by the late J. O'Neill as a *First Japanese Book*.

The Shingaku movement received a good deal of official support and countenance, and attracted much public attention, during the first half of the nineteenth century ; but it is not surprising that it ultimately proved abortive. The attempt to reconcile three such conflicting elements as Buddhism, Shinto, and Confucianism was in reality hopeless.

The Buddhist literature of Japan forms a separate subject, which I shall not attempt to deal with. Most of it is in the Chinese language, and that part which is in Japanese is not very important as literature. It consists chiefly of lives of the Buddhist saints, and of edifying tracts and stories all addressed to the more ignorant classes, and highly seasoned with a thaumaturgic element.

CHAPTER VIII

NINETEENTH CENTURY (*Continued*)—FICTION

Romantic School — Kiōden, Tanehiko, Bakin.
Humourists—Samba, Ikku. Sentimental Novels
—Shunsui. Works in Chinese of Yedo Period

THE eighteenth-century writers of Jitsuroku-mono or
historical novels did not attempt to invent plots for themselves or to introduce imaginary personages of importance, although in minor details they allowed their fancy
free play. SANTŌ KIŌDEN (1761–1816) was the first to
give to the world the romantic novel pure and simple.
He was followed by Bakin, Tanehiko, and a host of
other writers whose existence can only be indicated. It
is quite impossible to notice them or their numerous
works more particularly.

Kiōden was a genuine Yedokko or Child of Yedo, the
Japanese term corresponding to our "Cockney." He
was born in that city in 1761, of parents of the merchant
class. His youth was unpromising. He spent much of
his time in places of ill resort, sometimes remaining away
from home for weeks together. Books were his abhorrence, and all attempts to teach him a profession were in
vain. He took lessons in painting from the well-known
artist Kitawo Shigemasa, and it is stated by Mr. W. Anderson [1] that he has left many beautiful chromoxylographs,

[1] In his *Catalogue of Japanese Pictures in the British Museum.*

but his native biographers pronounce him a failure in this respect also. In 1790 he married a woman of the harlot class. Notwithstanding what has been asserted by some English writers, such unions are regarded in Japan with marked disapproval, and his friends augured little good of Kiōden's choice. His wife, however, proved an exception to the general rule. She made an excellent house-wife, and, the chief of virtues in a Japanese married woman, was unremitting in her dutiful attentions to her father-in-law. In short, she won respect from all Kiōden's acquaintances, and was spoken of by them as " the lotus-flower which has its roots in the mud." When she died he married another woman of the same class, who also made him a good wife.

Kiōden's place of business was near the Kiōbashi (a bridge) in the street called Temmachō. Hence the name by which he is known as an author, and which is composed of the first syllables of the names of these two places. His real name was Iwase Denzō, and he had half-a-dozen other appellations at various periods of his life and in various capacities. Kiōden sold smoking apparatus, such as pipes, tobacco-pouches, and the like, while he was also the inventor and compounder of a quack medicine, to which he gave the name of Doku-shogwan, or Reading Pills, the precise operation of which I have not been able to discover. He had the reputation of a shrewd and successful man of business, and was especially noted for his quickness at mental reckoning. He seldom bought books, but was always borrowing, and made it a rule when drinking with a friend that each should pay his own share, which, as we know from " Auld Lang Syne," was also the practice of Robert Burns. This became known as the Kiōden fashion.

Kiōden's first work (1782) was an imitation, more by way of joke than anything else, of some ephemeral publications describing the manners of the brothel-quarter of Yedo. It was successful to a degree which surprised no one more than the author. His next work was equally well received. Fortunately for his fame, his career as a purveyor of pornography was put a stop to by the police authorities. Kiōden, with many others, was prosecuted under the edict promulgated in 1791 for the suppression of such publications, and was condemned to fifty days' handcuffs (in his own house). The work which brought down on him this punishment he had had the audacity to describe on the cover as an "Edifying Story-book." He wrote no more books of this kind. In one of his later prefaces he protests strenuously that his works, although fiction, would be found to inculcate the highest morality. It is quite true that they are free from coarseness or licentiousness, although their moral tendency leaves something to be desired, at least from the European point of view. Kiōden lost nothing by his reformation. The bookshops were crowded by eager purchasers of his novels. The very horse-boys and cow-herds knew his name, and his house was besieged by rival publishers clamouring for manuscript. Kiōden took advantage of his popularity to insist on definite payment for his compositions. His predecessors, we are told, received nothing for their works but an occasional invitation to supper in some place of public resort, or presents of trifling value when their books sold well.

The first work for which Kiōden bargained for payment was an early production entitled *Shōgi Kinuburui*, a *share-bon*, for which he received the munificent sum of one rio.

Kiōden's best known stories are the *Inadzuma Hiōshi* (1805), of which some account is given below, the *Honchō Suibodai* (1806), the *Udonge Monogatari* (1804), the *Sōshōki* (1813), the *Chiushin Suikoden* (1798), a version of the forty-seven Ronin legend, and the *Fukushiu Kidan Asaka no numa*. He was also the author of two works of antiquarian research which are much valued by native specialists : these are the *Kottōshiu* and the *Kinse Kikeki Kō*.

Kiōden's writings would be classed by us among "sensation" novels. Wonder, amazement, and horror are the feelings which he aims, not unsuccessfully, at exciting. His style, however, is simple and straightforward ; and although he can be graphic and picturesque upon occasion, he is not fond of that superfine writing to which some of his successors and contemporaries were so prone, and which is so exasperating to European readers.

It is possibly a mere personal bias which leads me to prefer him to his pupil, the much-vaunted Bakin. If any Japanese novel deserves to be published complete in English dress, one of Kiōden's would, I think, be found the most suitable for this purpose.

His masterpiece is perhaps the *Inadzuma Hiōshi*, one of those tales of revenge of which the Japanese popular literature contains many examples. The characters are so numerous and the plot so complicated that it is impossible to give an adequate summary of it here. Amongst the incidents related are several murders and homicides, described with much vigour and an abundance of gruesome details, a *hara-kiri* and other suicides, thefts, sales of women by their relatives, terrific combats, hairbreadth escapes, dying speeches of great length, tortures, strange meetings, and surprising recognitions. There is an excellent description of a Japanese fair, with its booths of merchandise, its lecturers, quack-doctors, fortune-tellers, and shows of wonders. There are beauteous maidens at the sight of whom the moon hides her head for shame and the flowers close, demons of smallpox and of suicide, scenes of witchcraft and enchantment, with

> " *Dreams, magic terrors, spells of mighty power,*
> *Witches and ghosts who rove at the nightly hour.*"

This is surely a sufficient stock of material with which to furnish a novel of twenty chapters and about three hundred pages.

Each chapter, as is the custom with Japanese novelists, has a sensational heading, such as " The Hovel and the Strange Stratagem," "The Danger by the Wayside Shrine," "The Guitar's Broken String," "The Witchcraft of the Venomous Rats," "The Drum of Hell."

The following is part of the opening chapter of the *Honchō Suibodai :*—

" In the reign of Go Hanazono [fifteenth century] there was a pilgrim named Shikama no Sonematsu. He had been told in his youth by a soothsayer that his physiognomy indicated a danger by the sword, so in order to avoid such a calamity he entered the way of Buddha. He had no settled residence, but wandered about visiting one province after another. At length he arrived at a place called Rokudō, in the district of Atago, in the province of Yamashiro. Darkness came on. A wide moor stretched out before him which afforded no lodging, so he resolved to spend the night there, and take shelter under a tree. This Rokudō is a place of burial on the moor of Toribe, provided for all sorts and conditions of men. Here the monuments of the dead stand in long rows, some overgrown with moss, some freshly carved.

Not a day elapses in which some one does not pass to exile here. Dew [of tears] follows upon dew, one smoke [of cremation] succeeds another without an interval. The lines—

> ' The name remains, the form has vanished,
> The bones beneath the fir-clad mound
> Are changed to ashes in the grassy mead'—

must have been said of some such place as this. An utterly wild and dismal moor it was, the deep grass drenched with dew, and here and there a bleached bone showing among it. A weird, uncanny spot indeed, fit to inspire such sentiments as those of the poet, who says—

> ' He is gone to his long home,
> And we who now return
> Will one day follow him
> On the rugged path
> That leads to Hades.
> While in such gloomy thoughts immersed,
> The moon glimmering through the smoke [of cremation]
> Seems like a crag of the Eagle's Mount.' [1]

" Well, then, our pilgrim Sonematsu, brushing away the dew from the moss below an ancient fir-tree, put down his portable shrine. It was the season of the festival of the dead, so by way of a fire to light their path from Hades [the dead are supposed to revisit the earth at this time], he gathered some leaves and kindled them, the dew upon them standing for the offering of water. Then turning to the Buddha of the shrine which he carried with him, and striking his bell, he recited the prayer for the dead. Whilst he was thus deep in his devotions, the

[1] A mountain in India where Buddha preached—put for the other world.

moon was shedding a full flood of crystal light, and the lespedeza, the *Platycodon grandiflorum*, the *Anthesteria barbata*, the valerian, the pampas grass [or something like it], the *Dolichos bulbosus*, and such-like flowers[1] were blossoming luxuriantly and heavy with dew. The shrill notes of various insects piping with all their might, mingled with the chanting of the prayers and the sound of the bell, produced a sense of loneliness and desolation. There was borne on the wind the boom of a bell struck in some temple away on the moor, which by the number of its strokes indicated that the night was already far spent. His fire, too, had gone out, so the pilgrim thought to himself, ' I must snatch a short sleep.' He hung up a tent of oil-paper, and spreading on the grass his rain coat to keep off the dew of night, with a tree-root for his pillow he laid himself down. He was soon plunged in deep slumber, forgetful alike of past and future. But after awhile he woke, and pricking up his ears, ' Was that an insect's cry ? No ! it was a faint, far-off sound of music.' The pilgrim wondered how on this desolate moor, at this late hour of the night, such beautiful music could be heard. Was it not an enchantment by some fox, badger, or wild cat ? Presently he raised up his tent, and putting out his head, looked round. The weather had changed, and a night mist had gathered thickly, obscuring the moon. Even nigh at hand nothing could be seen. But the music came closer and closer."

The mist clears away, the moon again shines out, and a splendid palace is seen, which Kiōden describes with great wealth of language. It proves to be inhabited by the spirits of a wicked lady of noble birth and her equally wicked retainers, who use the brief respite

[1] Such are some of the difficulties of a translator from the Japanese.

granted them from the tortures of hell to plot further mischief against their former enemies in this life.

One of the few Japanese authors whose fame has penetrated to Europe is KIOKUTEI BAKIN (1767–1848). In his own country he has no rival. Nine out of ten Japanese if asked to name their greatest novelist would reply immediately " Bakin."

He was born in Yedo, and was the youngest of three sons of a retainer of an official of the Shōgun's Government, named Matsudaira Shinsei. When only eight, Bakin was appointed to attend upon the son of his lord, who was a boy like himself. At the age of thirteen, unable any longer to endure the tyranny of his young master, he ran away from home. His elder brother procured him several other situations, but he had not the patience to remain in any of them. He was also apprenticed to a physician, and became the pupil of a Kanga-kusha or Chinese scholar, but completed his studies with neither. At this period of his life he was for a short time a public fortune-teller at Kanagawa, close to the treaty port of Yokohama ; but having lost all he possessed by a flood, he returned to Yedo. Here he made the acquaintance of the novelist Kiōden, who received him into his house and showed him great kindness. It was while residing with Kiōden that Bakin produced his first novel (1791). Kiōden admired it so much that he exclaimed, " In twenty or thirty years I shall be forgotten." In the title-page of this work Bakin describes himself as Kiōden's pupil. It is not creditable to him that at the height of his fame he tried to destroy all traces of this fact, and with this object bought up as many copies of his early publication as he could find.

Through Kiōden's influence, Bakin obtained a position

as a bookseller's assistant, in which situation he remained three years. A novel which he wrote at this
period, and which was illustrated by Hokusai, was very
successful.

Bakin was a tall, well-built man. One day the manager
of a company of wrestlers came into the bookseller's
shop. He greatly admired Bakin's stature (over six feet),
and said, "Join us, my boy, and I promise you a reputation which will extend everywhere within the four seas."
Bakin laughed, but vouchsafed no answer. The old
Samurai pride still clung to him. The uncle of his em-
ployer, who kept a tea-house, supported by the custom of
an adjoining brothel, proposed to Bakin that he should
marry his daughter, a girl of considerable personal attractions. Bakin refused disdainfully to become connected
with a family which drew its income from this source.
Brothel-keeping, he said, was no better than begging or
thieving, and he must decline to disgrace the body he had
received from his parents by such a marriage. He left the
bookseller in order to marry the daughter of the widow
of a dealer in shoes in Iida-machi, becoming his mother-
in-law's adopted son and heir, as is the Japanese custom.
He was too fond of the pen and ink-slab, however, to
be a good business man, and as soon as his daughter
reached a marriageable age he provided her with a husband, to whom he handed over the shoe business. He
himself went to live with his son, who now held the
position of physician-in-ordinary to the Daimio of Mat-
sumaye. Bakin not only contributed to the household
resources by keeping a school, but earned a considerable income from the novels which he produced in
rapid succession. At the age of seventy he became
almost blind, but he still continued his labours, his

widowed daughter-in-law acting as his amanuensis. He died at the age of eighty-one, after a career as an author of more than sixty years. The amount of saleable "copy" produced by Bakin can have few equals in literary annals. His pen was never at rest, and the rapidity with which he composed may be inferred from the circumstance related by himself, that one of his novels (of about two hundred pages) was completed by him in a fortnight, "to stay the demands of an importunate publisher." He is said to have written no fewer than two hundred and ninety distinct works, many of which were extremely voluminous. Some authorities put the figure still higher.

Bakin was not an amiable man. He is described as upright, but obstinate and unsociable. A single word which offended him made of him an enemy for life. Even Kiōden, to whom he owed so much, could not get on with him. The famous artist Hokusai, who illustrated many of his novels,[1] had also reason to complain of his morose and intractable temper. Edmond de Goncourt, in his life of Hokusai, says that the quarrel between the painter and Bakin occurred in 1808, and was caused by the immense success of the illustrations to the *Nanka no Yume*, of which Bakin was jealous. It was smoothed over by friends, but broke out again with great violence in 1811, when a continuation of that novel was brought out. Bakin accused Hokusai of paying no attention to his text, and demanded that the drawings should be altered. But the publishers had already engraved both text and pictures.

It was in consequence of Bakin's recriminations on

[1] See Mr. W. Anderson's *Catalogue of Japanese Pictures in the British Museum*, p. 357.

this occasion that Hokusai turned his attention to publishing volumes of pictures without text.

It is impossible to notice more than a few of Bakin's publications. The early years of the century were a time of great literary activity with him. In 1805 he published the *Yumibari-tsuki* ("The Bow-bend or New Moon"), which is thought by some to be his masterpiece. It professes to be an imitation of the Chinese romantic histories, but departs far more widely from historical truth, and is indeed a romance pure and simple, though a few of the personages have names taken from real history.

The hero of this story is one Hachirō Tametomo, a famous archer of the twelfth century, whose adventures and exploits fill over eight hundred pages of the modern closely printed edition. For intelligence and valour he had no peer. His stature was seven feet. He had the eyes of a rhinoceros, and the arms of a monkey. In strength he had no equal, and was skilled in drawing the nine-foot bow. Nature seemed to have destined him for an archer, for his left arm was four inches longer than his right. His eyes had each two pupils.

Tametomo on one occasion was allowed to attend a lecture given before the Mikado by a scholar named Shinsei. The conversation afterwards turned on the great archers of ancient and modern times. Tametomo, at this time a boy of twelve, broke in with the following speech :—

"'It is useless to discuss the superiority of this one or that, for among archers of the present day I do not think there are any who excel Tametomo in repulsing myriads of stalwart foes.' Shinsei, on hearing this, was so taken aback that for a while he made no answer. Then bursting suddenly into a boisterous laugh, he said, 'An art requires months and years of hewing and polishing before it reaches perfection. Even if you had practised since your baby-hood, you are little over ten years of age. Bethink your-self. Men are not wooden figures. If you try to shoot them, they will try to shoot you. Those who are skilled in shooting should also learn to ward off the shafts. Are you prepared to catch the arrows shot at you?' Tame-tomo, without waiting for him to finish his speech, replied, 'Hoi, in his eighth year, acted as general for the Chinese Emperor Shun; Duke Yeki, in his fifth year, had the direction of fire. Wisdom and folly, skill, and the want of it, are not to be reckoned by years. Be pleased to summon archers the most nimble-handed. Even though it were the arrows endued with understand-ing of the goddess Kwannon, I will show you how easily I shall catch them.' Shinsei, who from the first had intended to give him a sharp lesson, at the unflinching attitude of Tametomo became highly exasperated. Pro-bably thinking it an opportunity for making a display of his own influence, he stood up abruptly and called out, 'Who are in attendance? Let them bring bows and arrows.' 'Your will shall be obeyed,' was the answer. Two of the Imperial Guards, named Norishige and Nori-kazu, now advanced with bows and arrows to the foot of the stairs [leading from the courtyard up to the hall where the Mikado held his court]. Shinsei, turning to them, explained the circumstances, and told them to have a shot at this youngster.

"Now, these two guards were originally soldiers of the Emperor Shirakawa, and skilled archers. When Gotoba no In came to the throne they were enlisted in the Imperial Guards. Once the Mikado gave them a target of $3\frac{1}{2}$ feet in diameter, telling them to shoot away its centre. The order was given at the hour of the Serpent [ten o'clock], and the target was returned without its centre at the hour of the Rat [two o'clock]. 'Yōyu himself could do no better,' exclaimed everybody in admiration. These men were now advanced in years, but their vigour had not failed. Even my Lord Yorinaga thought that Tametomo, had he six arms, could never escape the arrows of such archers. He could no longer bear to look on, and, turning to Shinsei, said, 'Tametomo, though he has a grown-up appearance, is still, so to speak, a yellow-mouthed boy. Even a joke should have some relation to the person it is practised on. This conduct is most unlike Shinsei.' Then turning to Tameyoshi [the boy's father], he advised him to retire at once and take his son with him. Tameyoshi, who up till now had remained silent, replied with deep respect, 'Tametomo is only twelve, but he is no longer a baby. If he does not stand the test on this occasion, I would call it worse than to turn his back on the enemy. I could bear the loss of one son without regret. What I should hate would be to disgrace the soldier-fame of the house of Gen, established for many generations. I earnestly beseech your Lordship to grant your permission, and allow the matter to proceed as Shinsei wishes.'

"Yorinaga offered no further opposition. Tametomo was delighted, and addressed Shinsei as follows : 'Norishige and Norikazu are peerless bowmen. To be a target for their shafts is an inappreciable boon. But if I fail to seize their arrows my life will end in a moment. I am therefore placing it in your hands. What will you give me if I succeed in catching their arrows ?' Shinsei smiled. 'If you succeed, this head of mine shall be your recompense. Shinsei belongs to the Gate of Buddha, and should you now be slain, he will not continue his revenge after your death.' Tametomo paid no attention to this taunt, but rushed down into the larger courtyard and stood up at the distance of a bowshot. . . . The two archers took two arrows each, and stood over against him. Not only the sovereign but all present wrung their hands till they perspired, expecting every moment to see Tametomo's life fade faster than the clear dew beneath the sunbeams. Norishige fitted an arrow to his bow, and drawing it till it bent into a full moon, let fly with an accompanying shout. With his right hand Tametomo caught the arrow in the nick of time, while with his left he stopped the shaft which Norikazu the next moment shot at him just as it flew close to his heart. 'A miss!' exclaimed the two archers, disappointed. 'We don't want to kill him, but this time he won't catch our arrows.' They drew their bows together, and watching a proper moment, let fly with a whiz. One arrow Tametomo stayed by entangling it in the sleeve of his garment; but as he had no other means of catching the second, he seized it firmly between his teeth, and at once crunched its head to atoms. All this was done with a rapidity which may be compared to the flickering air dancing over the hot ground, or to the lightning's flash. To all the spectators it seemed more than human. They felt as if intoxicated. It was beyond all praise, and no one said a word. Tametomo flung aside the arrows to right and left. 'Now, your Reverence, you will be so good as to give me your head,' he cried, and springing up the stairs, was about to take hold of Shinsei, when his father, Tameyoshi, interfered."

Tametomo has to leave Kiōto for political reasons. He

goes down to Kiushiu, where he has a number of surprising adventures. He becomes possessed of a wonderful crane, and an equally remarkable tame wolf. A strange hunter, who has neither bow nor shafts, but who brings down his prey by stones flung with marvellous precision to an incredible distance, attaches himself to his service. With him he proceeds to Loochoo, where, among other adventures, he falls over a cliff "several thousand feet" to the bottom. He is a little stunned, but walks home afterwards as if nothing had happened. He subsequently goes to Hachijō and other islands off the Bay of Yedo, and then again to Loochoo, where the principal events of the story take place.

Bakin's *Seiyuki*, or "Journey to the West" (1806), is not an original work, but an adaptation of the well-known Chinese romance *Siyuki*, in which a Buddhist ecclesiastic, attended by a magician-monkey and a semi-human hog, goes to India from China in order to procure Buddhist scriptures. It is full of supernatural occurrences from beginning to end,[1] and is wholly lacking in human interest.

He also translated the *Shui-hsü-ch'uan* (*Sui-ko-den* in Japanese), a much more amusing Chinese story, which fills over two thousand pages of small print in the modern Japanese edition. The influence of these and other Chinese romances is very noticeable in the works of Bakin and his school.

The *Nanka no Yume* (1807) is a story of fairyland in the Chinese manner.

The *Shichiya no Kura* ("Pawnbroker's Store"), 1810.—

---

[1] An episode of this story has been dramatised in Japan. A version of this in the Ingoldsby legend style is given in M'Clatchie's *Japanese Plays Versified*.

In this work a pawnbroker lying awake at night hears a noise in his storehouse. He peeps in and sees the pledges deposited there assembled in conclave. Each tells its story.

The *Musōbiōye Koshō Monogatari*[1] is an allegorical novel in which the hero visits the Land of Childhood, the Land of Lust, the Land of Drunkenness, the Land of Avarice, the Village of Lies, the Village of Sinful Desires, the Village of Grief, and the Village of Pleasure. The idea is borrowed from the older work *Wasōbiōye*, noticed in a previous chapter. It is very learned, intensely moral, and insufferably tedious. The same criticism will apply to the *Shichiya no Kura*.

The most famous of Japanese novels is the enormous work entitled *Hakkenden*. Begun in 1814, it was not finished until 1841. In its original form it consisted of one hundred and six volumes, and even in the modern reprint it forms four thick volumes of nearly three thousand pages.

The *Hakkenden* ("Story of the Eight Dogs") narrates the adventures and exploits of eight heroes of semi-canine parentage, who represent the eight cardinal virtues. After a perusal of some hundreds of pages of this work I can only express my amazement at its extraordinary popularity in Japan. It is full of physical and moral impossibilities, and, worse still, is often pedantic and wearisome. Yet it was greedily bought up by the public. The wood-engravers came daily for copy, and as soon as a part was ready it was printed off in an

---

[1] This work has been translated into English by L. Mordwin (Yokohama, 1881). An English version of Bakin's *Kuma no tayema amayo no tsuki*, by Edward Greey, was published in Boston in 1886. A French translation of his *Okoma* appeared in Paris in 1883.

edition of ten thousand copies, creating a demand for paper which, we are told, appreciably affected the market-price of that commodity.

In addition to his novels, Bakin wrote a miscellany entitled *Yenseki Zasshi*, which gives interesting information on such subjects as folk-lore and popular superstitions. His *Gendo Hōgen* is another work of a somewhat similar character. He also wrote an account of a journey to Kiōto in 1802, which was published long after his death.

Bakin's writings have some obvious merits. They prove, sometimes only too conclusively, that he was a man of great learning, intimately acquainted with the history, religion, literature, and folk-lore both of China and Japan. His style is usually flowing, perspicuous, and elegant, and he possesses a command of the resources of his own tongue unique among his contemporaries. His language is a happy medium between the purism of such writers as Motoöri and the semi-Chinese jargon of the later Kangakusha. It is honourable to him that at a time when pornography was the rule rather than the exception with writers of fiction, his writings are free from all indecency of language, and are invariably moral in their tendency. They alone were excluded from the sweeping prohibitive measure directed against light literature by the Shōgun's Government in 1842.

Perhaps the quality which most strikes European readers of Bakin's novels is his prodigious fertility of invention. The number and variety of surprising incidents with which they are crowded can have few parallels. On the other hand, his faults are as glaring as his merits are conspicuous. For the profusion of incidents with which he crowds his pages, he has recourse to his memory as well as to his invention, and, what is worse, he constantly overleaps the bounds of possibility to an extent which tries the patience of the most indulgent reader. The *deus ex machinâ*, in the shape of a ghost, demon, or supernaturally gifted animal, is in far too frequent requisition. His moral ideals are of the common conventional type of his day and country, the product of the teachings of China grafted on a Japanese stock. His power of delineating character is extremely limited, and reminds us very much of the portrait-painting of Japanese pictorial art. He has little or no humour, and his wit is mainly of the verbal kind. The sentiment of love is dealt with by him in a way which is to us very unsatisfactory. While he can describe the mischief produced by unlawful passion, and wifely fidelity and devotion are his frequent themes, such things as the gradual growth of the sentiment in man or woman, the ennobling influence of a pure love, and all the more delicate shades of feeling are wholly neglected by him. The pathos which native admirers find in his works fails to move his European readers, although they are not insensible to the same quality in other Japanese authors. In short, human nature as depicted by Bakin is far too sophisticated to appeal to our sympathies. He shows us men and women as they might be if constructed on principles derived from the Chinese sages and their Japanese expositors, and goes for his material to books rather than to real life. It is characteristic of him, that unlike many of the dramatists and novelists of his time, he avoids the common speech for his dialogue, and confines himself entirely to the more stilted literary language.

Bakin's style, which is his strong point, is occasionally disfigured by lapses into fine writing adorned with pivot-words[1] and other artifices of Japanese rhetoric irritating to all plain-minded people. Nor can he always resist the temptation of bestowing on his readers tedious displays of his erudition, or of introducing foreign or obsolete words not understood of the people.

It may be a question whether the rhythmical character of much that Bakin has written is a merit or a defect. It results from the more or less regular alternation of five and seven syllable phrases so often referred to, and produces much the same effect as the blank verse to which some English novelists are addicted. Bakin borrowed it from the popular dramatists of the preceding century ; but while it is obviously in its proper place on the stage, where the words are chanted to a musical accompaniment, it seems a more doubtful kind of ornament in an ordinary romance. Japanese critics have an unqualified admiration for this feature of Bakin's works, and suggest that it entitles the *Hakkenden* to be classed among epic poems.

---

[1] The more frivolous of my readers will perhaps pardon the following attempt to give an example of the sort of thing which we might have if the pivot style were adopted in English. It illustrates the mode in which Japanese novelists and dramatists frequently slur over the transition from one scene to another by a use of this device ; something on the same principle as their artists introduce a golden mist between different parts of the landscape in order to disguise defects of perspective.

" The sun went down, and the welcome, the thrice-wished for, the most fair, the best beloved night/knight sought a well-earned repose. On the morrow he rose from his couch at dawn/don ned his armour and sallied forth in quest of fresh adventuresome as was his bold spirit, his courage was now to be put to a testy old fool/full of meat as an egg-shaped domes, slender minarets, and square-built towers rose in picturesque confusion from the summit of a hill where dwelt," &c., &c.

It may be thought that the above is too low an estimate of a writer whose enormous popularity with all classes of his own countrymen is unquestionable. I therefore append the judgment of the authors of the only native History of Japanese Literature. It will enable the reader to correct any injustice which may have been done by the barbarous Western critic.

" Bakin was a man of immense erudition. His flow of ideas was profuse. When he took up his pen, a thousand words were quickly formed, long chapters fell from his hand. He, nevertheless, from time to time, used deep thought and mature reflection, giving profound attention to plot and construction. His pen darted hither and thither, following his thoughts wherever they went, accompanying his sentiments wherever they turned themselves. In describing men and events, his style changed with the change of subject. Many there have been in ancient and modern times who gave their attention to style, each of whom has his own particular merits. Some excel in depicting scenes of grief and affliction, some of gladness and jollity, while others possess unrivalled gifts of indignant or satirical language. But how many are there who, like Bakin, can build on so vast a scale, and include within their scope the billows of mankind with all their varied capacities and qualities ? How many possess the styles fitted for this purpose wherein are seen ever and anon magical things which far transcend our comprehension ? In short, Bakin comprises in himself the best points of many men. We see in him numerous resemblances to Shakespeare. It is not only women and children, tradespeople and peasants, who admire him. Even educated gentlemen are frequently moved to tears or laughter, or made to gnash their teeth and strain their arms [with rage] by his writings."

That there is some truth in this I am not concerned to deny. I nevertheless venture the prediction that when the Japanese people have more completely shaken off, as they are doing every year, the Chinese influences which have moulded their character and formed their tastes for centuries, Bakin's heroes and heroines will appear to them as grotesque and unreal as they do to us. His works will then be relegated to the same limbo which contains the romances of chivalry so dear to Europe before Cervantes, and be regarded merely as a document of a passing phase of the national development.

The best known of Bakin's contemporaries is RIUTEI TANEHIKO (1783–1842), a Samurai of the Tokugawa house, from which he received an annual allowance of two hundred bales of rice. Like Kiōden, he was in early life an artist. He also practised Haikai writing with some degree of success. As a writer of fiction he is best known for his romantic novels ; but he also published stories in dramatic form (*shōhonjidate*), meant only for reading, and not for the stage. Another kind of novel, of which he wrote a few volumes, was the *ninjōbon* or "sentiment book," which will be noticed presently. He was also the author of several works which are of a useful character, but have no pretensions to be regarded as literature.

Among his novels may be mentioned the *Awa no Naruto* (1807), the *Asamagatake Omokage Zōshi* (1808), and its continuation the *Shujaku Monogatari* (1812). The plot of the last two works is taken from an old play, and the scene is in the fourteenth century.

Tanehiko's principal work, the *Inaka Genji*, "A Rustic Genji" (in ninety volumes), is an imitation of the *Genji Monogatari*, the well-known romance of the Heian period. It was a great success, and other authors, by choosing titles which included the word Genji, endeavoured to persuade the public that their works were of a similar character. In 1842 the Shōgun's Government took measures to suppress publications of an immoral tendency. The *Inaka Genji* was considered objectionable on this score, and Tanehiko received a private intimation that he had better give up writing novels. He was only too glad to escape so cheaply, as any official condemnation would have entailed the loss of his allowance from the Government.

I have not had access to this work. It is much admired by native critics for its style and sentiment; and the illustrations, to which Tanehiko attached great importance, set an example to which was due a marked improvement in Japanese wood-engraving.

Tanehiko's *shōhonjidate* or dramatic stories differ chiefly from ordinary Japanese novels by the preponderance of dialogue over narrative, and by the choice of the ordinary spoken language for the speeches of the characters. They are also more realistic, and vary less violently from actual living manners, than the romantic novel.

The great defect of his books is their want of human interest. Like Kiōden, Bakin, and the other novelists of the romantic school, Tanehiko accepts implicitly the conventional standards of honour and morality, and deviates little from the types of character which were the common property of the writers of his day. Indeed he carries unreal sentiment and artificial rules of conduct to a more fantastic extreme than either of his rivals. Human nature is travestied by him in such a manner as to be no longer recognisable. How can one take any interest in a heroine of fifteen years of age who sets out to travel through Japan in quest of her father's murderer with the intention of making love to him and thus finding an opportunity for putting him to death ? Or in the murderer himself, who is a magician with the power of making himself invisible, but who finds no better use for such a gift than to rob unsuspecting travellers ? In another work of Tanehiko's the hero submits patiently to be insulted and beaten in the presence of his inamorata by her temporary owner, and then indemnifies himself by waylaying his enemy in a lonely spot with the intention of assassinating him. It is true that the author tries to save his credit a little by making him, in the first place, discharge his money obligations to his intended victim.

It is to be regretted that Tanehiko's writings should be marred by so vital a defect. They contain many interesting glimpses of manners and customs in a state of society which has now passed away, and his style, when not too ornate, is graceful and pleasing.

SHIKITEI SAMBA (1775–1822) — his numerous aliases may be omitted—was a native of Yedo. He belonged to the trading class, and in his boyhood was apprenticed to a bookseller. He subsequently opened a book-shop on his own account. His first work was written in 1794, when he was in his nineteenth year. In 1799 he was reported to the authorities by some person who objected to the immoral tendency of his writings. His parents and relatives, alarmed on his account, urged him to give up authorship, but he refused to do so. He was a prolific writer. Among his numerous publications he is now remembered chiefly by two—the *Ukiyo-furo* and the *Ukiyo-toko*. The *Ukiyo-furo* was first published in 1809; but the blocks having been burnt, a second enlarged edition was brought out in 1811. The name of this work means "The World's Bath-house." It consists of a series of realistic sketches of everyday life, something in the manner of Mr. Anstey's *Voces Populi*, a certain unity being given to them by assigning the dialogues to the frequenters of a public bath-house—an institution well known in Japan as a centre of gossip for the neighbourhood. In the preface Samba protests that he writes in the interests of morality. "In bringing up children," he says, "we give them bitter pills and sweet malt-extract. The Chinese classics resemble the pills, while novels and stories correspond to the sweet stuff. Both convey instruction, though in different ways." The edifying character of the *Ukiyo-furo* is not very obvious to a casual observer, but it is undeniably amusing. Some Japanese critics rank it even before the *Hizakurige*. If any one cares to know what subjects are discussed by Japanese of the middle and lower classes when they meet, he will find ample means of gratifying his curiosity in this work. Here is a conversation between two matrons at the bath-house :—

Mrs. A. Well! I have tried lots of servants, but I find that instead of their serving you, it is you who have to serve them.

Mrs. B. Really? But I thought the maid who was with you till last year was such an amiable girl.

Mrs. A. Yes, and she was bound over to me for a long term ; but as she had a good offer, I married her off and let her go.

Mrs. B. That was very nice of you.

Mrs. A. The one I have now has such a temper that I don't know what to do. If I reprove her she gets into a rage and smashes everything, and if I humour her it makes her so conceited. The worst of it is that when I lie down to sleep I cannot get that face of hers out of my mind.

Mrs. B. Our hussy Rin is just as bad. She is always putting herself forward, and talking when she is not wanted. So she gets the place to herself, and as soon as she has cleared away the breakfast things she goes upstairs and spends half the day doing her hair. Then, until I tell her to get dinner ready, she is always going out, as she says, to hang out the washing, but really for gossip. There is not a day that she does not excite herself about matters of course, crying and laughing over them, but grudging to take pains with her needful work. She will take up a pail, and with "I am going to fetch water, ma'am," off she goes to the well, and does not get back for a couple of hours. No wonder! When she is not making a fool of herself with all the young men in the row, she joins girls like herself in abusing the masters and mistresses. The other day I wondered what they were talking about, so I slipped behind the outhouse, and there she was praising her last master, &c., &c.

The *Ukiyo-toko* ("The World's Barber's Shop") is of a similar character. Other works of Samba are the *Kokon Hiakunin Baka* ("One Hundred Fools Ancient and Modern") and *Shijiuhachi Kuse* ("The Forty-eight Humours").

His works had a great popularity and have been often imitated.

JIPPENSHA IKKU (——?–1831) was the son of a petty official of Suruga. His early life was very unsettled. We hear of his holding small appointments in Yedo and Ōsaka, and his name appears with those of two others on the title-page of a play written for an Ōsaka theatre. He was three times married. On the first two occasions he was received into families as *irimuko*, that is, son-in-law and heir. In Japan such situations are notoriously precarious and unsatisfactory. "Don't become an *iri-muko*," says the proverb, "if you possess one *go* of rice." Ikku did not remain long with either of these wives. Very likely his parents-in-law objected to his Bohemian habits and dismissed him. In his third marriage he was careful not to sacrifice his freedom. Ikku's biographers relate many stories of his eccentricities. Once when on a visit to a wealthy citizen of Yedo he took a great fancy to a bath-tub. His host presented it to him, and Ikku thereupon insisted on carrying it home through the streets, inverted over his head, confounding with his ready wit the passengers who objected to his blindly driving against them.

One New Year's Day a publisher came to pay him the usual visit of ceremony. Ikku received him with great courtesy, and prevailed on him, somewhat to his bewilderment, to have a bath. No sooner had his guest retired for this purpose than Ikku walked off to make his own calls in the too confiding publisher's ceremonial costume, Ikku not being possessed of one of his own. On his return, some hours later, he was profuse in his thanks, but said not a word of apology.

When he was engaged in composition he squatted on the floor in a room where books, pens, inkstone, dinner-tray, pillow, and bedding lay about in confusion, not an inch of free space being left. Into this disorderly sanctum no servant was ever admitted.

Ikku's ready money went too often to pay for drink, and his house lacked even the scanty furniture which is considered necessary in Japan. He therefore hung his walls with pictures of the missing articles. On festival days he satisfied the requirements of custom, and propitiated the gods by offerings of the same unsubstantial kind.

On his deathbed he left instructions that his body should not be washed, but cremated just as it was, and enjoined on his pupils to place along with it certain closed packets which he entrusted to them. The funeral prayers having been read, the torch was applied, when presently, to the astonishment of his sorrowing friends and pupils, a series of explosions took place, and a display of shooting stars issued from the corpse. The precious packets contained fireworks.

Ikku's first work, exclusive of the dramatic piece above mentioned, was published in 1796 at Yedo, where he had then been settled for six or seven years. Others followed, but it is useless to enumerate them, as their fame has been eclipsed by that of the *Hizakurige*, the great work with which Ikku's name is always associated.

The *Hizakurige* was published in twelve parts, the first of which appeared in 1802, the last not until 1822. It occupies a somewhat similar position in Japan to that of the *Pickwick Papers* in this country, and is beyond question the most humorous and entertaining book in the Japanese language. *Hizakurige* means "knee-chestnut-horse," the Japanese equivalent for our "shank's mare." It is the history of the travels, mostly on foot, as the title indicates, of two worthies named Yajirōbei and Kidahachi along the Tōkaidō and other great highways of Japan, and of their manifold adventures and mishaps. Yajirōbei, Yajirō, or Yaji, as he is indifferently called, is an elderly man of the shopkeeper class, whom some Japanese insist on identifying with Ikku himself. There are points of resemblance, but this, like most such identifications, is in reality fallacious. Indeed there is a passage in the fifth part of the *Hizakurige* which seems intended as a repudiation of the suggestion. Yaji is here repre-

sented as involved in cruel embarrassments by an attempt
to impose himself on some provincial virtuosos as the
renowned poet and novelist Jippensha Ikku. Ikku says
elsewhere that Yaji was intended as a *tada no oyaji* or
" ordinary elderly man." But in truth he is neither
Jippensha Ikku nor yet a *tada no oyaji*. He and his
younger companion belong to that class who having
never lived can never die. They are humble but not
unworthy members of the illustrious fraternity which
includes Falstaff, Sancho Panza, Sam Weller, and Tar-
tarin—to us far more real personages than any originals
which may have supplied hints for them.

Yaji and Kida are by no means heroes. They are
cowardly, superstitious, and impudent. Lies, " gross as
a mountain, open, palpable," fall from their lips on the
smallest provocation or in mere wantonness. Yaji has
a certain share of good sense and *bonhomie* which goes
some way to redeem his character, but Kida is a fool
positive whose idiotic sallies and ill-advised amorous
schemes are continually entangling him in scrapes from
which it requires all the wit and *savoir faire* of his elder
companion to extricate him. Nor is Yaji, from a moral
point of view, much better. Both are, in sooth, shame-
less wights, whose moral principles are on a par with
those of Falstaff or Sir Harry Wildairs, and for whose
indecency of speech and conduct even Rabelais hardly
affords an adequate comparison. The most that can be
said for them is that their grossness is the grossness of
the natural uncultured man, and not the *con amore* con-
centrated filth which revolts us in some European authors,
and that with two continents and a wide gulf of social
and racial differences intervening, their indecency some-
how creates less disgust than if they were Englishmen

or Frenchmen. Still, people of nice taste had better not read the *Hizakurige*.

It is hopeless by translation to give any idea of the copious flow of rollicking humour which pervades every page of this really wonderful book. Those who have read it will not forget the scene in a roadside inn where some terrapins laid on a shelf overnight come out when Yaji, Kida, and their party are all sound asleep, and insinuate themselves among the bedding; or Kida's misadventure at the river ford with the two blind men who had agreed that one should carry the other over on his back. Yaji cleverly substitutes himself, and so crosses over dryshod. But Kida, in endeavouring to follow his example, is detected, and shot off in mid-stream. Then there is the scene in which a strolling medium (a young woman) delivers to Yaji a terrific but untranslatable message from his deceased wife, who adds a climax to his fright by proposing to come and pay him occasional friendly visits; and one where Yaji, fancying that Kida is a fox which has taken the shape of his friend, belabours him soundly to make him resume his natural vulpine form. Another amusing scene is one in which the owner of the pack-horse which Kida is riding, meets a man to whom the animal had been assigned as security for a debt. The creditor threatens to foreclose then and there. As the negotiations between the two sway backward and forward, Kida is made alternately to mount and dismount, until at last the situation is cleared by the horse bolting with debtor and creditor in hot pursuit, while Kida is left bruised and shaken on the ground where he had fallen.

The great drawback to the fun of the *Hizakurige* is that it is unrelieved by more serious matter. Doubtless

Bottom the weaver and Falstaff would still be amusing even if they stood by themselves, but they gain immeasurably by contrast with the poetry of fairy-land and the stately court of Theseus in the one case, and with grave political surroundings on the other. In the *Hizakurige* there is no suggestion of serious thought or feeling ; all is broad, frequently even farcical humour. It is, however, excellent fooling of its kind.

There can be no greater contrast than that between Ikku and the romantic school of novelists. He repudiates utterly their entire equipment of fantastic notions of right and wrong, artificial sentiment, supernatural interventions, impossible exploits, and euphuistic fine-writing. He is a realistic writer in the good as well as in the bad sense of the word. The *Hizakurige* is a picture of real life, for every detail of which Ikku has drawn on his own observation. We know that he actually travelled through the places which are the scenes of his heroes' exploits ; but even if there were no record of the fact, it is obvious to every reader who knows Japan. There is little word-painting or description of scenery, but the human life of the great highways is depicted with photographic accuracy, and with a verve and humour which no mere observation, however minute, could ever impart. We see the Daimio's train, slow-moving, silent, and imposing—but nevertheless containing a rowdy element—and hear Yaji and Kida's very free criticisms as they squat humbly by the roadside until the great man has passed. The religious processions, noisy and disorderly, are treated by them with more open ridicule. We meet provincial Samurai, the butt of the more quick-witted citizens of Yedo, obsequious innkeepers, facile waiting-maids, begging priests, Rōnins, Komusō (criminals

of the Samurai class who have been permitted to become
priests, and who lead a wandering life with their faces
wholly concealed under immense basket-hats), pilgrims
(who nowadays travel by excursion trains with tickets
available for two months from date of issue), boy pilgrims
to the shrines of Ise with all the precocious shrewdness
of a gamin or a street arab, Tome-onna or female touts
who beset the highway near their master's inn at sundown and wheedle or hustle the traveller into it, coolies
with their degraded dialect (all Ikku's personages use the
language and speak the dialect proper to them), thieves,
jugglers rustics, ferrymen, horse-boys, and many more.
Most of these have disappeared for ever, but they still
live in Ikku's pages to delight many a future generation
of readers.

It has been said that there are no terms of vulgar abuse
in the Japanese language. The compliments exchanged
by the coolies and pack-horse men in the *Hizakurige* are
a sufficient answer to this rash assertion. There is more
truth in the statement that profane language is unknown
in Japan. A European Yaji and Kida would certainly
have been as richly supplied with terms of this kind as
Ernulphus or our armies in Flanders, but the only oath
uttered by the heroes of the *Hizakurige* is the very mild
Namu San or *Namu Sambō*, that is to say, by the three
holy things, namely, Buddha, the Law, and the Priesthood. Paradoxical though it may appear, this is probably owing to the want of any very deep-seated
sentiment of piety in the Japanese nation. Their language is equally deficient in such phrases as "God
bless you," "Thank God," and "Adieu."

The Ninjōbon

All students of Japanese literature are familiar with the Ninjōbon or Sentiment Book, a species of novel which flourished most in the third and fourth decades of the nineteenth century. It was at last prohibited by the Government, like its predecessor and model the Share-bon.

The best known writer of this class of story was TAMENAGA SHUNSUI, who also called himself (after 1829) Kiokuntei. He was a pupil of Samba. Shunsui was a bookseller of Yedo. He began his literary career with some tales of an unedifying character, which he styled *Fujo Kwanzen no Tame* ("For the Encouragement of Women in the Paths of Virtue"). He died in 1842 whilst undergoing a sentence of confinement to his own house in handcuffs for publishing works of a tendency prejudicial to public morals. The blocks from which they were printed were at the same time destroyed. Even his admirers cannot say that Shunsui's punishment was altogether unmerited.

One of Shunsui's best known stories is the *Mume Koyomi* ("Plum Calendar"), with its continuation entitled *Shunshoku Tatsumi no Sono* ("Spring - Colour Eastern-Garden"), which appeared in 1833. It is a novel of low life, and the characters are singing-girls, harlots, Rōnins, professional jesters, and the like. Its morality cannot be defended, but in decency of language it is superior to the *Hizakurige*, and even to the *Ukiyo-furo*.

The *Iroha Bunko*, which is considered Shunsui's greatest work, is not a typical Ninjōbon, though from some points

of view it belongs to this class of literature. It is one of
the numerous versions of the story of the revenge of the
forty-seven Rōnins. Few worse arranged books have
ever been written. The scenes of which it is composed
have no sort of order, chronological or otherwise, and in
many cases have no obvious connection with the main
action of the book. Shunsui, in writing it, seems to have
had two objects in view, irreconcilable with each other.
One was to produce a historical narrative (he describes
it as a true record) enriched by matter drawn from
genuine documents ; the other to enhance the interest
of the story by the addition of imaginative details. As
a contribution to historical research the *Iroha Bunko*
is worthless. It is not always possible to distinguish
Shunsui the historian from Shunsui the romancist ; and
in order to comply with the edict forbidding novelists to
meddle with real personages of the Yedo period, he was
obliged to garble his materials, transferring the scene of
the story from Yedo to Kamakura, and from the eighteenth to the fourteenth century, and altering the names
of the characters. In this he was only following the
example of the *Chiushingura*, the famous drama which
deals with the same subject. The judicious reader will
skip his historical disquisitions, nor care, for example, to
follow him in discussing the question of the precise date
when shops for the sale of buckwheat vermicelli were
first established as separate institutions. He will turn
from such *muda-banashi* (vain talk), as Shunsui himself
calls it, to the scenes where he abandons his facts, and
endeavours by the help of a sympathetic imagination
to realise the feelings and emotions of the actors in the
tragedy, filling in their surroundings, supplying them
with parents, wives, sweethearts, or children, inventing

romantic incidents and passionate speeches, and, in short, converting them from vaguely outlined personages of history into real men and women.

The great service rendered by Shunsui and his fellow-composers of Ninjōbon was to recall the attention of writers and readers of fiction to human nature as the proper subject of the novelist's art. Since the time of Murasaki no Shikibu this branch of study had been sadly neglected in Japan. The novelists of the romantic school were too much occupied with sensational situations, hairbreadth escapes, and supernatural wonders, to study the human heart with its affections and passions; while Ikku and Samba, though excellent in their way, were humourists and nothing more.

The Ninjōbon, it is true, do not show us human nature at its best. The society into which they introduce the reader is far from select, and the morality sadly defective. But the vital element of fiction is there. We find in these works real human beings depicted in such a way that we can follow their fortunes with interest, and sympathise with them in their joys and sorrows.

The dialogue of the Ninjōbon is in the ordinary colloquial language of Yedo, the narrative portion in the written style.

Amongst other Ninjōbon may be mentioned the *Tsuge no Ogushi* (1834), by Jippensha Ikku the younger; *Imose-dori* (n. d.), by Tamenaga Shunga, a pupil of Shunsui; *Musume Setsuyō* (1831) and *Musume Taiheiki* (1837), by Kiokusanjin; and *Temari Sannin Musume*, by Shōtei Kinsui.

During the remainder of the Yedo period Japanese fiction presents no feature of special interest. A good many novels were produced in the several styles described above, but there was no new departure and no writer of conspicuous merit.

Works in the Chinese Language

During the Yedo period the Chinese language held a position in Japan similar to that of Latin in Europe during the Middle Ages. It was the vehicle of all literature of a serious kind, and more especially of history. Japanese scholars attained to great skill in composition in the literary dialect of the Han dynasty, a period which may be taken as corresponding for China to the Augustan era in Rome.

One of the chief historical works of this kind was the *Dainihonshi*, a history of Japan from the accession of the first Mikado, Jimmu Tennō, B.C. 660, to the abdication of Go Komatsu in A.D. 1413, which, with its numerous addenda, extends to one hundred volumes. It was written by a number of scholars engaged for that purpose by Mitsukuni, Prince of Mito, and was completed about 1715, although not printed until 1851. The *Dainihonshi* is much admired for its concise and elegant style.

The *Nihon Gwaishi*, which was brought out by Rai Sanyo in 1837, is probably the best known work of its class in Japan. It relates the history of the Shōgunate from its beginnings in the twelfth century down to the establishment of the Tokugawa dynasty of Shōguns under Iyeyasu in the beginning of the seventeenth century. Both this and the last-named work are invaluable for the study of Japanese history; but they present few attractions to ordinary European readers, who will heartily concur in the unflattering estimate of the *Gwaishi* contained in Mr. Chamberlain's *Things Japanese*.

Another important work by Rai Sanyo is the *Nihon Seiki*, a history of Japan in sixteen volumes.

Towards the end of the Yedo period there was a great falling off in the literary use of the Chinese language in Japan. At the present day it is employed only for a few special purposes similar to those for which Latin is still resorted to in Europe.

BOOK THE SEVENTH

TOKIO PERIOD (1867–1898)

BOOK THE SEVENTH

TOKIO[1] PERIOD (1867–1898)

SOME RECENT DEVELOPMENTS UNDER EUROPEAN INFLUENCE

THE first half of the present century was a time of profound peace in Japan, during which the feudal system, established by Tokugawa Iyeyasu, was in appearance as flourishing and efficient as ever; but indications were not altogether wanting that it was already tending to its downfall. The condition of the peasantry had become very unsatisfactory. They were grievously taxed and oppressed by the Daimios, who competed with one another in pomp and magnificence, and to this end maintained large numbers of sinecure officials and idle retainers. The military organisation was wholly effete, as some collisions with British and Russian men-of-war early in the century proved very clearly. The nation had become tired of over-government. The Shōguns, for want of general support, were obliged to relax their control over the Daimios, the more powerful of whom began to assert their independence in a way which was fatal to the maintenance of the old feudal government.

[1] The name of the capital was changed from Yedo to Tokio in 1869, when the Mikado took up his residence there.

The opening of Japan to foreign commerce in 1859 precipitated the inevitable struggle between the decrepit Shōgunate and its recalcitrant vassals. It resulted in 1867 in the complete downfall of the former, and the establishment of a new political organisation, presided over by the Mikado, and supported by the chief advisers of the Daimios who had been instrumental in restoring him to his rightful position in the State, so long usurped by the Shōguns.

These men, who combined political wisdom with ardent patriotism in no ordinary degree, built up on the ruins of the Shōgunate the new system of government which Japan now enjoys. It is the most highly centralised and efficient that the country has ever known, and has raised it to an unparalleled height of power and prosperity, liberty and enlightenment.

A very large share in this result was due to the influence of Western ideas. With the fall of the Shōgunate the moral, religious, and political principles on which it was based became more or less discredited, and the nation turned to Europe for guidance. The great political change which had taken place produced no immediate results so far as the literature was concerned. The reorganisation of the constitution, the reform of the laws, the formation of an army and navy, the construction of roads, railways, lighthouses, and telegraphs, and the establishment of a national system of education had first to be attended to. But the visible superiority of Europe in all such matters led to the study of European, and especially English books as sources of practical knowledge.

Before 1867, Dutch, which was studied by interpreters, and as a means of acquiring a knowledge of Western medicine, was the only European language known to the Japanese. About this time the nation was seized with a passion for more extensive European learning. In spite of many difficulties, numbers of young men of good family made their way to Europe or America for study, or were not ashamed to take service in the households of foreign residents in Japan in order to have an opportunity of learning English, even a slight knowledge of which was a sure passport to official positions and emoluments. The school of foreign languages in Tokio received substantial Government support, and flourished greatly. Presently a group of writers came forward who did their best by translations and original works to meet the general demand for information as to the learning, customs, laws, and institutions of Europe. Of these, Fukuzawa, with his *Seiyō Jijō* ("Condition of Western Countries"), was the most distinguished. Nakamura's translations of Smiles' *Self-Help* and Mill's *Liberty* also deserve mention. Kant and Herbert Spencer followed somewhat later. Their writings frequently supply texts for the Japanese able editor, instead of the works of the formerly venerated Confucius and Mencius.

Another sign of the renewed avidity for knowledge was the rise of a newspaper press and of a magazine literature. The first newspaper in Japan deserving of the name was published in Tokio by a Scotchman named Black about 1872. At the end of 1894 there were in existence, in spite of a rigorous censorship, no fewer than 814 different newspapers and magazines, with a total circulation of 367,755 copies.

With the exception of translations and works designed to make Europe known to the Japanese, the literature showed few signs of foreign influence until about 1879, when translations of European novels began to make their appearance. The first of these was Lord Lytton's *Ernest Maltravers*. It produced a profound sensation, and was followed during the next few years by a number of others.[1] A pronounced reaction against the methods and principles of the Bakin school of fiction was the consequence. TSUBOÜCHI YŪZŌ was the principal promoter of the new movement. In a work entitled *Shōsetsu Shinzui* ("Spirit of Fiction") he denounced the artificial morality of Bakin's writings. More recently he became editor of a literary magazine called *Waseda Bungaku*, the organ of the newer school of criticism, which derives its principles and standards entirely from European sources. In his *Shosei Katagi* ("Types of Students"), 1887, Tsuboüchi has given an example of a realistic novel. It is well written, and contains some graphic and humorous sketches of modern student life viewed from the seamy side, but has little plot, portraiture of character, or dramatic incident. Tsuboüchi has also tried his hand at drama. I have not seen his *Julius Cæsar*, which Dr. Florenz describes as a version of Shakespeare's drama thrown into the form of Jōruri, that is, with a thread of poetical narrative and description woven into it ; but I have before me two others of his plays, the *Maki no Kata* (1897), and the *Kiku to Kiri* (1898).

The *Maki no Kata* is in the Kyakubon style, that is, it depends almost wholly on dialogue. The small element

---

[1] Among European writers of fiction whose works have been translated into Japanese may be mentioned Dumas (*Trois Mousquetaires*), Cervantes, Rider Haggard, and Jules Verne. *Télémaque* and *Robinson Crusoe* (commended for its excellent moral teaching) have also been translated.

of Jōruri which it contains is limited to one of the seven acts of which this play is composed which seemed to demand a more poetical treatment. It is one of a trilogy which deals with the history of the Hōjō regents. The time is the beginning of the thirteenth century, and the subject the crimes and intrigues into which Maki no Kata, the wife of the Regent, was led by her ambitions on behalf of a favourite son. The *Maki no Kata* is decidedly melodramatic. There are several murders and bloody combats, and two *hara-kiri* by women. But there are also some really forcible scenes, and although no supreme height of excellence is anywhere attained, there is careful workmanship and a gratifying freedom from the extravagances of the earlier school of Japanese dramatists. Of pivot-words and such-like rhetorical devices there are the merest traces. Most writers of the Tokio period show a marked tendency to dispense with these contrivances.

The specialty of SUDŌ NANSUI is the political novel. This author belongs to the progressive party in politics and social science, and his pages bristle with allusions to "things European." He quotes glibly, "To be or not to be, that is a question" (*sic*), and talks familiarly of Shakespeare, Dumas, Gladstone, and O'Connell. The extent and variety of his reading may be inferred from an airy reference in one of his prefaces to Lytton, Bakin, Scott, Tanehiko, Hugo, Shunsui, Dickens, and Ikku.

The Ladies of New Style (1887) is a good example of his works. It is a novel of the future, when Tokio shall have become a great port, with all the appliances of an advanced civilisation, such as wharves, docks, tramways, and smoking factory chimneys. The heroine, whose charms are depicted with a profuse expenditure of ornate diction, is a dairymaid. Let not the reader suppose that this occupation is meant to suggest pastoral simplicity. On the contrary, it indicates to the Japanese public that the lady is in the forefront of the progressive movement. Formerly cow's milk was not used as food in Japan, and when this novel appeared none but a truly enlightened person would dare to affront the old-fashioned prejudices against it. This dairymaid's favourite reading is Herbert Spencer's treatise on education. She is a member of a ladies' club where croquet and lawn-tennis are played and women's rights discussed. Other characters are—an adherent of Arabi Pasha, who, after his leader's defeat by the "great warrior General Wolseley," was banished from Egypt and took service with a Japanese gentleman ; a Chinese cook, who is naturally assigned the rôle of a subordinate villain, and a number of politicians of the Conservative and Liberal parties. Among the incidents we have a balloon ascent, a contested election, and a dynamite explosion, which is prevented from doing harm by the sagacity of a dog of European breed. All this, it will be observed, indicates a high degree of civilisation.

In the last chapter the dairymaid is married to the advanced politician, who, on the auspicious occasion, wears a clean standing-up collar and a white silk necktie, with white gloves, and a small white orange blossom in the left button-hole of his coat.

The Ladies of New Style has really considerable merit. There is plenty of incident and a coherent plot, and the writer can not only quote Herbert Spencer and Mill, but, what is more to the purpose, has an excellent command of his own language, more especially of the

Chinese element in it, which is so prominent at the present time.

The Local Self Government (Sudō affects English titles) is a work of a similar character.

YAMADA TAKETARŌ, a contemporary of Tsuboüchi's, is the principal champion of an attempt to substitute the modern colloquial grammar for the grammatical forms and rules of the traditional literary dialect. He has produced a number of novels and stories written on this principle, which, if universally adopted, would save the Japanese nation the trouble of mastering a second grammar for purposes of reading and writing, in addition to that of their ordinary speech. His *Natsu Kodachi* ("Summer Trees") is a series of short stories which bear numerous traces of the author's studies of European literature. One is a Japanese version of the story of *Appius and Virginia*, and another a pastoral idyll obviously suggested by a European model. Yamada's later writings I have not seen. Dr. Florenz describes them as "cleverly written, the characters well and naturally drawn." This is high praise to give a Japanese novelist.

YENCHŌ, a blind story-teller of Tokio, also composes in the colloquial style. Indeed his novels are first delivered in a spoken form, and are taken down in writing by his pupils. Their language is simple and easy, and they may be recommended to any European who is beginning the study of Japanese. Some of his plots are said to be taken from the French.

One of the most popular and voluminous novelists of the present day is OZAKI TOKUTARŌ (KŌYŌSAN). In his earlier works, which I have not seen, he made great use of the pivot style, but his *Tajō-takon* (1897) is written in the colloquial language. An acquaintance with English is evinced by the short sentences, the copious use of personal pronouns, and the frequent introduction of words which, although composed of Chinese elements, can only be fully understood when we have recognised the English word which they are intended to represent. Such English-Chinese-Japanese words are by no means peculiar to Ozaki. They now form a considerable part of the vocabulary of newspaper and magazine writers. Ozaki frequently gives the impression of having thought in English, and then presented his readers with a literal translation into Japanese. He is said to be an admirer of M. Zola.

The *Tajō-takon* ("Much Feeling, Much Hate") is a study of sentiment. It opens with the lachrymose lamentations of a disconsolate widower. At the eightieth page the hero is still plaguing his friends and exhausting the reader's patience with a maudlin grief, which must be even more obnoxious to Japanese feeling than to our own. One weary reader left him at this point, wiping his streaming eyes with a borrowed pocket-handkerchief, and complaining that he had now nobody to wash his own dirty ones for him.

One of the most considerable literary figures of the present day is KŌDA NARIYUKI (pseudonym, Rohan). He writes in the ordinary literary dialect, using the colloquial speech only for the dialogue, and in some of his writings not even for that. He has imagination, lofty aims, and a fine flow of language, never descending to vulgarity, and rising frequently to poetical descriptions of a high order of merit. But the action of his stories moves slowly, and the speeches of his personages are terribly lengthy. His *Hige-otoko* (1897) is a historical

novel of the civil wars which preceded the establishment
of the Tokugawa Shōgunate.

The general impression left by a very imperfect examination of the drama and fiction of the last twenty years is
on the whole favourable. The moral standards are less
artificial, there are fewer offences against good taste and
decency, and there is a prevailing sobriety of tone and
an avoidance of the glaring improbabilities of every
kind which abound in the writings of such authors as
Chikamatsu and Bakin. We no longer meet with such
monstrously long drawn-out stories as the *Hakkenden*.
Comparatively much shorter than its predecessor, the
recent novel shows more signs of conscientious care in
its composition.

The social position of Japanese writers of fiction has
of late been completely revolutionised. In the Yedo
period they were Bohemians or *hommes déclassés*, who
were in constant trouble with the police, and were classed,
along with actors, among the lowest of the people. Now
they are respectable members of society ; some of them,
like Tsuboüchi, being graduates of the Imperial University. Notwithstanding the low prices at which their
works are issued,[1] a popular novelist now commands a
fair income from his works. Yano Fumiō, out of the
proceeds of the sale of his *Keikoku Bidan* (a novel of
Theban life, with Epaminondas for the hero), was able
to treat himself to a tour in Europe, and to build a fine
house with the balance.

The art of writing history has not made much progress in recent years. Modern methods of investiga-

[1] The *Tajōtakon*, of five hundred pages, with illustrations, is published at
about 1s. 6d. of our money.

tion and principles of historical criticism are known and accepted; but a great sifting of the existing heterogeneous material must be done before history, as we understand it, can be written. Nobody has yet made any serious attempt to distinguish the true from the false in the old Japanese annals, though it is pretty generally acknowledged that this process is indispensable. Philosophical history is still in its infancy. The numerous historical works which have appeared during the last twenty years are chiefly uncritical epitomes of Japanese, Corean, Chinese, and European history, and simple *mémoires pour servir.* Shimada Saburo's *Kaikoku Shimatsu* (1888) is one of the most important of the latter class. It is a collection of material bearing on the opening of Japan to foreign trade in 1859.

The *Shōrai no Nihon* ("Japan of the Future"), by Tokutomi Iichiro, is an attempt to forecast the future of Japan by an examination of its past history. Mr. W. Dening describes it as "more philosophical in conception than most preceding publications of its class, and surpassed by none of them in point of style. This work, in the space of two years, ran through five editions, and competent Japanese critics pronounce it to be one of the most remarkable books of the age. The writer is a Christian."

Among other works of a serious kind may be mentioned Marquis Ito's *Commentary on the Constitution*, and a treatise by Ono Adzusa on the same subject. Mr. Dening gives high praise to Nose Yei's *Kyōikugaku*, a work on education. The author's aim is to adapt Western principles and ideas to the local requirements of Japan, and in this he has, according to Mr. Dening, achieved a high degree of success.

It can hardly be maintained that the Japanese nation has up to the present time produced much poetry of striking merit. The Naga-uta of the *Manyōshiu*, notwithstanding its limited resources and confined scope, gave a promise which was not destined to be fulfilled, and the tiny Tanka which succeeded it in popular favour was precluded by its very form from being a vehicle for the utterance of any but the merest atoms of poetical thought or sentiment. Again, the poetical element to be found in the Nō and Jōruri drama is so disfigured by ornament of questionable taste, and so imperfectly freed from prosaic dross, that we can only allow it a very modest place in the history of the art. Its importance lies rather in its keeping alive the national taste for imaginative writing than in any intrinsic merit which it possesses.

The conditions of the present day are more favourable than those of any previous time to the production of good poetry in Japan. The ordinary language, by the more thorough assimilation of its Chinese element, has gained considerably in fitness for poetical purposes, and its phonetic capabilities are now appreciably greater than in the time of the *Manyōshiu*. Still more important considerations are the great stimulus which the national life has received from the introduction of European ideas, and the attention which has been recently directed to the poetry of Europe, especially of England.

The credit of being the first to recognise the advantages which the Japanese poet might derive from a study of European models belongs to TOYAMA MASAKAZU, a Professor of the Imperial University, Yatabe Riōkichi and Inouye Tetsujiro, whose joint publication, entitled

Shintaishishō [1] or " Poetry of New Form " (1882), marks an epoch in the history of poetry in Japan. It is a bold attempt to revolutionise the art. The writers ignore the Tanka altogether, and set an example of a kind of Naga-uta adapted to modern conditions. The old principle of the alternation of phrases of five and seven syllables is re-tained, the seven-syllable phrases, however, being usually put first. A decided improvement is the division into verses or stanzas of equal length. But it is chiefly in the language employed that the new style is distinguished from the old. Toyama and his colleagues, finding the ancient classical language unequal to the expression of the new ideas, and largely unintelligible to a modern public, frankly adopted the ordinary written language of the day, which had hitherto been only used for popular poetry of the humblest pretensions. In their choice of themes, in the length of their poems, and in the general tone of thought, the influence of European models is plainly traceable.

Some experiments in rhymed verse by poets of the new school confirm the opinion already expressed of the unsuitableness of the Japanese language for this form of poetical ornament.

The *Shintaishishō* contains nineteen poems of no great length. Of these only five are original, the remainder being translations from English poets. Bloomfield is represented by "The Soldier's Return," Campbell by "The Mariners of England," and Tennyson by "The Charge of the Light Brigade," of which two versions are given. The same compliment is paid to Gray's

[1] Dr. Florenz, Professor of Philology in the Imperial University of Tokio, has given an interesting account of this movement in a paper contributed to the German Asiatic Society of Tokio, March 1892.

" Elegy " and Longfellow's " Psalm of Life." Shake-speare is represented by four extracts, and Charles Kingsley by his "Three Fishers."

The original poems include verses written before the colossal image of Buddha at Kamakura, an ode to the four seasons, and a war-song. Neither the original poems nor the translations have striking merit in themselves, but they attracted a large measure of public attention, and gave rise to a lively controversy between the adherents of the old and new styles. They also produced a school of imitators, among whom the novelist Yamada was one of the most eminent.

More recently (1891) Toyama, the chief originator of the movement, brought out a poem on the great earth-quake of 1855, which has not only considerable merit in itself, but occupies a unique position in Japanese litera-ture as a descriptive poem of some length.

Dr. Florenz, writing in 1892, says that 1888 may be taken as the culminating point of the favour shown to the new style of poetry. A reaction then set in, which, however, was of short duration. The last two or three years have produced a considerable quantity of verse more or less in the new form, of which all that can now be said is that, on a hasty examination, it reveals some promising features. Regularity of form is more carefully attended to—a great desideratum in the longer kinds of Japanese poetry.

The day of Tanka and Haikai seems to have passed. These miniature forms of poetry are now the exception and not the rule.

The following specimen, which may be taken as characteristic of the vague and dreamy style of most recent Japanese poetry, is translated from a little volume of prose and verse by three authors, entitled *Hana Momiji*, or "Flower and Autumn Leaves" (1898) :—

THE BAMBOO FLUTE BY THE SHORE

I

" *In the shade of the firs of the craggy cliff,*
    To-night again a bamboo flute is heard :
Is it some fisher-boy, solacing his heart
From the woes of a world bitter with salt and seaweed ?

Moonlight or dark, he little cares,
    Night after night he visits these fir-trees' shade.
In the music of his bamboo flute
There may be heard cadences which tell of yearning love.

A day had passed since the courtiers of the lord of the land
Held night-long revel here, wandering forth upon the beach,
    While the bark of the autumn moon
    Pursued its crystal course ;
When the fisher's flute was for the first time heard.

A day had passed since the ladies of our lord,
Mooring their gay pleasure-boat, held revel here,
    Attuning the music of their golden lutes
To the song of the breeze through the fir-trees on the cliffs ;
When the fisher's flute was for the first time heard.

II

On nights when the dew lay heavy on the reeds of the chilly shore,
And the wind of the firs came in gusts down from the crags,
He never failed to come—this fisher-boy :
His bamboo flute was heard in clear-sounding notes.

On nights when the rattling of the hail was loud,
And the ripples on the beach were changed to ice,
He never failed to come—this fisher-boy :
His bamboo flute was heard in subdued tones.

On nights when evening fell, wild with mountain blasts,
And the sand was whirled up into the air,
He never failed to come—this fisher-boy :
His bamboo flute was heard in confused notes.

On nights of rain, when darkness came down with a sound of
*   moaning waves,*
And the rocks were steeped in moisture,
He never failed to come—this fisher-boy :
His bamboo flute was heard, languid and faint.

III

To-night the autumn moon has changed,
So long his yearning love has endured.
Still his bamboo flute is heard,
Its tune and measure ever more entrancing.

With the storm from the cliff it was troubled,
With the echoes from the fir-trees it became clear,
With the surges from the deep it was frenzied,
With the waves on the rocks it became choked.

Even the clouds over Onoye [1] paused to listen
To its notes, now calling clearly, and now with strangled utterance.
What wonder then that some one descends from the bower above,
And comes forth absorbed in reverie !

For awhile the flute ceased its importunities ;
But hark ! louder than before
The music of the bamboo bursts forth, making the sky resound,
And in accord with it, how sweet !
Are heard the notes of a golden lute.

Sometime the wide-spreading clouds descending from Onoye
Bore away with them the musicians of the fragrant rocks below,
Up to that region where the bark of the moon,
With altered helm, steered straight to meet them."

—SHIWOI UKŌ.

[1] The mention of this place shows that the scene is the same as that of Takasago. See above, p. 207.

Thirty years is far too short a time for the seed sown at the Revolution of 1867 to grow up and ripen literary fruit. We have seen that the intellectual movement to which Iyeyasu's establishment of the Yedo Shōgunate led, did not reach its climax until a century later. No doubt things move more rapidly in the present day, but it seems reasonable to believe that what we now witness is only the beginning of a new and important development.

The process of absorbing new ideas which has mainly occupied the Japanese nation during the last thirty years, is incomplete in one very important particular. Although much in European thought which is inseparable from Christianity has been freely adopted by Japan, the Christian religion itself has made comparatively little progress. The writings of the Kamakura and two subsequent periods are penetrated with Buddhism, and those of the Yedo age with moral and religious ideas derived from China. Christianity has still to put its stamp on the literature of the Tokio period.

There are some considerations which tend to show that important results in this direction may be expected during the century which is nearly approaching us. The previous religious history of the nation has prepared Japan for the acceptance of a higher form of faith. Buddhism did not a little towards fostering ideals of holiness, humanity, and detachment from worldly things. Confucianism provided high, though it may be somewhat distorted, standards of morality, and a comparatively rational system of philosophy. Shinto taught a reverence for the Divine powers which created and govern the universe and man. But none of the three sufficed by itself to meet the heart, soul, and mind want of the Japanese nation. Can it be imagined that when a religion is presented to them which alone is adapted to satisfy far more completely all the cravings of their higher nature, the Japanese, with their eminently receptive minds, will fail in time to recognise its immense superiority?[1] They have already accepted European philosophy and science. It is simply inconceivable that the Christian religion should not follow. Probably, as was the case with Buddhism, it will not be received without some modification. Their previous history suggests that this may take the direction of a more rationalistic form of Christian belief than that which prevails in Europe. Ἀλλ' ἤτοι μὲν ταῦτα θεῶν ἐν γούνασι κεῖται. The historian of the Japanese literature of the future will have more to say on this subject.

---

[1] There are even now 113,000 native Christians in Japan.

BIBLIOGRAPHICAL NOTE

IN regard to bibliography, the writer of the present volume of this series finds himself in a very different position from his predecessors. He has no *embarras de richesses* to contend with. The only survey of the whole field of Japanese literature which has hitherto appeared in any European language is an article by Sir E. Satow, in vol. ix. pp. 551–565 of *Appleton's American Cyclopædia* (New York, 1874), excellent as far as it goes, but owing to the brevity inseparable from such a form of publication, more fitted to excite than to satisfy the reader's curiosity. It will be found useful by any one who wishes to extend his knowledge of the subject, as it mentions a large number of Japanese books which have been entirely passed over in the preceding pages.

Mr. B. H. Chamberlain's *Classical Poetry of the Japanese* (1880) contains translations into English verse of a number of poems from the *Manyōshiu* and *Kokinshiu*, with selections from the *Nō* and *Kiōgen*, and an appendix of very short biographical notices of the more ancient Japanese poets. There is a similar work in French by M. Léon de Rosny.

Some interesting glimpses of the popular literature and folk-lore of the Yedo period are given in Mr. A. B. Mitford's *Tales of Old Japan* (1871).

Mr. William Anderson's *Catalogue of Japanese and Chinese Pictures in the British Museum* (1886) deals with the literature of Japan viewed as a source of supply of subjects for the artist.

The *Transactions of the Asiatic Society of Japan* contain a number of translations and notices of Japanese books, by Sir E. Satow, Mr. B. H. Chamberlain, and others; and Dr. K. Florenz's contributions to the *Journal of the German Asiatic Society of Japan* should also be mentioned.

In addition to the above, there exists in various European languages a considerable mass of translations from the Japanese, published either separately or in magazines and journals of learned societies, of which it may be said—

"*Sunt bona, sunt quædam mediocria, sunt mala plura.*"

The more important have been indicated in the body of this work, and it is believed that little inconvenience will be caused by the omission of all reference to the remainder. Those who wish to prosecute their researches further in this direction will find the means of doing so in Mr. Fr. von Wenckstern's comprehensive and useful, though not particularly accurate, *Bibliography of the Japanese Empire* (1895). A *Catalogue of Japanese Books and Manuscripts in the British Museum*, by Mr. R. K. Douglas, is also useful for reference.

The contributions of the Japanese themselves to the materials for a history of their literature are naturally much more important than anything which has been written by Europeans. The labours of Mabuchi and his greater pupil Motoöri have been already noticed, and good work has been done by a multitude of native editors and commentators towards clearing up the obscurity which even to Japanese surrounds many of their older authors. Nothing, however, which deserves the name of a History of Literature appeared until 1890, when Messrs. Mikami Sanji and Takatsu Kuwasaburo, of the Imperial University of Tokio, brought out their *Nippon Bungakushi*, which is by far the most valuable work on this subject. The critical judgments of the authors may not always commend themselves to Europeans, but they have succeeded in setting forth the leading facts of the history of their literature in a clear, methodical manner. I gladly acknowledge my very considerable obligations to their work.

A history of fiction, entitled *Shōsetsu Shikō*, by Sekine Masanao (1890), should also be mentioned.

The most useful bibliography in the Japanese language is the *Gunsho Ichiran*, by Ozaki Masayoshi, six volumes (1801), and the best biographical dictionary is a bulky work by a number of authors, entitled *Dai Nippon Jimmei Jisho* (1886). A list of other works of this class may be found in the article in *Appleton's Cyclopædia* already referred to.

Monographs on Hakuseki, Sorai, Chikamatsu, and other eminent authors, have been lately published, and a good deal is being done at the present time in the way of re-editing and annotating the monuments of the older literature.

The Hakubunkan publishing house of Tokio have reprinted most of the fiction and drama of the Yedo period under the description *Teikoku Bunko* or "Imperial Library." As an illustration of the cheapness of books in Japan, it may be mentioned that each volume of this series contains about one thousand octavo pages of reasonably good print, on tolerable paper, in neat binding, and is sold for the equivalent of about one shilling of our money.

A LIST OF DICTIONARIES, GRAMMARS, AND OTHER WORKS OF REFERENCE USEFUL TO STUDENTS OF JAPANESE

A Japanese-English and English-Japanese Dictionary, by J. C Hepburn (fourth edition, 1888).

A Dictionary of Chinese-Japanese Words, by J. H. Gubbins (1889).

A Chinese-English Dictionary, by H. A. Giles (1892).

A Native Chinese-Japanese Dictionary, such as the *Gioku-hen*.

One of the following native dictionaries of the Japanese language : *Nippon Daijirin; Genkai; Nippon Daijisho.* Of these, the first-named is the fullest and most elaborate. But even in the best dictionaries, whether by Japanese or foreigners, vast numbers of words are not to be found.

A Grammar of the Japanese Written Language, by W. G. Aston (second edition, 1877).

A Grammar of the Japanese Spoken Language, by W. G. Aston (fourth edition, 1888).

Or, *A Handbook of Colloquial Japanese*, by B. H. Chamberlain (third edition, 1898).

A Romanised Japanese Reader, by B. H. Chamberlain (1886).

A Manual of Japanese Writing, by the same author, is in preparation.

Japanese Chronological Tables, by E. M. S. (Sir Ernest Satow), (1874), or a similar work by W. Bramsen (1880), will be found necessary.

INDEX

Other TUT BOOKS available:

UNBEATEN TRACKS IN JAPAN: An Account of Travels in the Interior Including Visits to the Aborigines of Yezo and the Shrine of Nikko *by Isabella L. Bird*

ZILCH! The Marine Corps' Most Guarded Secret *by Roy Delgado*

Please order from your bookstore or write directly to:

CHARLES E. TUTTLE CO., INC.
Suido 1-chome, 2–6, Bunkyo-ku, Tokyo 112

or:

CHARLES E. TUTTLE CO., INC.
Rutland, Vermont 05701 U.S.A.